How to
Prosper
in Your
Own Business

Brian R. Smith

**Management Consultant
and Director of Education
COUNTRY BUSINESS SERVICES**

How to Prosper in Your Own Business

Getting Started and Staying on Course

The Stephen Greene Press
Brattleboro, Vermont

To Elizabeth, my daughter

How to Prosper in Your Own Business by BRIAN R. SMITH

This book has been produced in the United States of America.
It is designed by IRVING PERKINS ASSOCIATES and published by THE STEPHEN GREENE PRESS, Fessenden Road, Brattleboro, Vermont 05301.

Library of Congress Cataloging in Publication Data

SMITH, BRIAN R.   1939–
  How to prosper in your own business.

  Bibliography: p.
  Includes index.
  1. Business.   2. Small business.   3. Self-employed.   I. Title.
HF5351.S68   658.1′141   80–19917
ISBN 0–8289–0408–1

Contents

Acknowledgments

As is the case with any book, large or small, there are usually a host of people who help the author go from the original idea to the sale of the first volume. Such is the case with this book—many helped.

Probably the largest body of praise goes to Jim Howard, the president of Country Business Services in Brattleboro, Vermont, for his inspiration, constructive criticism, and actual technical knowledge. Without his overall guidance and support, the book would never have been completed in its present form. Other staff members of Country Business Services who deserve noteworthy mention are Sarah Howard, for the research on husbands and wives as entrepreneurs; Bruce Pernie, for the data on taxes; Milt Eaton, for some of the financial information; Phil Steckler, for the methods of assessing a small business's capabilities; Bill Oates, for general hints on what makes a business successful; and Linda Remy and Sue Laware, for their administrative support and coordination.

Special thanks go to Virginia Page of Brattleboro, Vermont, for her research into women as entrepreneurs.

More thanks go to the faculty and staff of Franklin Pierce College in Rindge, New Hampshire: to Denise Labrie, for typing and not complaining about the lunch she was supposed to get; to Bob Coburn, Division Director of the Economics and Management Division, for constantly flooding my desk with every known article on small-business management; and to Dean Clifford Coles, for helping to resolve some problems that I had while writing the book.

The reader will find a number of references to business plans in Chapter 4, "Business Planning"; these were taken from student papers which the author deemed to be worthy of note. Gratitude for these references goes to the following individuals:

"Sports World"	Mike Mattos
"The Sturbridge Glass Shoppe"	Joe Codderre
"Twin Dragon Frozen Foods"	Pradit Phataraprasit
"Cheshire Trophies"	Tim Hunt
"Well Strung"	Bob Strandfeldt
"OAICP"	Roy Pressimone and Karen Melikian
"Teddy Bear"	Jeff Katz
"Farmer's and Garden Supplies"	Walt Shine
"Recycled Records"	Bob Roth
"Autoword Services"	Dave Voss
"Tim Bruder, Electrical Contractor"	Tim Bruder
"Sportster's Sporting Goods"	Kevin Delaney
"Smilin' Pete's"	Pete Wood
"Creative Forms"	Ed Niskanen

"Tower's Marina"   Bill Bernard
"B & T Marina"   Bob Vitelli and Patricia Reilly

The business plans in Appendix I are reproduced almost exactly as they were written, and thanks go to their authors for their help.

Another group to which I am indebted are those who helped me shape my general thoughts about the entrepreneurial function: Jeff Timmons at Northeastern, who first made me aware that I was an entrepreneur, not a company executive; Bob Schwartz of the Tarrytown Executive Conference Center; and Joe Mancuso of the Center for Entrepreneurial Management.

I would like to especially acknowledge the grand folks at The Stephen Greene Press, with unique praise for Castle Freeman, who worked steadily with me from the dream to the reality.

Introduction

The following is a quote from *Maximum Performance* by Laurence E. Morehouse and Leonard Gross:

> Years ago, Eugen Herrigel wrote a little book called *Zen in the Art of Archery*. When it appeared it was viewed as a far-out philosophical tract that had nothing to do with performance. But subsequent readings gave the book the credit it deserved. The book mightily influenced me. Its central idea was that man, the bow, the arrow, and the target could be made to interrelate until all were a harmonious whole. It offered the first glimpses of feedback phenomena: You are affected by your target, just as your target is affected by you. You're going to pierce the target with an arrow, but the target is organizing you by its presence.

As I was reading the passage it struck me how much this description was so akin to the entrepreneur and his or her small business. The two are one. Each affects the other in an inseparable, interrelated way. Using this as a springboard, I tried to make this book *one*. Both my colleagues and myself in our consulting and educational efforts in small business found ourselves suggesting three or four books to would-be entrepreneurs, where one should have been sufficient. We would recommend one book for fundamentals, one for planning, one for an analysis of the entrepreneur as a unique individual. This book is my attempt at unification and hopefully provides a single work to help entrepreneurs and small business owners to prepare for the 1980's and beyond.

The book has an unmistakable rural caste to it. There is a definite reason for this. Most books on entrepreneurship are slanted towards high-technology manufacturing operations. I, and those who advised me on the material included in the book, wanted a broader appeal, and one that would point itself toward some of the emerging trends of right-thinking individuals who are beginning to wonder if the corporate life in the large metropolitan areas hasn't shattered some of their earlier hopes and aspirations. We are not in any way advocating the overthrow of the corporate life, but we have an extreme sensitivity to what these large institutions can do to one's state of mind and physical well-being.

The book is intended to be a guide, a helpmate, and a way-to-do-it. Use it as a traveling experience; you can proceed directly through the material or you can wander at random, selecting those areas that interest you or that you feel you are extremely weak in. You can do this because the book is modular in nature; the chapters stand alone, just like the cheese in "The Farmer in the Dell."

The book is laid out in what we believe to be the simplest manner possible. If an entire subject is new to you, we suggest you proceed through the text one chapter at a time. Chapter 1 discusses our concept of the new entrepreneur, with a brief history of entrepreneurship. Chapters 2 and 3 prepare the reader to enter business ownership. Chapter 4 discusses the business plan, and how to prepare one; excerpts from actual plans are included to give concrete examples of what we are talking about (more plans appear in Appendix I). Chapters 5 through 10 are the "nuts and bolts" of running your own enterprise. In addition to being much like other "how to" books on the subject, these six chapters contain some of the systems used by big business. Chapters 11 and 12 are devoted to areas which concern women and couples in small business. Chapter 13 talks about the future of small business as we see it.

The book is intended to be rather light in nature—and it is where it has to be. It's pretty hard, however, to be jocular when explaining discounted cash flow or internal rate of return.

Sticking to our intended theme, then, the following story will drive home our advice to anyone thinking about getting into their own business:

> A young man in his late teens was discussing his problems inherent in dating the opposite sex with his father. Although this usually touchy subject was being handled easily and without embarrassment to either party, the son was apparently anxious to bring up one particular subject. Finally, during a lull in the conversation, the son cleared his throat and asked his father what his opinion was of the son's deflowering his girlfriend. The father said simply, "Son, if you don't do it, someone else will."

Have fun!

"I have these nightmares every so often," said the restaurant owner.

"Nightmares about what?" I asked him.

"About losing it all," he answered.

"You mean, the business failing?"

"Well, not that exactly . . . See, we could lose our shirts; the whole thing could go down the drain. The family'd simply pack up into the van and we'd take off into the sunset . . . No, that's not exactly what; it's about . . ."

He squinted one eye, then stared at the sun-washed walls of the restaurant. "I mean losing working for yourself . . . God forbid you should ever lose that . . ."

From an interview with an entrepreneur.

CHAPTER ONE

The New Entrepreneur

The gull sees farthest who flies highest.
Jonathan Livingston Seagull

Overview

This book is about small businesses and the people who own and operate them. The first chapter describes the people, the *entrepreneurs.*

The word *entrepreneur* has become a very popular, almost faddish term used to describe business owners. In most common meanings of the word, an entrepreneur is a person who starts a business, especially a manufacturing company, from scratch (as opposed to an individual who buys an existing business). However, in this book we will use the terms *entrepreneur* and *small-business owner* synonymously and interchangeably, and the terminology will reflect the people—men, women, and couples—who have chosen the ownership and operation of an independent business as both a life-style and a career.

The word *entrepreneur* comes from the French verb *entreprendre* which means "to undertake." There are two basic definitions of the term, (1) the character or disposition that leads one to attempt the difficult, and (2) one who assumes the risk and management of business. The key phrases from each definition are *attempt the difficult* and *assume the risk.* These are the two criteria which set the entrepreneur apart from his or her counterpart in corporations, government, labor, education, and social service, for not everyone is willing either to attempt difficult tasks or to assume risks. But we are dealing with a unique individual, one who willingly assumes the risk of enterprise so that he can reap the rewards, and who then attempts the difficult so that achievement and accomplishment and success can be his. For, after all, if the true entrepreneur seeks one thing above all others, it is the achievement of goals that he has set himself. Without risk, there is little or no return, and it is the risk-reward balance that the small-business owner lives with every day.

Many authorities have said that entrepreneurs are "do-ers." Some years ago, when the television series "The Man from U.N.C.L.E." was popular, someone asked the spy Ilya Kuriakin (played by David McCallum) what his occupation was. He replied, "I go, and I do." Entrepreneurs, too, go and do. They are accomplishment-oriented and achievement-motivated. The successful ones function best as doers. They work hard and long to attain their objectives, but they also work *smart.*

The successful entrepreneur possesses some unique traits and answers some unique demands. He or she must exert great effort, expend astounding amounts of energy, operate at a frightening pace, and be ready to look potential failure square in the face and laugh. In other words, as Sir Lancelot's song in *Camelot* suggests, he succeeds "where a less fantastic man [*sic*] would fail."

The reward for the entrepreneur is not always monetary, although personal wealth may come as a by-product of drive and ambition. Much of the entrepreneur's reward comes from the fact that the business becomes an extension of himself, something that he has done with his own hand and his own efforts. The business reflects his character, his spirit, his moral values, and his life choices. The business *is* the entrepreneur.

Who Are the Entrepreneurs?

Entrepreneurs come in all sizes and colors, span the age continuum from teenager to golden-ager, have a variety of educational and ethnic backgrounds, and may have lived in the summer homes of Newport or the slums of Bedford-Stuyvesant. The founder of the company that makes Parks' sausages was black; the builder of one of the most successful bakeries in the world, Pepperidge Farm, was a woman; and Colonel Harland Sanders opened his first Kentucky Fried Chicken stand when he was sixty-seven, living on Social Security, and had $100 in the bank. The only real barrier to small-business ownership is the lack of desire.

Entrepreneurs are an inventive lot by nature, and the most successful ones have a natural curiosity that makes them seek out answers and then use their natural initiative to solve problems. Ray Kroc, who has amassed a personal fortune that some people estimate at close to a billion dollars and who has been the chairman of the board of a major United States corporation for a number of years, was, at one time, a salesman for a company that sold mixing machines which could make six milk shakes at one time. One day he received in the mail an order for eight such machines, and he simply had to see what kind of business establishment needed to make forty-eight milk shakes at once. There, in California, he saw two golden arches and found a thriving hamburger stand operated by two brothers from Bedford, New Hampshire. Their last name was McDonald.

Wealth is not, however, the *sine qua non* of business. Many privately owned and operated businesses stay relatively small by design since that is the desire of the entrepreneur. As E. F. Schumacher in his book *Small Is Beautiful* said, not everything has to or should continue to grow every year so that, in each successive period, we outproduce ourselves and use as a primary goal that next year must be bigger, faster, and presumably better than last year. If we continue on the collision course that we have mapped for ourselves, we'll be out of food and fuel in thirty-five years. Very few modern small-business owners look upon growth as an objective in itself.

A Brief History of Entrepreneurs

Some historians tell us that America attracted both the best and the worst of the cultures to its young, growing, and energetic society. If this is true, both groups had a duality of purpose in making the geographic and cultural shift from their native environments to one of a new and different structure. They went *from* the land of their birth because they lacked personal fulfillment, suffered overcrowding and disease, were denied what they felt were their rights as citizens, or were afraid of prosecution or persecution. They went *to* a land that offered them the basic freedoms humanity had yearned for since man formed societal groups, and an opportunity to rise above their classic and assumed level in life.

We tend to suspect that, by and large, the best of foreign societies came to our shores and that the criminals, the malcontents, and the misfits were a minority. Even the ancestors of today's black Americans were not originally captured in Africa because they were physically or mentally the weakest of their society; and even if some were weak, they surely would have failed to survive the horrible voyages to the slave markets of Savannah and Charleston.

Consider the following two points:

First, imagine you are a Spaniard living in a small town outside of Madrid in the early nineteenth century. The chances are that your father, your grandfather, and your great-grandfather were born, lived, and were buried in the same town in which you now live. Your style of life, although arduous at times, is regulated and predictable. Yet you make a decision to leave your heritage behind and journey to a new land thousands of miles distant, where you are ignorant of the customs and can't speak the language. Worse yet, you will be discriminated against by others that have preceded you. This type of individual does not appear to us to be the worst that their society had to offer.

Second, when political unrest or war comes to a nation, this tends to drive away the cream of its society. Albert Einstein came to us from Germany, and Enrico Fermi from Italy, both during governmental upheaval and turmoil. Whether or not we advocate nuclear energy, either controlled (a reactor) or uncontrolled (a bomb), its discovery is regarded as a momentous technological development, in this century, second only to the computer. More recently, many emigrating Cubans have achieved levels of success not attained by most Americans.

If we accept the fact, then, that the majority of immigrants were the best that their various countries had to offer, what did they find in America? They found the opportunity to do whatever they wanted.

Many became entrepreneurs. Anyone who takes a pleasant summertime walk through Williamsburg, Virginia, or Sturbridge Village, Massachusetts, will delight in the restorations of ancient, quaint shops that produce basic daily necessities. The butcher, the baker, and the candlestick maker are still there. These were the early entrepreneurs, plying their trade, earning a living, and supplying a needed commodity. This earliest group we shall call the *craftsman-entrepreneur.*

Many immigrants to our country took a slightly different route. These were the *retail-entrepreneurs.* The Italian grocer in Boston, the Jewish jeweler in New York, and the Dutch milliner in Philadelphia were part of a vast and growing number of small businesses throughout our country in the nineteenth century. Often these businesses were of the "mom and pop" variety, and many stayed that way. On the other hand, Jordan Marsh of Boston, Macy's of New York City, and John Wanamaker's of Philadelphia became enterprises of significant size.

Another interesting fact is that this period saw a proliferation of inventive, creative minds that carried through to the twentieth century. These *inventor-entrepreneurs* produced startling devices to accomplish a necessary task, and many also built businesses to produce and market their products. It is also worthy of note that some of the best of these individuals went beyond their original inventions. Probably the best example of this was The Wizard of Menlo Park, Thomas Alva Edison. His first patent, issued in 1868, was for a device that would display the "aye" or "nay" vote of a legislator. Edison believed that the machine would greatly reduce the time that government bodies spent in session because the tally of a vote would take seconds rather than hours. When he proudly showed the device, one congressional chairman commented that it took, on an average, forty-five minutes to call the voice roll, and, in that time, votes could be traded. Because Edison's machine would not allow that to happen, no legislative body would buy it. Edison made a solemn and private promise never to invent anything again that nobody would buy.

Another example was Eli Whitney, who, after inventing his cotton gin, organized a factory that manufactured, among other things, rifles for the army. Alexander Graham Bell made several aircraft in 1909 which employed both ailerons and tricycle landing gear, two items which modern aircraft still employ.

Around the turn of the century, three developments in business occurred almost simultaneously and on parallel paths. Many economists feel that, without these events and without their simultaneity, the United States would never have "arrived." Whether one happened because of or in spite of the other two is somewhat of a mystery. The fact is that they did happen. These events were (1) America developed the capability of producing large numbers of goods in a single facility, (2) the economy could generate sufficient amounts of capital to finance these vast ventures, and (3) businessmen learned how to communicate and market the items that were produced in such prodigious numbers. The visionaries who took advantage of these changes were the *enterprise-*

entrepreneurs such as J. Pierpont Morgan, Andrew Carnegie, John D. Rockefeller, and Andrew Mellon.

Beginning early in the twentieth century and continuing to this day are the *technology-entrepreneurs* who have the great visionary genius to see an idea, a technology, or an entire enterprise that will serve a market need both today, tomorrow, and far into the future. David Sarnoff of RCA and Thomas Watson of IBM are examples of the earlier group, but Kenneth Olsen of DEC and Edson DeCastro of DGC remind us that this group has not died. Because of the cost of capital the deserved conservatism of venture capitalists, and the concerns of commercial banks, these types of entrepreneurs may diminish in total number, but they will never cease altogether. To join their ranks from a start-up venture is now difficult indeed, but this may change in the future as a function of an ever-growing desire on the part of many individuals to experience independence.

The New Entrepreneurs

Now we have the new entrepreneurs. They are a combination, a synthesis, of all five of the earlier types.

Craftsmen

They are not like the village smithy standing beneath the spreading chestnut tree, but they do bring to their enterprises the expertise of some kind of craft.

Retailers

These new entrepreneurs understand the retail method; that is, they have a well-defined notion of merchandising and economic values. They understand that any business must also be a delivery system. An old saw in the marketing game says that nothing happens until a sale is made, and that is correct. An entrepreneur can possess all the required traits and characteristics of his business, but without the grasp of the profit motive—or, more simply stated, without being able to sell goods or services for something more than they cost—he will eventually fail.

Inventors

This type is not as unfamiliar as it may seem. Many of us know a true inventor who, because of his or her technical capabilities, became an entrepreneur; the invention was so unusual that venture capital was attracted to it. But consider for a moment the premise that all successful entrepreneurs are really inventors. They *do* change the world around them. As a matter of fact, they have been and will be the instruments of change. Big business, big labor, big government, and big education do not manifest major changes. They can't. Basically, they only *maintain*. The entrepreneur is an inventor by nature, being both creative and innovative.

Enterprisers

By definition, entrepreneurs can't be otherwise. The enterprising person can't last more than a year's time with larger institutions. Either he quits in total desperation because of bureaucratic methods and executive gamesmanship or else he is fired for disrupting and circumventing the established order. The petty procedures, the boring meetings filled with inane conversation, and the useless politics are simply too much for the entrepreneur. If the large institution could learn how to become creative, enterprising and fun, the new entrepreneurs wouldn't run screaming for the exits. But our large institutions have become massive graveyards for the time-servers. The entrepreneurs could never be part of a large enterprise run by other people because they cannot be an agent of change in that organization; they feel disenfranchised, at odds with how the big business is run.

Technologists

Modern entrepreneurs are technologists by the very nature of today's society, and this technology is used two different ways. The new entrepreneur is, more and more, bringing the systems approach to his small business. The reason for this is that the entrepreneur realizes that the small enterprise has all the functions—marketing, operations, and finance—of GM or IBM. Whereas, in the massive organization, thousands of individuals may be devoted to some task such as quality control or purchasing, in the small business, all the functions of a business may be performed by a single individual.

The successful entrepreneur looks on his business as a total system (a delivery system) composed of a legion of subsystems; this entire mechanism is held together and driven forward by a management information system and pure love. To aid the operation of the information system, entrepreneurs are turning in large numbers to the use of technical aids. The first round of change for the entrepreneur came about with the use of the electronic cash registers. These devices, as we have all seen, do simple calculations, like computing a customer's change, and they also classify sales by department or by any category of product or service that has meaning for the entrepreneur. These devices will get more and more complex until they begin to resemble the one that is just beginning to help serve the entrepreneur—the computer.

Our technological age has brought with it the phenomenon of *information.* In centuries past, power accrued to those who owned the land. Around the turn of the century in this country, assets and control of finance meant power. We suspect that, now and in the future, the power will go to those with information and knowledge. Those are available to all, not just the large concerns.

The New Entrepreneur and the Corporation

The new entrepreneur is often an alumnus, or refugee, from the management hierarchy of a large corporation or other bureaucracy (government, education or nonprofit institutions). These organizations have been supplying a significant number of the new entrepreneurs and will probably continue to do so for many years to come. One major employer in the state of Massachusetts, according to a study conducted in the early seventies, had supplied so many entrepreneurs to the local economy that the combined sales of all these new ventures had reached a total greater than that of the multibillion dollar firm that once held these individuals as employees. A career with a large employer provides a multitude of security blankets, including a predictable paycheck delivered to the employee on a regular basis as well as a host of other benefits and perquisites. There is, however, no independence, little freedom of choice while on the job, and, in many cases, no feeling of self-fulfillment or self-actualization. Many people in this situation feel trapped and victimized. Their dreams may have come true in terms of financial success, but happiness has somehow eluded them. An article entitled "Chucking It" in the November 1978 issue of *The New Englander* magazine stated:

> Reappraisal has become an all-American activity, and many an executive who never thought to doubt his aims and goals now finds himself high on the corporate ladder, but low in what are increasingly coming to be understood as the satisfactions of life.

We are in an era of self-discovery, and, with that discovery, are coming the realizations that what was once thought to be one of the most desirable career patterns is not providing many individuals with all that they want.

Traits of the New Entrepreneur

Experts have studied the entrepreneur from many viewpoints in order to compose some kind of a picture of this individual. What turns him on (and off)? What is he like? Why does he do what he does? Both college professors and successful small businessmen have written about the entrepreneur. The problem with the former is that some well-educated teachers have had little practical small business experience, and the latter is too often using his book for exposition and exploitation as well as a vehicle for literary bragging and personal back-patting. Also, most books talk about male entrepreneurs involved with high technology ventures. Although these cases are the most complex of the entrepreneurial situations, requiring product development, the building of the managerial team, and the raising of venture capital, they represent only one subdivision of a large number of individuals. This book is intended for all entrepreneurs. As a matter of fact, we have reserved later chapters for married couples in their own businesses and women entrepreneurs since (1) we suspect there may be several million enterprises of this type, (2) there is apparently little or nothing written on the subject, and (3) they both face somewhat unusual situations.

This book is a compilation of some things we suspect will help to bring success to entrepreneurs of all types. The items that we talk about are the result of the four following different activities:

- Teaching small business management to undergraduate and graduate students, aged sixteen to seventy-six.
- The reading and analysis of much of the written work concerning the entrepreneur.
- The observation of hundreds of active business owners and would-be entrepreneurs from every stage in life.
- Personal experience in starting and operating businesses.

The various traits and descriptions that have been used to describe entrepreneurs are legion, indeed. Almost every positive-sounding adjective has been used over the past thirty years or so. The terms are often confusing and intertwined. What one explication, we wondered, would totally describe the entrepreneur? Of all the terms and phrases used, is there one that stands out as the most important? Almost every knowledgeable person in the field seems to agree that the best description would be *achiever*.

David C. McClelland at Harvard has done a vast amount of research into achievement motivation and the entrepreneur, as has Jeffrey A. Timmons at Northeastern University. Their findings concur with what we have found. Most entrepreneurs that we know are singly, above everything else, achievers. *Achievement* is defined as the successful completion of something that usually requires skill and perseverance.

Personality

There are "achievers" in many careers, however. What traits of character or personality make the new entrepreneurs different from their counterparts in other careers? In writings on the subject over the last twenty-five years, a profile of the new entrepreneur has emerged.

New entrepreneurs' personal and business lives tend to be highly integrated. They make few distinctions between work and recreation. To the outsider, they appear to work all the time. In reality, though, they don't consider their activities work as work is usually understood. They view the business as an extension of their senses and capabilities. The business is first a means of fulfilling themselves, and only secondarily a source of money.

New entrepreneurs tend to be motivated by what psychologists have called higher needs, including personal fulfillment, recognition, knowledge, understanding, rather than the basic needs of shelter, food, safety, companionship, and ego satisfaction.

New entrepreneurs tend to accept technology, not to be threatened by it. They will generally employ fairly advanced means of goal-setting and planning. They naturally gravitate toward fairly advanced knowledge concerning the management systems approach to business.

New entrepreneurs have a basic need to change the world, even though they may focus only on a small corner of it. They are not likely to acquire a business and allow it to remain someone else's creation. They will ultimately rebuild it to make it the lengthening shadow of their own image. They have been, during most of their lives, winners, not losers. They chose small business ownership because their individual needs could not be fulfilled in a large organization or in working for someone else.

New entrepreneurs have the qualities that studies have indicated are part of entrepreneurship—dedication to playing by the rules, honesty, and personal integrity. They do not like to take shortcuts, because the results are not valid measurements of their capabilities.

Many successful entrepreneurs also have a well-developed spiritual awareness. Life, to them, is a full, rich experience. They are in control of themselves and their emotions. Many become depressed over various events, but this does not immobilize them. They reflect on their setbacks, revel in their accomplishments, and, above all, have a mature sense of humor.

Since they are "inward-looking" individuals, luck is not a part of the new entrepreneurs' working vocabulary. They take the responsibility for setbacks and failures. Failure is not an event that brings them to a complete halt; it is a learning experience. *Failure* can be defined in many ways. To an entrepreneur, it may be simply having something turn out differently from the way it was planned. Many entrepreneurs do not attach value to failure, as so many other people do. Failure is neither right nor wrong—it is simply failure, not a good enough reason to stop trying.

Finally, many authors on entrepreneurs and entrepreneurship have observed that successful entrepreneurs aren't in it for the money. Eventual financial security is a strong goal of the entrepreneur, but for many new entrepreneurs money is a by-product of drive, energy and initiative.

Brains

Conflicting data about the mental abilities of the entrepreneur make some generalities necessary. Most researchers agree that intelligence is a plus, and we suspect that is true. There are, however, two points to consider. First, having a low intelligence score as measured by our standard I.Q. tests does not necessarily mean failure as an entrepreneur. Many successful small business owners could never qualify for membership in Mensa, but they know what needs to be done, and they work with goals and objectives in mind. Second, the true genius may have some difficulties being an honest entrepreneur. This is, of course, a generality and is open to some argument. Geniuses may get involved in side issues not germane to the operation of the business. Usually, the resident genius needs a partner or a team who are what we normally think of as business people. If you can combine these two traits in one individual, you have something very explosive indeed.

There is, of course, that rare quality called common sense which, unlike intelligence, cannot be quantitatively measured; it can only be observed. Common sense, it is said, is so named because it is so uncommon.

Needs

Many authors suspect, and we endorse the fact, that the entrepreneur simply cannot work for someone else. Not only that, he disdains organizational politics, laughs at the idiocy of the paperwork snowstorms that hierarchies seem to generate and, in general, does not conform. In the early sixties, Tom Watson, Jr., then the chairman of the board of IBM, made the outlandish statement that what the company needed was a few "wild ducks." Having a covey of wild ducks was just what IBM could not tolerate. Nor can the entrepreneur tolerate all that goes with what is expected of the modern manager, including such compulsory social events as the boss's cocktail parties.

Security

Nevertheless all of us, including entrepreneurs to one degree or another, have a need for security. The security issue is always one of the most important topics in union-management collective bargaining, and, if you want to send a government employee into blind panic, suggest that the department is going to be phased out. The security-conscious middle manager has a great deal of difficulty understanding the motives of the entrepreneurs, for he sees them as people who forsake the monthly paycheck and all the other warm, womb-like protectors such as company life-insurance and paid medical benefits. Entrepreneurs are not without a security need; far from it. The difference is that, for the entrepreneurs, the security is self-made. Because successful entrepreneurs have assurance and confidence in their own abilities to be an agent of change, they create their own security by building an enduring enterprise. When we ask entrepreneurs to tell us their life goals, over 35 percent mention leaving a legacy for their children in terms of a going business concern. (If we separate women from the group, the percentage goes over 50 percent.)

Other People

Like so many successful individuals in all pursuits, the new entrepreneur is a communicator, and we mean this in terms of two-way communications. We know that good entrepreneurs are users of information, and therefore we suspect that they are good listeners. The information provided to them becomes the instrumentality of potential change: pure data. In terms of clear outward communication, both verbal and written, this trait has several results.

First, information is passed along with a minimum amount of "noise" (or unwanted signal); successful entrepreneurs are clear about what they want. In addition, customers, the lifeblood of all business enterprises, are informed and made more amenable to buy. Team members, be they hourly-paid employees or equal partners, feel more of an integral part of the business. Listeners, too, are more comfortable in engaging in their own outward communication.

Allied with this high communicative skill is the orientation of the entrepreneurs toward their fellow humans. McClelland calls this a need for affiliation. How many of us have gone into a business establishment in which the proprietor appears to be a brusque, surly individual to whom meeting people is a distasteful task? (In many cases, this is probably true.) Naturally, as customers, we do not wish to return to that punishing environment.

Contrast the negative atmosphere with a pleasant one. Even the unethical entrepreneur has staying power in business (including some of the biggest swindlers of our time) if he has learned that a smile, a kind word, and some understanding will overcome most unpleasant situations. To say that successful entrepreneurs are people-oriented understates the situation.

Peter Drucker, the noted author and consultant, in his book *Managing for Results,* has a very important chapter entitled "The Customer Is the Business." The entrepreneur realizes this concept and acts accordingly.

Successful entrepreneurs can deal easily not only with situations that are ill-defined and uncertain of outcome, but they can also handle failure reasonably well up to and including the failure of the business itself. Many entrepreneurs do not build their lasting venture on the first try; often one, two, or even three failures are necessary before sufficient knowledge is gained to assure success. Unfortunately, our nation's banks rarely recognize this fact.

Being Onstage

Although the only evidence on the matter comes from observation, we suspect that many successful entrepreneurs like to be "onstage." Their strong theatrical need is coupled with a natural, well-developed, mature sense of humor. We have seen and observed many small-business owners tell jokes to strangers, wear outlandish costumes, or pull pranks on customers. We know an owner of an office supply business who has been known to burst into songs and routines from Broadway musicals. A fellow in a neighboring town who runs an auto dealership wears a white ten-gallon hat and spats. A proprietor of an inn often serves a joke-store rubber chicken.

Knowledge of the Particular Business

That knowledge is a required trait of the successful entrepreneur can hardly be disputed. There is some conflicting evidence that knowledge of the specific business that an entrepreneur wants to enter is a requirement for success. As the song from Porgy and Bess goes, it ain't necessarily so. To be sure, some knowledge of that particular business is probably better than none at all. This is uniquely true for the high-technology venture, but not equally valid for less complex operations. Consider the following actual examples.

A salesman working for a medium-sized manufacturer of precision metal products was becoming more and more dissatisfied with his job. The money, the benefits, and the nearly unlimited use of the company car were not sufficient to compensate the salesman for what he felt were the many frustrations he faced each day, such as being gone from his family for weeks at a time, lack of recognition for landing a large account, and spending weekends writing sales reports. He wanted to be in business for himself but couldn't decide what to do. He made a few tentative fits and starts—a small plastic molding operation, a Jeep dealership, and a bar. Nothing seemed to fit.

He described his situation to the author. The simple advice offered to him was the apparent catalyst that he needed. It was suggested that he (1) list *all* the businesses he would like to enter without giving any thought for the time being to potential stumbling blocks like financing; (2) list the things he liked to do personally, professionally, socially, and avocationally; (3) look for any kind of match.

It worked! His real love in life was the outdoors. He was a fisherman, an avid hunter skilled with both the bow and the rifle, an expert skier, and a hiker and camper. He not only tied his own fishing flies but had taught many others to do the same. The choice of a business, so obvious but yet so elusive, was a sporting goods store. Now he is having fun and making money.

The second case involves a fellow who was an engineering supervisor with a major manufacturer of pumps and compressors. He also felt unfulfilled in his position, and offered the comment that he spent more time protecting himself and "playing the game" than he did doing his job. He resigned and bought a large, nineteenth-century inn which needed extensive repairs. To worsen the prospects of future success, there were only a handful of permanent tenants occupying a few of the sixty-seven rooms, and transient tourist traffic had all but ceased.

His only experience with the hospitality field had been his one-night stays in the Holiday and Ramada Inns of the Northeast, but he was confident of his own abilities, and, more than anything else, he wanted his inn to succeed where it had almost failed. The other big plus was that he understood systems and the concept of wholism. The venture would not grow and prosper unless all the subsystems were working properly.

He decided not to renovate the inn to look like the modern, plastic hotels that are so common everywhere, but to keep the colonial charm and to build the future reputation of the establishment on that basis. While the necessary renovations were underway, he began an extensive advertising campaign. As the first new guests began to arrive, he reopened the dining room and built a cocktail lounge in the basement.

It wasn't very long before the rooms were fully occupied and the inn was a thriving venture. As the business grew, more systems were added. For example, our entrepreneur calculated that, at an average monthly occupancy rate of 65 percent or better, it would be more economical to build a laundry facility on the premises rather than to use a linen service. He bought some used equipment, poked around in a couple of junkyards, and built, from scratch, such a unique laundering plant that it was written up in a national hospitality magazine.

There is a rather tragic end to this story. Because of a careless smoker on the fourth floor, the inn burned to the foundation. Luckily, no one was injured, but the business was a total loss.

Our entrepreneur, being true to form, moved to a neighboring state, bought another old inn, and started again. He did do one thing differently. He installed an intricate fire alarm–smoke detector–fire sprinkler system.

Motivation of the New Entrepreneur: Theory

We have analyzed the writings of several of the foremost thinkers on management and motivation to see if what they said has any meaning for the new entrepreneur. After all, if the metamorphosis of corporation employee into entrepreneur takes place, what is said about motivation in the corporation may be relevant.

Three prominent authors and thinkers who most impressed us, as they have many other readers, are Frederick Herzberg, Abraham Maslow and Douglas

McGregor. Most of the work of these outstanding researchers has described the managerial process in large organizations. We will see how their basic material applies to the motivation of the new entrepreneur.

Herzberg

Frederick Herzberg, studying the work situation for many years and interviewing thousands of people, isolated certain factors of the work situation and combined them into what he called the "motivation-maintenance model." [1] He defines two sets of factors, the first of which he defines as *motivation factors*. Motivation factors, when present, help to bring about job satisfaction. They are what workers and managers like about their jobs. Motivation factors include: the job itself, recognition by superiors, responsibility, advancement potential, and achievement.

The second set of factors Herzberg calls *maintenance* or *hygiene factors*. Maintenance factors, when present, cause a neutral feeling about the work situation, but, if they are removed or are perceived to be insufficient, they will cause a negative feeling about the job. These maintenance factors, which also represent what many Americans dislike about their jobs, are money and benefits, human relations, working conditions, nature of supervision, and company policies.

In very few of our major companies can it be said that these five maintenance factors exist at a satisfactory level. Company policies are arbitrary, even foolish. The author once worked for a company (but not for long) where even top level managers could drink coffee only during the ten-minute morning or afternoon coffee break. Inflation places continuous pressure on wage and salary levels. Table 1.1 shows one theory for fleeing the corporate trap. The perceived maintenance factors degrade to such a level that more and more people leave the organization to increase the motivation factors and to reestablish the maintenance factors *which they now can control!* The point is that motivation can operate more effectively in your own small business than in the large institution, because, although motivation is internal in nature, it does seem to require a conducive environment.

Maslow

Now we turn to Abraham Maslow and his world-famous (and almost overworked by now) hierarchy of needs. His general theory states that we have five levels of needs, basic or physiological, safety, companionship, esteem (ego),

---

[1] Frederick Herzberg, *Work and the Nature of Man* (World: New York, 1966).

TABLE 1.1

Herzberg's Motivation and Maintenance Factors

Motivation Factors	*Maintenance Factors*
Work itself	Money
Recognition	Human relations
Responsibility	Working conditions
Advancement	Supervision
Achievement	Company policies

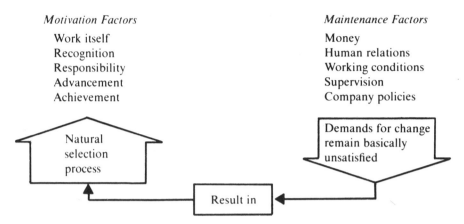

Natural selection process

Demands for change remain basically unsatisfied

Result in

and self-realization/actualization.[2] Maslow says that, as each need in the list becomes satisfied, we move to the next (higher) level. Accordingly, once our basic needs of air, food, and water are fulfilled, we seek needs at the safety level. Once we are convinced that we are safe from mental and physical harm, we arrive at the companionship level. (See Table 1.2.)

TABLE 1.2

Maslow's Hierarchy of Needs

Level	*Needs*	*Example*
5	Self-actualization and realization of total needs for self-fulfillment and for becoming everything one is capable of	Entrepreneur
4	Esteem needs for self-respect, prestige, recognition, and the respect of others	Corporate manager
3	Companionship and belonging needs for attention and affection, need for becoming a respected member of a group	Typical work group
2	Safety needs for protection against mental and physical danger	Coal miner
1	Basic needs for food, water, air, sex, rest	Primitive tribe

[2] Abraham H. Maslow, *Motivation and Personality* (Harper & Row: New York, 1954).

It appears that a large percentage of American workers today stay pretty much at the companionship level. They are reasonably free from physical danger, although some of the mental pressures may be severe. It is the fourth level, the need for ego-fulfillment and status, that seems to separate the manager from the worker. The person who aspires to management apparently has a higher level of need than his counterpart who chooses not to accept managerial responsibility. The problem for many managers, though, is that esteem does not automatically come with a higher rank. Esteem has to be earned, and a great number of corporate executives fail to appreciate the difference between that and status.

But if workers are trapped in level three (companionship), most managers are held prisoner at level four (esteem). Maslow says that, once one level is fully satisfied, the individual strives for the next level. If you accept the thesis that many managers are held at the fourth level because the large organizations simply will not allow them to self-actualize, you can understand the frustration that often takes place. The fourth level has been attained and satisfied, but the natural move that should take place to the fifth level *cannot take place*. Part of the self-actualization process involves total self-expression and gratification which the large institutions will not tolerate. People have to play by the rules and stay between the lines. Going the route of one's own business will allow a greater degree of self-expression since there is no one around to watch.

McGregor

Douglas McGregor, a number of years ago, introduced *Theory X* and *Theory Y* as basic working postulates about how organizations operate.[3] A firm operating on Theory *X,* the way that large business has operated for years, assumes that people are lazy and will not work unless forced to do so; that workers will not seek responsibility on the job beyond that which they must do; and that the manager's job is to control and direct the people that report to him or her. The newer, more desirable type of organization operates under Theory *Y,* assuming that work is as natural as play, that people will seek responsibility in the work environment and will work toward goals and objectives that they feel are important, and that the basic task of the manager is to create a climate where motivation can take place. Interestingly, most large organizations still operate primarily under Theory *X* assumptions, even though many of them proclaim that from a McGregor standpoint they are "liberated." It is easy for an entrepreneur to create Theory *Y* in his own venture, however.

If you consider Table 1.3, you will not wonder why there is a coming entrepreneurial revolution.

[3] Douglas McGregor, *Human Side of Enterprise* (McGraw-Hill: New York, 1960).

TABLE 1.3

Comparison Analyses of Maslow, Herzberg, and McGregor

Researcher	Large Business	Small Business
Maslow	Level 3 (companionship) attained by most workers, Level 4 (ego) by most managers	Level 5 (self-actualization) possible, even highly probable and desirable
Herzberg	Both motivation and hygiene factors probably absent, at least beyond the control of many	Motivation and maintenance factors to be designed-in and kept under control
McGregor	Primarily Theory *X*	Can be made into Theory *Y* relatively easily

Big Business and Small Business

Consider, if you will, the following summary comparisons about big business and small business:

Creativity. In the usual big business or corporation way of life, there is relatively little room for creativity for anyone below top executive status. Individual creativity can even be a disruption to others, so it is either barely tolerated or actively discouraged. The nature of small business is that it depends heavily upon the creative input of its owner.

Game-Playing. An important part of the politics of corporate life is learning to avoid blame for mistakes. Over a period of time, this leads to complex game-playing, which is almost obligatory among corporation people and bureaucrats. In small business, it is almost impossible to blame other people for failures. The successful small-business owner, over a period of time, learns to accept failures and triumphs as normal parts of the operation of his business. He is never permanently discouraged by failures and is able to exult in triumph. This is impossible in corporate life, where every triumph is shared by every person.

Breadth. As a rule, management responsibilities are fragmented in corporations due to the vast complexity of the job to be done. In a small business, the owner does everything, though, if he is wise he seeks help when it is needed. On the scale of things, the duties of the middle management corporation executive are the most fragmented; the duties of the owner of small business are least fragmented. The successful small-business owner becomes a person of greater breadth in every way than the successful corporation businessman because this is the way he is trained to be.

Reaction Time. Large corporations are cumbersome. Everything has to be approved by committees, often a waste of time, and reduced to the lowest common denominator. The small-business owner must be fast on his feet. This is an important competitive advantage. The successful entrepreneur learns to carve out a position for himself that is impossible for the large corporation to fill, simply because the corporation cannot be fast enough. Small business is far more fun!

Personal Effectiveness. The same differences exist in personal dealings. In a corporation the individual loses his or her identity, and the views and contributions of individuals are subordinate to the needs and wants of the group. Small businesses, in contrast, directly reflect the actions and decisions of their owners.

Three Strikes and . . . . In a large corporation, a failure usually becomes a part of the permanent record of the business executive. In a small business, the owner learns from failures, and eventually expects them as part of the learning and building process.

The Real Risks. We hear repeatedly about the inordinate risks in small business; yet we hear of career tragedies from people in large corporations far more frequently than we hear of small businessmen going "bottoms up." We consider the risk of being fired, demoted, robbed of an expected pension or other benefits, "squeezed out," or literally driven to emotional disaster far greater among corporation executives than we do among small-business owners.

Earnings. The earnings of the small-business owner may be a well-kept secret. Counting all earnings, including tax savings (which are major), capital gains (which are often major), fringe benefits from paid expenses, and other factors, the entrepreneur is often much better paid than his or her friend who is well up the ladder in big business. Much more self-sacrifice may be required at first, however, and not everyone can tolerate this.

The Pygmalion Effect

Most people strive to make things come out as they expect they will. There is a term that characterizes this fact as it applies to entrepreneurs and others—the Pygmalion Effect, or the self-fulfilling prophecy. The force of the Pygmalion Effect is important to the success of anyone who owns his own business.

Most readers will remember the myth of Pygmalion, who attempted to create a statue of the perfect woman. He succeeded, and he fell in love with his creation. He was rewarded when his statue came to life.

In George Bernard Shaw's *Pygmalion* which, as most of us know, became the musical hit *My Fair Lady,* Professor Henry Higgins successfully transforms Eliza Doolittle from a flower girl to a woman of breeding. Eliza says to her teacher, ". . . the difference between a lady and a flower girl is not how she behaves, but how she's treated."

Robert Merton of Columbia University describes a bank failure that occurred in 1932 not because the bank was financially unsound but because the depositors *thought* the bank was unsound. They began withdrawing their savings, and the bank failed. Self-fulfilling prophecy!

In a landmark book, the results of a classroom experiment in a San Francisco school district is described in great detail.[4] Teachers were given lists of students in their classes who were known to be gifted. These children were actually chosen at random. However, these chosen students improved markedly in their schoolwork over the students who were not on the list.

A McGraw-Hill film about the Pygmalion Effect suggests that the ultimate self-fulfilling prophecy is demonstrated by nations that prepare for war.

If the Pygmalion Effect is as staggering in its impact as we suspect, it could be used to change our perception of our own world.

What does Pygmalion and the self-fulfilling prophecy mean for the entrepreneur? Everything, we think. If a person about to start or buy his own business can become convinced of his ability to make the venture a success, the chances are that it will. Reaching that emotional and intellectual stage can be accomplished either by one's self or with the help of others. The writing of the business plan is a part of the total process. Reading such books as Eric Berne's *I'm O.K., You're O.K.,* Wayne Dyer's *Erroneous Zones,* and Maxwell Maltz's *Psycho-Cybernetics* is a part of the process, as is formal education in courses and seminars. The preparation process for small-business ownership, then, means more than just learning how to control inventory or how to read financial statements. It also means self-analysis, self-improvement, and nurturing a positive attitude toward success, making it a self-fulfilling prophecy. "Nothing is so good or bad as thinking makes it so."

In Conclusion

Technological change, counter cultural movement, and even *revolution* are phrases that have been used too frequently in discussions about what will happen in the future. Most of us have some difficulty understanding where one starts and the other leaves off. But one thing is fairly certain. It will be the entrepreneurs who will spearhead these changes in our life-styles, our resources, our products and services, and, indeed, our very existences. The large institutions are already showing dangerous signs of decay such as shrinking profit margins, creation of intense dissatisfaction among the working classes and the managerial ranks as well, and the inability to adapt rapidly. The pyramid appears to be buckling, and the structural cracks are rising to the capstone. If the corporation continues to rob its people not only of their basic individual rights to freedom and self-expression, but also of their will to create, then the logical alternative will become small-business ownership by those courageous enough to try it.

---

[4] Rosenthal and Jacobson, *Pygmalion in the Classroom* (Holt, Rinehart and Winston: New York, 1968).

Robert Schwartz, executive director of the Tarrytown House Executive Conference Center, Tarrytown, New York, who is probably the foremost authority on the future role of the entrepreneur in American society, suggests that the entrepreneur is the only work-related individual who can, by and large, satisfy the Buddhist concept of Right Livelihood. In Schwartz's words, this is "the fullest use of one's total self in the pursuit of a noble concept." This also fits Maslow's hierarchy of needs, in which the fifth and most rewarding need is for self-fulfillment, becoming all that we are able to become.

The last analysis of whether an individual becomes an entrepreneur or not has to do with choice. We have all been told that we are free to make choices, even though we don't often feel that way. If we let it happen, we can become overwhelmingly victimized by everyone—the government, our employer, our spouse, and our friends. But free choice is itself the ultimate choice. We can choose choice as a way of life. The major problem is that we have been taught to think that we shouldn't want things that we think are impossible. This is incorrect thinking. We can want and choose things that appear totally unattainable. If we don't get what we want, that isn't failure at all. We just didn't get what we wanted. At least we didn't lie by telling ourselves that we didn't want it anyway. Too many of us play the game of "Yeah, but . . ." to talk ourselves out of what we want.

If you think that having your own business is what you really want, then go to it! Nothing in the world—not money, not assets, not your friends, not your relatives, not your spouse, and not the government—can bring you to a halt if you know that the entrepreneurial life is for you. What *will* stop you is *you*.

Many books that have been written about entrepreneurship and small-business ownership include tests or self-evaluation exercises to help you determine whether or not such a career pattern is where you should be directing your efforts. We did not put such exercises in this book. They aren't needed. The only questions to be answered are, "Do you want to do it? If someone could give it to you, would you take it?"

If so, get started.

Get started now.

CHAPTER TWO

Small Business Defined and Discussed

Business? It's quite simple. It's other people's money.
Alexandre Dumas

Small Business, Big Business

The common belief that small business is nothing like big business is partially true and partially false. The area of commonality is that both the large and the small businesses of this country have the following basic concerns about the functional areas of the enterprise:

Area	*Main Concern*
Technical	How do I remain in business facing an uncertain and rapidly changing future? How must I adapt?
Operations	What problems and opportunities do I see as I convert my raw materials to finished goods that can be sold?
Marketing	How do I attract the maximum number of potential accounts?
Administrative	What must I do in terms of reports, payments, and conformance with the law?
Personnel	How do I find and hold the best people possible?
Financial	Does the return on my investment make all this worth it?

Small businesses and big businesses, then, must ask themselves some of the same questions. The differences between them are differences in scale rather than differences in kind.

But, then, when does an operation become a big business? These are questions that are not easily answered because so many things are relative. Obviously, American Telephone and Telegraph Company, with over one million employees, is a large concern, and junior's lemonade stand is small. General Motors, with annual sales in the area of $50 billion, is large. Is American Motors small? In 1966, the Small Business Administration (SBA) said it was. The point is that the perception of size is relative. The proprietor of a corner grocery store looks on the town's supermarket as large, whereas The Great Atlantic and Pacific Tea Company (A & P) sees that same supermarket as small. Depending upon the industry, the SBA will allow a company to grow to $15 million in annual sales and still be categorized as small for loan purposes. One source has suggested that the line of demarcation between small and large business is 100 persons employed.[1] Depending upon the industry, that would place maximum annual sales at $2–10 million.

After World War II, the Committee for Economic Development stated that for a business to be designated as a small business, it should meet at least two of the following criteria:[2]

1. Management is independent. Usually, the managers are also owners. (This means that the business is not a subsidiary of another company. Also, notice the use of the word *usually;* there are many absentee owners across the country.)
2. Capital is supplied and ownership is held by an individual or a small group. (The current Internal Revenue Service guideline allows a corporation to file as a small business when it meets several criteria, one of which is having less than fifteen stockholders. See Chapter 9 for the definition of a Subchapter S corporation.)
3. The area of operations is mainly local. Workers and owners are in one home community. Markets need not be local.
4. The business is small when compared to the biggest units in its field. The size of the top bracket varies greatly, so that what might seem large in one field would be definitely small in another. (The Lukens Steel plant in Coatesville, Pennsylvania, although physically large, is small compared to Jones and Laughlin, Bethlehem, or U.S. Steel.)

Even the SBA's own definition, taken from the Small Business Act of 1953, needs interpretation. The act states that, to be a small business, the operation must be "one which is independently owned and operated and not dominant in its field of operation." Up until a few years ago, Coors Brewery in Golden, Colorado, would have fit that definition.

Profitability of Small Business

Tables 2.1 and 2.2 show analyses of some types of American business, and their profits. Table 2.2 reveals some very interesting data. Partnerships, on the whole, are about 50 percent as profitable as proprietorships, and corporations are only about 40 percent as profitable. Business size appears to be inversely proportional to profitability. It might be argued that the profit figures for proprietorships and for partnerships do not reflect owners' salaries, but this effect may be offset by two other factors.

First, in many partnerships and proprietorships (more in the latter than in the former) "skimming" takes place. Small-business owners pocket cash that is never reported to the Internal Revenue Service. Some entrepreneurs do not

[1] H. N. Broom and Justin Longenecker, *Small Business Management* (Cincinnati: Southwest Publishing, 1975).
[2] *Meeting the Special Problems of Small Business* (New York: Committee for Economic Development, 1947), p. 14.

TABLE 2.1

Breakdown of United States Business by Legal Form and Receipt Size—1975

Size of Receipts	Proprietorships		Partnerships		Corporations	
	Receipts (billions)	Percent	Receipts (billions)	Percent	Receipts (billions)	Percent
under $25,000	$ 48.3	14.2	$ 4.0	2.7	$ 2.4	0.1
$25,000–$49,999	42.6	12.6	5.1	3.5	5.4	0.2
$50,000–$99,999	59.6	17.6	9.6	6.6	17.1	0.6
$100,000–$199,999	63.4	19.0	16.2	11.1 ⎫	154.7	5.2
$200,000–$499,999	68.2	20.1	27.7	18.9 ⎭		
$500,000–$999,999	26.4	7.8	17.4	11.9	124.9	4.2
$1,000,000 or more	30.7	9.0	66.0	45.4	2,657.2	89.7
TOTAL	$339.2	*	$146.0	*	$2,961.7	*

* Total does not add up to 100 percent because of rounding.
SOURCE: U.S. Department of Commerce, *Statistical Abstract of the United States—1979*, p. 555.

view skimming as a mortal sin. There is, however, a real financial reason not to skim. If you report, and pay taxes on, all revenue, then total revenues of your business will be reflected in the operating statements, and, thus, in the future selling price of your business.

A second observation on Table 2.2 concerns the figures given for corporate profitability. This figure does not reflect dividends yet to be paid to stockholders, in effect, a cost of doing (corporate) business. This cost, too, is a double whammy for the corporation, since dividends are paid *after* profit calculations, and are not a deductible expense.

The comparison between proprietorships and corporations becomes even more startling when one notices that the corporations take in almost ten times

TABLE 2.2

Distribution of United States Businesses by Type—1976 (preliminary)

	Proprietorships	Partnerships	Corporations
Number of Businesses (thousands)	11,358	1,096	2,105
Business Receipts (billions)	$375.0	$157.6	$3,341.7
Net Income (billions)	$ 49.5	$ 10.4	$ 184.8
Percent Net Income to Receipts	13.2	6.6	5.5

SOURCE: U.S. Department of Commerce, *Statistical Abstract of the United States—1979*, p. 553.

as much revenue, but, with it, can produce only about three and one-half times as much profit. In terms of sheer numbers, only about 1 percent of all United States businesses of any type could be classified as big businesses.

Small Business Failure

Businesses fail. That is simply a fact of life. More small businesses fail than large businesses. When a small business becomes insolvent (unable to pay its bills), it must usually cease operation eventually. A large business may weather a temporary storm because of its staying power and its ability to raise additional capital. One rather disappointing factor is that, if a small business has incompetent management, it is very likely to fail. If a large business has the same incompetence, it is likely to be helped out by the government. (Lockheed, Penn Central, and Chrysler are three recent examples.) This appears disappointing to many small-business owners especially when there is an entire governmental agency, SBA, devoted to helping small business. Some entrepreneurs say that the initials SBA stand for "Small Business Annihilators." This attitude is usually sour grapes, however, and not an accurate reflection of the SBA's fine role in small-business support over the years.

Although we will touch again on the process of business failure in Chapter 10, some interesting data from Dun and Bradstreet's study of business failure might be of interest here. Approximately each year, Dun and Bradstreet studies the underlying causes behind the cessation of operation of American businesses. For example, in 1977, 7,919 businesses failed (a 25-year low); the average liability of these firms was nearly $400,000 (with some running into millions). Table 2.3 classifies reasons for these failures.

TABLE 2.3

Classification of Business Failure

Reason for Failure	Percent of Failed Businesses
Management incompetence	44.6
Unbalanced experience	22.6
Lack of management experience	14.6
Lack of experience in particular line	11.3
Neglect	0.9
Disaster	0.5
Fraud	0.4
Unknown	5.1
	100.0

Another breakdown of failures using a different set of reasons than Table 2.3 showed that nearly all of these failures could be ascribed to inadequate sales

(62.3%), competitive weakness in the firm (17.5%), difficulty in collecting receivable accounts (13.5%), and operating expenses that produced a constant loss (19.3%). (The values in parentheses do not total 100% because some failures were attributed to multiple causes.) The remainder can be ascribed to miscellaneous reasons, from bad health to poor location to marital difficulties (only 0.3% for those of you who worry about this) to fire. But the ultimate cause of failure—the final reason that a business ceases operation—is the inability of the business to generate cash.

Factors in Failure

From the Dun and Bradstreet information, from personal experience, and from actual observation we see business failure occurring because one or more of three factors was missing or weak: (1) the Idea, (2) the Money, (3) the Team (which can be one person). Which is the most important? The team. It has been said that good people can succeed with a poor idea, but the reverse is not true. If you have a seminal mind, good business ideas are not hard to come by. Notice that we say *good* ideas. By that, we mean products and services that others will buy and that will yield you a profit. Beware of things like the air-conditioned sauna (although you could probably even sell a few of these). Use good marketing research techniques and listen to people; we were all given two ears and one mouth, and we should use them in that proportion. See the section on new product planning in Chapter 6 for some useful techniques for coming up with ideas for new things to sell.

Good people are harder to find than good ideas. The team is all-important. Good people can find a viable idea, and, if enough honest effort goes behind it, they can find the money to make the idea work, as well.

Businesses that fail are not necessarily bad or unworkable businesses. Unforeseen things can go wrong, a practice may be instituted that the entrepreneur and his or her advisors never knew was wrong, or their attitude may have predicted doom at the outset.

Forty Ways to Fail

It is said that a certain percentage of compulsive gamblers consciously or unconsciously want to lose. If you're an entrepreneur who wants to lose, be sure that you do one or more of the forty things listed below. You'll get your wish beyond your wildest dreams:

1. Don't bother to increase your knowledge about entrepreneurship or small business fundamentals. Ignore the hundreds of courses in small business that are offered at colleges and community colleges all over the country; ignore the many good books on small business; ignore the small business seminars, some of which are listed at the end of this chapter.

2. Don't research the business you are about to start or buy—just plow right in. Damn the torpedoes!

3. If you have partners, don't consult them. If your spouse offers advice forget it. What do they know?

4. Fool everybody—your friends, your partners, your banker, your employees, your suppliers, your customers, your competitors. Most of all, fool yourself.

5. Be sure to accept any financing the bank will give you, even if it's far short of what you really need.

6. Don't write a business plan. Your grandfather didn't, and he made a killing in the alfalfa business.

7. Pay no attention to anyone else—brokers, consultants, relatives, friends, customers, suppliers, lawyers, competitors, accountants, ad agencies, insurance people. In fact, don't use any outside services.

8. Spend like crazy. There's no tomorrow.

9. Don't advertise. People will find you.

10. Overorder. Do everything that the fast-talking salesperson tells you. Shelves look better when they're full, anyway.

11. Since you are invulnerable and indestructible, don't get any kind of insurance.

12. Ignore any outside (usually free) information and data available from governmental bodies, business groups, and professional associations.

13. Don't check for hidden problems, like the old septic tank or the new highway that will bypass your business. As the line from *Jesus Christ, Superstar* says, "Everything is fixed and you can't change it."

14. Get into a business where the market is either glutted or declining. Jump on fads at the end of the demand cycle. Who knows? Pet rocks may yet return.

15. Look on your customers as unknowing fools who can't appreciate a good thing when they see it.

16. Never change, adapt, or alter your venture. As Descartes said, "Everything is known now."

17. Financial statements are meaningless. Don't read them. Better yet, don't even have them prepared.

18. Pay no attention to competitive moves.

19. Treat your employees simply as physical assets of the business. Pay them the minimum wage and don't ever involve them in your decisions. So what if they leave? There's more where they came from.

20. If economic conditions worsen, don't react. The government advisors will tell you the economy is wonderful.

21. Cheat on your income tax. Keep two or more sets of books.

22. Cash registers are expensive. Use a shoe box.

23. Work at a leisurely pace about four hours a day. Take long vacations.

24. Keep a large, ferocious dog right near the front door.

25. Let your equipment fall to rack and ruin. After all, old is quaint. Do business in a condemned building. Forget maintenance.

26. Don't pay your bills on time, especially electricity and telephone.

27. Become a recluse. Don't join the Lions Club or Rotary. Don't donate to deserving charities. Pass up chances to talk to civic groups. Forget trying to get a news article in the local paper; they wouldn't print it anyway.

28. When customers come in or call, be surly and rude. Chew tobacco and smoke Parodi cigars. Spit on the floor. Burp. Baths are for the rich—forget them.
29. Be certain that your physical layout causes the maximum confusion on the part of your customers. Get them lost up blind aisles.
30. In summer, turn on the heat. In winter, open the windows. Play loud music. Have the dog bark a lot.
31. If you buy a going concern, find out all the things that existing customers liked and eliminate them. They probably only cost the previous owner precious money.
32. If credit accounts are overdue, write them off. Don't bother to collect them; it's a waste of time.
33. Constantly be on the lookout for drastic cost-saving measures regardless of their impact. If you run a restaurant, reduce the food portions and switch from butter to oleo. If it's a motel, use the sheets, pillowcases, and towels three or four times over.
34. Be blatantly discriminatory in your selection of employees and your treatment of customers.
35. Don't file legally required reports. Better yet, take your employees' withholding taxes and spend them.
36. Pay no attention to your neighbors. Saw wood at 2 A.M. Dump all kinds of nasty things in the river. Belch black smoke into the air. Pollute!
37. If your employees are attempting to form a union, fight it. Tell them you'll fire everyone connected with organizing.
38. Don't bother to budget cash flow for the future.
39. Do a little bit of everything. If you've got a shoe store, put in a soft–ice cream machine. You'll never know how many people want an ice cream cone while trying to lace up a pair of boots.
40. If a new and exciting opportunity comes your way, don't analyze it.

Well, there are some of our rules and, of course, each one has an exception. But just follow them faithfully, and your wish to fail will be granted marvelously and quickly.

We've had a little fun with our list of don'ts, but it makes a very strong point. The team—whether it's just you alone, you and one other, or you and a whole gang—is the pivotal key to your entire venture. We said earlier in this chapter that it took the team, the idea, and the money. There abide these three, but the greatest of these is the team. To reiterate, if the team is a good one it can find the good idea and raise the money.

Small Business Success

Before embarking, in succeeding chapters, on practical guidance for the adventure of entrepreneurship, we'll consider, in summary, some benefits and headaches of owning your own successful business.

Advantages of Owning Your Own Business

- You set the terms of your own employment.
- In a family business, your family can be fully employed in a family environment.
- You are free to build your business in a manner compatible with your own talents and tastes.
- You will get the fruits of your own hard work; they will not go to a boss or a remote shareholder.
- You will be less vulnerable to outside forces beyond your control such as mergers, layoffs, transfers, firing, mandatory early retirement, poor management beyond your control, or company politics.
- If you are truly successful, you have the opportunity to earn more money than you can as an employee.
- When you have the business operating well, you can choose your own time off.
- You will experience business from a very broad viewpoint. You will no longer be involved in a single specialty.
- A successful business is an exceptionally good tax shelter, probably the best legal one in existence. You will have the benefit of depreciation shelter, and, when the business can afford it, pretax payments for life insurance, medical care, pension fund, travel and entertainment, auto expense. If you have living quarters in the business property, a substantial portion of your living expenses can be used as a business expense.
- You will have the opportunity for large financial gains if you build the business competently.
- You will have the status and respect due a successful entrepreneur.
- Most of all, the business will become a reflection of you, not the lengthening shadow of some other person.

Disadvantages of Owning Your Own Business

- Usually, you will have to work harder and longer hours than you would as an employee.
- If you fail, it will probably wipe you out financially.
- You will have to spend a great deal of time learning about every facet of business management and the science of your field of business if you want to be successful.
- You will probably have to make sacrifices in your living standards until you are through the survival period.
- If you make a bad mistake, you will have to pay for it.
- You will not have the backing of the large amounts of money involved in a corporation. If you find you are undercapitalized, it will be very difficult to raise funds.
- Your business will have to come first, at least until you are out of the survival stage, which may last years.

- You will have to attune yourself to the marketplace. If you are not the kind of person who can adjust willingly to other people's needs, even when you don't especially like them, don't even consider being in business for yourself.
- For a period of time, you may have to give up many forms of security provided by corporate employers (medical-hospital plans, retirement, vacation pay, expense accounts), at least until your own business can pay for them.
- If your family life is weak, the responsibilities of your business will put an additional strain on it. Your family must willingly and actively support you.

Small Business Seminars

For seminars available for entrepreneurs, contact the following individuals:

Donald M. Dible
The Entrepreneur's Press
4422 Fairfield Circle
Santa Clara, CA 95051

James S. Howard
Country Business Services
12 Linden Street
Brattleboro, VT 05301

Joseph R. Mancuso, Ph.D.
Center for Entrepreneurial Mgt.
American Management Association
311 Main St.
Worcester, MA 01608

Robert L. Schwartz
The School for Entrepreneurs
Tarrytown House
East Sunnyside Lane
Tarrytown, NY 10591

Each of these seminars has a slightly different emphasis, cost, content, and length, but all are excellent and will be worth much more than the expense to you and your business. Write to each one asking for the basic information, available dates, and meeting places before you enroll.

CHAPTER THREE

Preparing for Business Ownership

Those who can, can and will. Those who can't, can't and won't.

Virgil

An old Chinese proverb says that a journey of a thousand miles begins with a single step. The single step is your decision to become an entrepreneur, and can be taken at any stage in life. Some latent entrepreneurs don't bloom until their seventies, whereas, with others, the operation of their first lemonade stand triggers the decision never to work for anyone else except for pure survival. By the way, don't discount working for a large company before starting or buying your own venture. But, while you work, do the following:

1. Save every dollar you can. If possible, live on half what you make.
2. Observe everything that your employer does. Make notes. Keep the useful, discard the wasteful and silly.
3. Constantly learn about small business. Read this book and others. Attend seminars. Take a course in small business management. Visit the SBA office in your state. Talk to entrepreneurs.
4. Any time that you get an idea about a venture, write it down. Think about what you like to do. Is there a viable business idea there?
5. Make all the personal contacts that you can. Catalog people that can help you. Keep an especially sharp eye out for people you might want as partners or employees.

Use all your spare time working for yourself. Many people are able to start their ventures on a part-time basis while still using a large employer to provide their daily bread. This is an excellent way to start, because the basic business idea can be tried with minimum financing and risk, and the switchover is usually easy.

You can also buy a going concern, but know the risks. To be most successful you should devote full time when you buy an existing operation; absentee ownership is dangerous.

Targeting Where to Operate and the Business to Enter

Location

One important consideration for operating a small business is its location. You have three areas to consider, urban, suburban, and rural.

An *urban* location has one major advantage over the other two, and that is traffic. It is a pure fact of life that the maximum density of people per square mile occurs in the cities. This means more business and more money. We think, however, that the city is not the place to go. Many downtown businesses are robbed more than once a year, and the police either don't care or are helpless because of the amount of work they have to do in a day. A store in a city may have a nearly impossible task in getting vandalism insurance. Taxes are atrocious and getting worse. Air, water, and noise pollution take a daily toll. On top of all this, consider the fact that cities depersonalize the people who live and work there. This means that not many of your clients will have winning personalities, and you will have to deal with them, day in, day out, for life. Some cities have begun to change, however, and you should not use what we say as an absolute rule.

The second area to consider is *suburban,* and that ordinarily means the shopping center. You usually lease the facility in which you operate. Certain covenants are put upon you by the leaseholder, which can restrict your flexibility. On the other hand, traffic is high, and most suburban centers are located near or within relatively affluent areas. Residents are earning well above a subsistence wage, have a high net disposable income, and are impulse buyers. The purchase of a $100 or $200 item is relatively easy for them. It is in such areas that an elegant restaurant, a fine gift store, or a home electronics center (including a mini-computer store) can flourish. Expect competition, however.

The third location is the *rural* or country setting. There are drawbacks to be sure, such as antiquated septic systems, town ordinances, and the lack of cultural activities, but we think the quiet and clean air more than make up for the disadvantages. In the country the business can really become *you,* and the relative absence of some restrictions and regulations means businesses can reflect more completely the image of the owner. There is more freedom. The wayside inn, the country gift shop, and the general store are all ways for total fulfillment without the hassles of the city. The country life is, in most respects, a heck of a lot of fun living.

Your Attitudes and Desires

Once the general location has been selected, if you haven't already done so, list five businesses that you'd like to enter. Then select and list five businesses that you wouldn't want to own. These lists should begin to narrow your choices. What kinds of businesses dominated the positive and negative list? Goods? Services? One interesting fact is that services (consulting, chimney-sweeping, home improvement, lawn care) will grow more rapidly than goods (food, shoes, hardware). The reason for this has to do with an increasing demand by American consumers for services of many different kinds.

Prerequisites

Now look at the first business that you put under the ones that you'd like to enter. The chances are that it is really your first choice. If it isn't, select the one from the list that most interests you and answer the question, What do I need to enter this business? (The answers can be anything that makes sense to you, from money of a certain amount, to a skill that you now don't possess, to a unique location.) Then, consulting the above list of answers, write down the obstacles to entering this business. Once you have delineated these factors, you can begin working on what you need to solve to start or buy your own business.

Pitfalls

Before starting any new venture, answer the question, "Why hasn't anyone done this before"? There may be a very good reason why no one has done what you plan to do and it may be sufficient to put you out of business quickly. Some of these reasons could be:

Geography. Beware of locating in areas with high unemployment and low disposable income. Beware of the local sentiment; an X-rated moviehouse wouldn't last long in the heart of Amish and Mennonite country in Pennsylvania. Beware of pure errors in judgment; you wouldn't sell many ski parkas in Key West, Florida.

Location. It might be just lovely to open an inn on a quiet, little-traveled country road, but, unless you have a four-star rating from Duncan Hines, forget it. People won't seek you out.

Competition. The market may be well serviced by existing firms. There are numbers available from the government of the approximate resident population that you need to support any type of business. Of course, tourist businesses depend more on traffic count. Analyze existing competition carefully.

Fads. We Americans are addicted to fads and rapid change. When we discover a song that we all like, our radio stations favor us by playing the song every twenty minutes until we can't stand to hear it anymore. If you plan to cash in on a fad (discos, restaurants constructed from old railroad rolling stock and memorabilia, "head" shops), be ready to change quickly.

Capital Required. We have a rule for entrepreneurs to follow when they plan their cash needs. First, figure every item in that you can and be as accurate as your best estimates will allow. Then double the amount. Then double it again. It's always going to be more than you thought. Sometimes the capital needed to get into a business doesn't justify it. Every five years or so, someone, somewhere tries to get into the automobile business. It's always a big flash, a bunch of people get suckered out of their money, a few models get sold, and the company folds. It would probably take at least $2 billion to launch a profitable car company, and then you'd still be behind American Motors, which struggles to survive. It doesn't make any sense, but it happens.

Economic Conditions. Learn to interpret the economic state of things. Buy and read the *Wall Street Journal.* We know people that have started businesses during recessions and succeeded, but it's difficult.

One valuable exercise to play before starting your venture is the "what if" game. Assume that Murphy's Law will hold—"If anything can go wrong, it will." And remember O'Brien's Law, "Murphy is an optimist."

Starting Your Own Business

Starting your own business is the height of entrepreneuring. A new venture springs up every day. It can be the local corner gift shop or it can be the next Federal Express. Starting your own business means taking an idea and creating something where there was nothing before. Of course, it is also the riskiest way to go. There is no certain way to know whether a new venture will make it or not. Whims of the buying public, local laws, competition, all can work against the new enterprise. The business can be poorly timed, too bizarre, out of step with the area (what works in Des Moines may not go in Manhattan and vice versa), and the wrong business for the right reasons. And then, on top of everything else, some completely unforeseen factor can come out of nowhere and put the business under. A true story bears re-telling. We are all familiar with Ralph Waldo Emerson's maxim, "If a man makes a better mousetrap, the world will beat a path to his door." It ain't necessarily so since it assumes

1. That there is a need for a different kind of mousetrap.
2. That catching mice is, in and of itself, a desirable thing.
3. That alternative procedures—cat, poison, and anti-mouse programs are ineffective.

The Woodstream Corporation of Lititz, Pennsylvania undertook to build the better mousetrap. The device was marvelous! It caught every mouse who had the unfortunate experience of wandering close to the trap. So the company sent out samples of the new twenty-five-cent trap and waited for the orders to roll in. No orders. Why? The reason was basically quite simple. The company had spent a great deal of research time on the habits of mice but not much on the lifestyle of the American consumer. It's always easy to use hindsight (which has 20-20 vision), but here's the basic scenario:

1. In the typical American household, who sets the mousetrap?
   Answer: The wife
2. What do American housewives hate?
   Answer: Mice

3. What do American housewives hate worse than mice?
   Answer: Dead mice.
4. What does this mean in relation to the American mousetrap market?
   Answer: That the housewife, upon finding the dead mouse in the trap throws out
   the mouse while still in the trap.

The company found out (too late) that their twenty-five-cent trap could not compete with the two-for-fifteen-cents trap that people could throw away, mouse and all.

The lesson to be learned is: Spend lots of time researching your market before starting your own venture from scratch. Be certain that the market can bear your product or service. Be certain that you can react to change.

The one nice thing about starting your own business is the total independence that you are allowed. You can dream up the name, pick the location, hire who you want. Since there is no past equity, you do not have to worry about losing any.

Buying a Going Concern

Buying a going concern has many distinct advantages. The major one is that there is a track record. The business has been in operation for a period of time, and it is possible to determine at least its present profitability. It's a little less enterprising than starting something on your own, but, on the other hand, there is less risk involved and you can change the character of the business to suit your own needs.

One very nice advantage of buying a going concern is that the owner(s) will often stay on after the sale to help in training. Even if you have to pay a consulting fee, it is well worth it. Also, if you have narrowed your choice of types of businesses (small manufacturing, hospitality, hardware store) you can visit a number of them and make comparisons.

Before you get serious, consider the *right* way to buy a business outlined as follows:

> *Make certain you are prepared to leave your present situation.* Before you go to the time and expense of trying to find a business, think carefully whether you would be better off if you made a greater effort to improve the situation where you now live. Perhaps, with a much smaller risk, you can make a job change or alter your personal situation to solve problems that are troubling you. Do not hide your discontent with a long business search that is really an excuse for not taking steps that you should be taking. This is a very common psychological ploy. Avoiding problems that can be solved by straightforward action is never a good idea. If you can't make difficult decisions now, you will not be able to make them when you own your own business.
>
> *Be sure your motivation is right.* If you do not have a basic motivation to run your own show, you probably should not own your own business. Equally important,

how does your wife or husband feel about it? Is there general agreement in your family that you should take this step? If not, talk it over more and try to get together on what you really want.

Learn about the business you are interested in. Take a course in the type of business you want to enter if you don't have specific experience. Get some books from the library. Write the SBA. If you have made no effort to learn about a business you want to enter, you are probably fooling yourself about really wanting to do it. Serious people often take night courses, correspondence courses, get a part-time job, talk with people already in the business, and do anything possible to gain some knowledge and experience. If you haven't done any of this, it is a sign you are not ready or that you are fooling yourself.

If you use a business broker, work with experienced brokers only. It is always a good idea to check bank references of a broker that you contemplate dealing with. Does the broker work exclusively in businesses and related properties? It is unlikely that any broker who splits his time among businesses, commercial properties, and residential properties can effectively help you. Do not hesitate to ask a broker for the names of people he or she has sold businesses to. Do not hesitate to ask those people their opinion of the broker involved. Once you have decided that a broker is reliable, place your confidence in him or her. No broker can be expected to help you unless he has financial data on your capabilities and knows your work or professional background. Do not expect to play games with the broker. There is such an intense demand for businesses that this will simply turn him off. If it doesn't, he probably isn't worth working with.

Start with a business conference. A business conference with your broker is the first step. This permits a relaxed exchange of ideas and opinions. Expect a good broker to be forthright about his opinions. A broker can often add insight. This type of personal acquaintance with your broker is important. If there is mutual feeling of trust and understanding, he will give you his support.

Expect to devote the required time to finding what you want. Once a broker is convinced that a buyer is serious, he will spend a good deal of time with you. Brokers are usually not impressed with people who repeatedly ask for volumes of information and never bother to make a trip to see properties. They are glad to give you the full resources of their organization, but only when you take the time and effort to use them properly.

Inquire about sales prices of comparable properties. A broker should be happy to review with you, on a confidential basis, the sales histories of comparable properties. They will point out significant comparisons and where adjustments should be made. Where possible, meet people who have recently purchased the type of business you are interested in. Their experiences will be meaningful. One purpose of this is to help you recognize an overpriced property and a well-priced property no matter where you see it. It is very common to hear months later the regrets of someone who passed up what he wanted because he couldn't see that it was advantageously priced.

Look for a property you "feel" right about. That may sound unbusinesslike, but it is important. Before you do the work required to find out whether something will produce the financial results you want, find out if you and your family feel good about it. One of your motivations for moving is to find a better life-style than you have now. You will be working terribly hard, so be sure you can do it in an enjoyable environment.

Find out if it will accomplish your financial goals. You can easily make a preliminary investigation into the financial feasibility of a business you are seriously interested in. A good broker will help you do this. Eventually you will have to do a detailed feasibility study if you want to be certain, but at this point you are working with preliminary data to see if you should go to the time and expense of a feasibility study. It is always a mistake to go 100% on the basis of past operating statements. There are many reasons for this. Small businesses are virtually always run for the tax benefit of the owner. There may be several sources of income buried in an income account. These include owner's salary, reported profits, depreciation (or at least a portion of depreciation), and living expenses. Interest rates must be adjusted to your basis. Operating conditions will change when you acquire the business, and so will a hundred other things. Of course, it is of interest to know how the past owners did, but it means little when you are the one who has to live on income from the business. Every good broker is experienced in making such adjustments.

Draw up a letter of intent. When you know that you are working with a property you like and that it probably will do what you want financially, there are still many unsolved problems. These include legal questions such as purity of title and market questions such as possible future competitive changes. (Is a Holiday Inn going next door to your twenty-unit motor inn?) The answer to these is that you draw up a letter of intent. This document passes between the buyer and the seller. A letter of intent says to the broker and the seller that you will purchase the property at a stated price and terms if certain stated conditions are satisfied. One such condition is obtaining a commitment for your financing. Another is usually agreement on the terms of a Purchase and Sale Agreement on both sides. Another may be the completion of a feasibility study that shows the property will support you. There may be still others. A letter of intent should never be used to take a property off the market while you make up your mind. It should only be done to accomplish the purposes stated. It should last for a specified period of time while these questions are cleared up. Usually, a relatively small deposit is given with signing of a letter of intent—from one to five thousand dollars. This is returnable to you without penalty if the questions are not resolved.

Obtain competent advice. After the preliminaries are completed, you begin spending money. You should retain an attorney skilled in business matters and an accountant who can help you structure the contract and examine and verify past figures. You may want to obtain a special consultant who can prepare a complete feasibility study, up to and including interviews and market profiles, study of competitive properties, analysis of pertinent census data, study of traffic counts, and preparation of one- to three-year forecasts, based on the assumptions you give him. The size of the fees will depend on the size and complexity of the transaction. The total can easily amount to $5,000, and it will be more on a larger transaction. In so many cases, early entrepreneurs turn pale when someone mentions spending $5,000 for a consulting study. Consider, however, this actual statement from an entrepreneur who nearly lost his business: "If I had spent $5,000 two years ago, it would have saved me $50,000 last year." It is the attorney's job to prepare the final Purchase and Sale Agreement. It is both the attorney's and the accountant's job to analyze the tax and financial position to see that the final deal is good for all parties. Often the structure of a transaction can severely affect the tax position of the buyer or seller. We will not go into such ramifications here. But every buyer should be aware that it is vitally important to get top-flight help.

Shop for financing. You will want to get the best available financing. Often, there will be partial or full financing from the seller, and the terms offered can be as important as the price. Usually, however, bank financing will be needed. Brokers can help extensively with this, even up to virtually packaging the financing. Unless you are skilled at such matters, rely on assistance. Brokers know how to package an application, how to approach banks, and what to ask for. Some markets are competitive, and you can apply to several banks and shop for rate and terms. In other markets, you go to one bank at a time and take what you can get. Sometimes mortgage brokers can help with out-of-state or private lenders who can give better terms. This will involve paying *points,* but the net package can be to your advantage. You will want to have financing secured before the final contract is signed. If it isn't, you will want a contingency in the contract which protects you in case you can't get needed financing. This clause will last for a specified number of days.

Use a final contract. Both the letter of intent and the final contract will often involve much negotiating. While you will govern what is offered, expect the broker to do the actual negotiating. A good broker is very skilled at this. Never attempt to deal directly, since it is both unethical and dangerous, except with the consent of the broker. Trying to do so almost inevitably ends up with your losing the negotiating position you have. The broker's motivation is to achieve agreement. He should also be responsible enough to see that both parties are fairly and realistically dealt with. If you have started with a letter of intent, the final contract will usually be easy, since the difficult part of the negotiating has already been done. But there are always many important details on which agreement must be reached. Some of these will have important long- and short-term tax consequences.

Prepare for closing. If everything above has been well done, closing the sale will be virtually an anticlimax. Just before closing, inventory (if there is one) will be taken. That is always a nuisance, but it must be done. At closing, dozens of documents will be signed, much money will change hands, the broker will be delighted, and you will depart as a new business owner. That's when the fun starts!

Pricing a Going Business

Putting a price on a business is often a difficult task indeed.[1] Very often, the seller has an inflated idea of what the business is worth. He or she (or they) may have spent years building the enterprise and may feel that all this effort is worth some financial return. Rightly so. But, as we will show later, when you buy a going concern, you are usually getting a bargain. You actually spend

[1] For a very complete treatment of the subject, see James S. Howard, *The Business Appraisal Workbook* (Portsmouth, NH: Upstart Publishing, 1980).

```
                        INCOME STATEMENT
                              OF
                         XYZ BUSINESS

              for the year ending December 31, 19XX


    Net sales                                    $100,000

       Cost of goods sold
          Inventory January 1      $10,000
          Purchases                 40,000
          Goods available          $50,000
          Inventory December 31     15,000

             Cost of goods sold                    35,000
    Gross margin                                  $ 65,000


    Expenses

          Rent                     $ 6,000
          Wages                     17,000
          Supplies                   2,000
          Advertising                1,000
          Insurance                  1,000
          Delivery cost              2,000
          Depreciation               1,700
          Taxes paid                 1,000
          Utilities                  2,000
          Maintenance                1,000
          Miscellaneous              3,000

             Total expenses                      $ 37,700


    Net profit                                   $ 27,300



    Note:  Owner took $18,000 for himself.
```

Figure 3.1 *Income Statement of a Hypothetical Business*

```
                    BALANCE SHEET
                         OF
                    XYZ BUSINESS

              as of December 31, 19XX


Current assets                      Current liabilities

    Cash                 $ 3,000        Accounts payable      $1,500
    Accounts receivable    5,700        Notes payable          1,000
    Inventory             15,000        Other accruals         2,000
                         _____                            _____

    Total current assets $23,700        Total current         $4,500
                                          liabilities


Fixed assets                        Fixed liabilities

    Equipment and Fixtures $18,200       Long-term debt        $5,000
    Depreciation           (1,000)       Total liabilities     $9,500
    Truck                   4,900
    Depreciation           (1,500)       Net worth
Total fixed assets        $20,600          proprietorship     $34,800

                         _____                            _____


Total assets             $44,300     Liability and net worth $44,300
```

Figure 3.2 *Balance Sheet of a Hypothetical Business*

much less to buy an operating business than to start one, even considering the salary paid to yourself and the profits.

Figures 3.1 and 3.2 present the financial statements of a hypothetical business. (If you are unfamiliar with either the terms or the construction of these statements, turn to Chapter 7.) Assume that you are interested in the XYZ Business as a purchase and wish to find a fair price. The simplest method is to get an independent, objective appraisal of the business. Good appraisers do this all the time, and they have developed methods for it. Be certain, though, that the appraiser has experience in business, not just residential, property.

In working with business appraisals, here are some areas to watch out for.

An appraiser, in many states, does not have to be licensed. Therefore, you stand the risk of reading a report that has no professional basis for its findings. Most appraisers, however, have wide experience in business and real estate, and their analysis is the best that can be had. Beware of appraisals done by banks and appraisals done by real estate agents. In most cases, neither has had any business experience. Thus, they can only look at land and buildings. Their estimate of the "business" portion can be significantly different from its actual value. (In our example, the XYZ Business, there is no real estate to be considered—see the balance sheet under Fixed Assets.)

The most obvious way to purchase a business is simply to buy the assets. If you and a buyer decide that is the best way to go, you have three prices that might be established as a starting point: (1) Assets as shown on the balance sheet; (2) Assets at replacement value; (3) Net assets (owner's equity).

The first item, total assets, would be the $44,300 shown as the last line in Figure 3.2. This price is easy to compute and is logical from the standpoint that actual things of value are changing hands. For one thing, you will receive title to a checking account that has $3000 in cash on deposit. Not all of the accounts receivable will be collectible (some will be bad debts), but most will.

Pricing the business by calculating assets at replacement value will add back into the sale price the depreciation of $2500 ($1000 plus $1500), resulting in a sale price of $46,800. Naturally, the seller would opt for this method, as it yields a higher price for the business.

If "going concern value," or earning power, or "goodwill" is not going to enter into the price negotiation process, then the third pricing method, calculation of net assets, is the fairest of all. This method takes into account the fact that when you take over the business, you not only own the assets, but you assume the liabilities as well. In this example, the current (short-term) liabilities as well as the long-term debt ($4500 plus $5000), when subtracted from the total assets, yield the value of the *net* assets, or the net worth, of $34,800.

These pricing methods are practical from an accounting standpoint, but fail to reflect either the earning power of the business or the sweat and toil of the owner that resulted in an enterprise that has enduring value. This extra factor has been termed goodwill, but we would just as soon see this term retired along with single-entry bookkeeping. Three methods of pricing that deal with the earning power of the business are: (1) "Times earnings"; (2) Bank of America scheme; (3) Going concern value.

The "times earnings" approach has long been used by major corporations when they are considering acquiring a small company. They examine the accounting profit of the firm in question and then try to estimate a number, expressed in years, that they would use to multiply by the net profit to arrive at the purchase price. The problem here is selecting the appropriate multiplier. The seller wants it as high as possible (rarely above 8) and the buyer wants it as low as possible (never below 2). In the example shown in Figure 3.1 we must first "back out" (subtract) the owner's salary of $18,000 from the total net profit of $27,300 to arrive at the actual (not taxable) profit of $9300. If we use an average multiplier of 5, the sale price would be (5 × $9300) $46,500.

The Bank of America, headquartered in San Francisco, has long had a dedicated interest in small business. They developed a pricing scheme which seems to work pretty well. Refer to Figure 3.3. In line 1, we take the net worth of XYZ at $34,800 and in line 2 we take the annual earning power at some appropriate percentage—in this case 10%. To this we add the annual salary of the owner, $18,000 resulting in a total of $20,660 on line 3a. In line 4, we enter the total taxable income of $27,300, and subtract the value on line 3a, giving the net earning power of $6640 on line 5. (Notice that we could have arrived at the same figure by subtracting the earning power of $2660 from the "real" profit of $9,300.) Now we must try to estimate the appropriate time frame over which to schedule the intangible of earning power or goodwill. Here again, this is open to interpretation, but the usual range is one-to-three years. We have chosen two years in this case, resulting in a value of (2 × $6640) $13,280. This is added to the net worth, giving a sales price of $48,080.

The final pricing method to be discussed is our favorite: calculating the *going-concern-value*. This method reflects some of the costs of building the business to a saleable state.

"Going concern value" (GCV) is not so much a way of actually setting a price on a business as it is a way of analyzing a particular asking price to determine whether or not that price is a fair one as compared to what it would take to re-establish the business from a start-up situation. GCV is an intangible, like "goodwill." The term goodwill is an accounting category only; one expert (Robert Townsend) calls it "capitalized crap," and in most cases it is little else, especially in the big companies who load up this asset account with things like patent development expense. (Don't ever let patents fool you. Most realists will tell you that a patent has no value until it is tried in court.) In reality, however, a business does have a dollar value connected with the fact that certain things the business has developed have value beyond what can be seen on the balance sheet: a particular customer's loyalty; the name of the business (which may or may not be yours to keep); a long-term sales contract with a valued customer;

1. Tangible net worth $34,800

2. Earning power at 10% $ 2,660

3. Salary for owner   18,000

3a. Total $20,660

4. Annual net profit (gross)   27,300

5. Earning power
    (line 4 - line 3a) $ 6,640

6. Value of intangibles using
    a 2 year basis   13,280
    (2 x line 5)

7. Price (line 1 + line 6) $48,080

Figure 3.3 *Bank of America Pricing Scheme*

supplier terms which may go beyond normal arrangements granted other customers. These are GCV. They all have value, but the value is impossible to establish from an accounting standpoint.

If an unsophisticated business owner tries to sell you a business, he or she (or they) will talk about this elusive intangible called GCV or goodwill. Remember two things: No one can set a monetary value on this, and you may get yourself into an awkward tax situation regarding any payment for this will-o'-the-wisp. But, on the opposite hand, there is some GCV created by the very fact that the business has been in operation, even if the operation shows an accounting loss!

Let's look at an actual example of GCV that occurred in the real world. A restaurant was for sale for $375,000. It could very easily be projected that the next year's profit on its gross sales (and we don't even need that value) would be $100,000 based upon past history, expected growth in dollar volume, and the reputation of the restaurant itself. The present owner invested $225,000 in land, building, equipment, advertising to get the business started. In his first year of operation, he showed a loss of $20,000. In the second year, he showed a profit of $35,000, and, in the third, a profit of $60,000. After the sale was consummated at $375,000, he would realize a net cash price to him of $335,000, subtracting broker's fees, legal expenses, and miscellaneous taxes.

The owner's flow of investment and earnings are as follows:

Initial cost	$(225,000)
Year 1	(20,000)
Year 2	35,000
Year 3	60,000
Final sale	335,000
Net	$ 185,000

For all his efforts, he would realize a "profit" of $185,000. (Note: We fully understand, for the knowledgeable reader, that we did not do a Discounted Cash Flow (DCF). The subject is treated in Chapter 7, Financing.)

Now, suppose that the owner, instead of starting the business, had acquired it at its present condition of profitability and growth. The price of the business is $375,000, and we will assume that profit increases the next year to $100,000 and then stays constant for the next two years. We will make the outlandish assumption that he sells the business for exactly what he paid for it and experiences the same selling net return of $335,000. The income flow would then be as follows:

Initial cost	$(375,000)
Year 1	100,000
Year 2	100,000
Year 3	100,000
Final sale	335,000
Net	$ 260,000

Thus, by doing nothing other than caretaking the business, he would have made $75,000 more ($260,000 − $185,000) by buying a comparable going business than by starting one. And the risks are much less in taking over an enterprise that has an established track record than in starting one from scratch. Buying a going concern, therefore, you normally benefit from the previous owner in ways that can't be calculated from either the income statement or the balance sheet.

The $75,000 can be thought of as the GCV of the business and all, or part, or none of it may wind up being negotiated as a part of the purchase price.

Franchising

We regard franchise owners as sort of half-entrepreneurs, but they are entrepreneurs nonetheless. They desire business ownership but want the security of an established business. Franchising is a way to enter small business ownership and, at the same time, to minimize the risks of starting a business.

A *franchise* is a legal relationship between the national organization itself (the franchisor) and the owner of the establishment (the franchisee). The franchisee has the right to use the name and products of the business (McDonald's, Kentucky Fried Chicken, Midas Muffler, Texaco, Pizza Hut), and, in return, agrees to conduct the business along certain guidelines and to meet the requirements of the franchisor. (You can't paint a Howard Johnson's roof green.) The legal relationship is expressed in a contract between the parties spelling out the terms and conditions of the franchise agreement.

The Franchise

The franchisor agrees to let the franchisee operate as a privately owned and operated business (meaning that the franchisee hires the help, pays the utility bill, pays local taxes) with the benefit of the use of the name, trademarks, and logos of the franchisor. In many cases, the franchisee agrees to purchase supplies from the franchisor. This is usually to the franchisee's advantage since he can take advantage of the national purchasing power of the franchisor.

The Expenses and the Fee

The contract spells out the fee, usually a one-time payment, that is to be paid by the franchisee to acquire the franchise. McDonald's Corporation estimates that it costs a franchisee about $250,000 to open one of their restaurants. The franchise fee is $12,500, and the balance goes to cover the actual assets of the facility. McDonald's now requires a cash payment of from $105,000 to $125,000 down, and there is a waiting list of applicants. Although a quarter of a million dollars seems like a lot of money, the average McDonald's that has been open for at least thirteen months grosses about one million, and nets the owner in the neighborhood of $75,000 to $100,000 per year.

Franchisors naturally prefer to have the franchise fee paid in a lump before the operation opens its doors, but, in many cases, franchisors will aid in new-owner financing. In the case of newer, untried franchises, any potential buyer should thoroughly investigate the fee and what he will get for it. Plenty of people have lost their nest eggs pursuing phony or shaky franchise deals.

The Royalties

In addition to having to purchase goods and supplies from the franchisor, the franchisee may also be expected to pay a certain royalty fee. In the case of McDonald's, this amounts to 11.5 percent of monthly gross sales. A portion of the royalty goes to support McDonald's local and national advertising program. Therefore, this expense has a direct, traceable benefit for the franchise owner.

Training and Support

Any good, reputable franchisor will want to provide training to assure success on the part of the new owner. A McDonald's franchisee attends Hamburger University for two weeks of intensive training and schooling and then receives a comprehensive operations manual that is so complete it even spells out how often to empty the wastebaskets. (The manual supposedly states, "When they're full.") Later on, the franchisee can call upon various personnel within McDonald's for continued support and can elect to attend the post-graduate course.

Exclusivity

Nearly all franchisors will grant an exclusive territory to a franchisee, defined either in terms of geography (a town or a county) or population. McDonald's will grant an exclusive franchise for a minimum population of 25,000.

Franchising is here to stay. It has been estimated that it now contributes 10 percent of our Gross National Product. Anyone seriously considering a non-proven franchise should read Dias and Gurnick's book, *Franchising: The Investor's Complete Handbook* (Hastings House: New York, 1969), which has an excellent checklist on pages 38–41. As an absolute minimum effort, anyone considering buying a franchise should do the following:

a. Visit existing franchisees to determine the viability of their operations.
b. View the business as an entrepreneur. Does the idea make good sense now and for the future?

   c. Check with such organizations as the Chamber of Commerce and the Better Business Bureau to see if any complaints have been lodged against existing operations.

   d. Visit the franchisor's headquarters. If there is none, forget the deal.

   e. Have a lawyer review any contract for legal implications. (NOTE: Be very careful about opinions rendered by a lawyer regarding the business as a business. If you want that kind of opinion, pay a consultant. Lawyers tend to be overly cautious.)

   f. Be sure that nothing is left unresolved before signing the contract.

One final caveat. Somewhere, sometime, someone is going to erect the very last fast-food restaurant because only so many pasty hamburgers and spicy chicken wings can be consumed by the 225,000,000 or so Americans. Don't you be that someone.

Starting a Cottage Industry

Many entrepreneurs simply do not have and cannot raise sufficient capital to start a business as a full-time venture. One possibility is to start a *cottage industry,* a very small, part-time business, and then allow the business to grow as time and cash flow will allow. As the venture grows to self-sufficiency, the entrepreneur can choose to run it full-time, or he can hire someone to run it (possibly a member of the family) or he can even sell it. One entrepreneur we know runs a small market and decided to offer sandwiches made on the premises to shoppers. In several weeks, the market down the street asked to buy a supply of wrapped sandwiches. This snowballed. In three years, the sandwich operation was grossing $300,000 and earning a handsome profit.

Starting as a cottage industry has some distinct advantages over starting a normal business. Since growth is financed strictly with owner capital and cash flow, no debt is created. The risk factor involved with a business failure and the subsequent financial loss is minimized; and changes can be made quickly and easily.

Mental and Physical Requirements of Business Ownership

The physical requirements in small business ownership can be substantial. If you want to save money and you don't detest doing it, you will want to take care of many of the repairs to the physical plant yourself. This requires various skills (carpentry, plumbing, wiring) which can drain energy and wear you down. If you are a person who needs ten or twelve hours of sleep a night, then the rigors of small business operation are probably not for you. The more successful entrepreneurs, especially in the early years, work very long hours, sometimes from seven in the morning until nine at night, seven days a week. One thing to remember is that, even though eight hours in your Manhattan office may totally exhaust you and make you unable to do anything but gulp four martinis, fourteen hours in your own business may simply be fun. You don't have all the worries about superiors, colleagues, and subordinates. There are no games to be played and there are no politics. But if you are inherently lazy (and you know whether you are or not), don't try your own business.

The mental requirements are more complicated but are part of one all-encompassing characteristic—the possession of a *right attitude*. In Chapter 1, we talked about some of the qualities that successful entrepreneurs possess and, in the end of that chapter, we discussed motivation and the Pygmalion effect, or the self-fulfilling prophecy. The right attitude is as much a part of the self-motivation process as the business plan that creates the physical vehicle of expression for the self-fulfilling prophecy. This self-motivation, an inwardly directed process, has something to do with what Timmons calls the "internal locus of control" or, more simply, internalization.[2] There is a maxim (borrowed from Dick Gariepy of Motivation Associates Inc.) that says, "All individuals are self-made; only the successful admit it." Before you start or buy a business, you must have total confidence in yourself that you can bring it off. Why not? After all, millions of others have done it before you. Furthermore, don't forget choice. If you want it, you want it. Never mind how you will get it, and, whatever you do, don't start analyzing why you want it.

Another thing to keep in mind is that, even if you fail miserably, all you will lose is money—and maybe it won't be all yours. There are no more debtor's prisons, and no one can sell your mother or your children into slavery. By all means run your business as a business, but don't take yourself too seriously. Don't underestimate the value of having a sense of humor and being able to laugh at yourself when you do something silly.

Sources of Information and Help

There are many sources that entrepreneurs can consult for help. Some are one-time contacts, others are continuing. Some are free; some will cost you money. Some you will find invaluable; others may be worthless or even harmful. Since good entrepreneurs use available data well, this information-gathering is critical to your success. Research should be done well in advance of joining the entrepreneurial ranks. If you are working for (being subsidized by) a large concern, you can use days off and weekends to build your data file. If you consult a source verbally, make a sales report. Write it or dictate it onto a cassette tape as soon as the call is over, when things are freshest in your mind. The more sources you consult, the better your knowledge.

[2] Jeffery Timmons, Leonard Smollen, and Alexander Dingee. *New Venture Creation* (Homewood, Ill.: Richard D. Irwin, 1977).

One other item to consider—don't assume that people are reluctant to talk with you. That's far from the truth. People will often feel flattered that you consider them experts.

Small Business Administration (SBA)

The SBA was chartered by Congress in 1953 specifically to aid small businesses (see Chapter 2 for more discussion). The SBA should be the first of your field visits. A list of all SBA offices is in Appendix B.

The SBA has been criticized over the years for failing to really serve the needs of small business and entrepreneurs. In some cases, criticism has been warranted, and, in others, it has not. One thing that is true is that one SBA office can be filled with ex-entrepreneurs and ex-managers who have been through the mill and understand the problems, while another SBA office a hundred miles away is populated with career government employees who only care about their paycheck and their next jump in grade.

Make an appointment with one of the SBA counselors before you go. Tell him what you're planning to do and that all you are seeking is basic information about the SBA. When you get there, ask about their various services—counseling, publications, seminars, loan guarantees, direct loans. Be sure to get two free documents, SBA Publications 115A (free material) and 115B (for-sale publications). Read them at your leisure and order the ones that pertain to you. Be sure to get *Checklist for Going into Business.* Use their Service Core of Retired Executives (SCORE) with extreme caution. The author has rarely encountered a success story that could point to SCORE's help as the critical element.

United States Department of Commerce

Visit your local Department of Commerce field office. (A list of Field Offices is in Appendix C.) Ask the agents to explain the publications that they and their subsidiary sister agency, the United States Bureau of the Census, produce. The census data is invaluable for your initial market research on the location of your enterprise. (See the initial section of Chapter 5 for some uses for this data.)

Two books, produced every year by the department that should become part of your personal library are *U.S. Outlook: Projections to 19XX,* which discusses the future of certain businesses five years out, and costs about $10; and *Statistical Abstract of the U.S.,* which contains a host of numerical values about all kinds of things, and costs about $8.

If you plan to manufacture a product, ask the department about exporting. There are lots of free aids to consult, and an inexpensive service to find you foreign sales agents through the various United States Embassies. Some of the larger offices have a small business specialist whose job it is to visit businesses in his region. Although these specialists rarely call on retail establishments, a brief chat can't hurt.

Federal Bookstores

In most of our larger cities, there are government bookstores which sell the publications of the United States Superintendent of Documents, Government Printing Office (GPO). Browse around. Talk to one of the people working there. Get on the mailing list of the GPO.

General Services Administration

If you have any product or service that might be of use to our government, the world's largest purchasing agent, visit the General Services Administration (GSA). There are eight regional offices located in our larger cities, and the people are extremely helpful. They will explain the government bidding and contract process and will either give or sell you (at a nominal fee) basic purchasing directories of United States governmental and military agencies. One publication lists the name and telephone number of every Small Business Advisor at all the military installations; another book lists what they buy.

State Industrial Development Agencies

Each state has a department dedicated to business development within the state. These departments are primarily interested in big business, but they may have some individuals that specialize in smaller organizations, especially one with possibilities of substantial growth. Tell them your story and see what counsel they can offer.

Local Chambers of Commerce

Some general philosophy holds for local Chambers of Commerce. You want information, but this time on a local level. Tell them what you plan to do and see what they tell you. Watch out for political motives and potential conflicts of interest, however. If the executive director of a local chamber sees you as a threat to the established order, you may have some uphill sledding awaiting you.

Successful Entrepreneurs

Successful entrepreneurs are the best sources available, and this includes potential competitors. Pick a time when they can spend an hour with you. Ask them how they got into the business, what unforeseen problems they encountered, and how they solved those problems. Ask them about professional services, who has helped them, and who has cheated them. You might want to be a little cagey talking with people who will be your future competitors. If you want to stay "blind," call them on the phone and say you're a consultant investigating the market; you'll find 75 percent of people called in this manner will tell you nearly everything you want to know. For more discussion of this, see the marketing research section of Chapter 6.

Professional Associations

For almost any business that you want to enter, from a hardware store to research in ion physics, there is probably a professional association. Your local library probably has a copy of the two or three publications that list all the professional associations in the country. You may find several of interest to you. Write to them. See what you can get free. Ask how much membership fees are per year and what you get in return. If all one gives you for a $100 fee is a brochure about the annual convention, forget it. You want an association that gives help in the form of prewritten documents or periodic literature. Possibly a visit to their facilities would be in order. If you go, bring lots of questions with you.

College Faculty

Most colleges and universities that have a business administration or management department have a concentration, a major, or at least a course in small business. Get to the faculty member in charge of the program, or to the professor teaching entrepreneurship. Tell him your ideas. Let him look over your business plan as if he's correcting a student paper. Harken to his comments, especially substantive comments. If you're really lucky, the professor might retain a copy of your plan for closer scrutiny. Bring a large, stamped, self-addressed envelope with you just in case this offer is extended. Let the professor "grade" the plan. Many management professors today have had real experience in their own businesses, and teach as a professional hobby.

Lawyers and Accountants

Many lawyers and accountants specialize in small business, and have amassed a great deal of experience in legal and financial aspects of the field. Most professionals will give you an hour or so of their time in an initial meeting without charge. Ask about their fee structure and their small business clients for reference purposes. Solicit their advice during this first meeting in a general way, asking what things you should watch out for that fall in the lawyer's or accountant's field of expertise. Remember that you are also looking for a lawyer and an accountant that you will use later on, and you want individuals whom you can work with and who will respond to your needs.

Keep in mind that lawyers and accountants, like other specialists, operate most efficiently when they are confined to their fields. Do not assume that lawyers and accountants are business consultants, even if they purport to have broad business experience. Your business should be run by you, not by outside professionals.

Bankers

Introduce yourself to a number of commercial loan officers. Sit down for a chat, and ask them if the current money supply is loose or tight; what the prevailing interest rate is on commercial loans; and what down payments and security (including personal guarantees) are required. Find out who some of the bank's customers are, and inquire about special bank services, including trust management, Keough plans and Individual Retirement Accounts. Check the bank's attitude on additional financing, and ask about availability of different types of mortgages (floating interest rates, mortgages with balloon payments, prepayment penalties). Ask about the bank's relationship with the SBA.

In this initial visit with a prospective banker, don't bring out your business plan. Simply use the time to gather facts about the particular bank and what kinds of deals appeal to it. Have the banker relate some success and failure stories for you. Study him from a personal standpoint. Could you like him? This will become important to you in the future when you can't meet Friday's payroll without a short-term loan (it will happen).

As with lawyers and accountants, exercise caution in taking *business* advice from a banker.

Once you've selected a bank, give it all your banking business, including your trust account and your estate planning. Have lunch with your banker at least once a month and keep asking about interest rates and the money supply.

Investors

It is possible that your business will attract investors. Although this subject will be treated in more detail in Chapter 7, a brief word is in order here. If you are seeking investors, private individuals who might think of providing debt (a loan, to be repaid) or equity (ownership, not to be repaid) financing, you have another opportunity to gather information. Question potential investors. If no investor seems interested in your project, find out why. Maybe your business plan has serious flaws in it. The final test comes when that investor reaches for his checkbook.

Consultants

Anyone can call himself a consultant. As a result, consultants are a maligned bunch. Unlike a CPA, CLU or real estate broker, a consultant has no regulation whatever. There is no minimum education or training, no experience requirement, no qualifying exam. Therefore, as one might suspect, there are a number of incompetent consultants doing a real disservice to their clients. The best way to screen a consultant is through past clients. Good consultants will be delighted to tell you whom they have worked for.

Stay away from the McKinsey's and the Booz Allen's. Find a consultant who is in sole practice.

If you are going to use a consultant for any purpose (such as for a review of your business plan), be certain that you *know* (not *hope*) the consultant is qualified; that he or she has had experience with small business; and that you know the cost of the consultant service. Get the consultant to formally quote a not-to-exceed price. Rates should run from $100 to $350 per day plus expenses, but the first visit is almost always free.

One final note about business advisors. Anyone can be a free consultant if you let him. Some of your friends and family might be able to give you good advice. Let them. They'll be flattered.

During this data-gathering stage of your enterprise, keep a folder, or, better yet, a notebook of the information that you collect. At first this may consist of sheets of foolscap on which you have scribbled a few bits of practical wisdom. As the file grows, the various subject headings—accounting, competition, money supply, professional services—will begin to fall into a natural kind of order. At that time, sit down and organize the data into the proper categories. You will be amazed to find that after only a few months' time you have gathered a veritable encyclopedia of small business topics, better than any textbook.

Many Other Sources

As you continue your quest, you will find more sources of information and data than you can possibly ever use in a lifetime. There are nonprofit groups that have been established to help special groups of would-be business owners, especially women and ethnic minorities. Some of these organizations are helpful and dedicated; others have no idea what they're doing. Beware of groups that have a "cause" first and help for you only secondarily. Dun & Bradstreet, 99 Church St., New York, NY 10007, has a number of free booklets that are of great help; one of them is a bibliography of small business sources. There are, by now, probably ten magazines dedicated to small business and entrepreneurship. The three best seem to be *Inc., Venture,* and *In Business.* Think about subscribing to them, or at least go to a large news dealer in your area and buy one of each. There are newsletters, too. The best of these costs less than $100 per year and comes from The Center For Entrepreneurial Management, American Management Association, 311 Main St., Worcester, MA 01608. Another source is *Common Sense,* available from Upstart Publishing Co., P.O. Box 323, Portsmouth, NH 03801.

CHAPTER FOUR

Business Planning

It is a bad plan that admits no modification.
Publilius Syrus, c. 42 B.C.

Introduction to Planning[1]

Motivation and success begin with the determining of goals and objectives. The underlying assumption of the goal-motivation-success cycle is that a plan is necessary to reach the goal and to achieve the desired success. In a small business, whether that business is begun as a new venture or purchased from a previous owner, the entire process is accomplished with the preparation of a *business plan.* This plan is a written document which describes the basic elements of the business (marketing, operations, personnel, finance, management) and projects future events and needs so that the entrepreneur can anticipate the future. If you've never prepared a business plan before, the task is not as difficult as it may first appear. Its creation will involve making assumptions about the future and building a hypothetical business operation on those assumptions. If the assumptions prove to be incorrect as the future becomes the present, they may be changed and the plan altered to conform to those changes. Don't let us lull you into thinking that the preparation of a business plan is a simple and quick job; this is far from the truth. It will be time-consuming, and success will require careful thought. It may exhaust you, shake your self-confidence, and tear your guts out. But it should be fun! Once the job has been completed, you will not only realize a great sense of personal accomplishment, but you will have been forced to learn your new business in detail. One reminder is necessary, however. When the business plan is finally prepared, your job is not over; it has just begun. For the plan to be an effective instrument, it must become a document that is examined and reexamined. The plan, to be fully usable, should be revised continually. Rockwell International, the massive aerospace/machine-tool empire, uses the following rule to govern its planning: the business plan for the company is rewritten every six months on a revolving, five-year basis, unless it is felt that the financial projections for the next twelve months will create more than a 10 percent deviation from the existing plan. In that case, the plan is rewritten within six months.

Many people, entrepreneurs included, fail to plan at all. Their lives and their businesses are a random walk. Many people can get through life without a plan and never experience serious difficulty; to do so in a business is to invite finan-

[1] For a complete and excellent treatment of the subject, see David H. Bangs and William R. Osgood. *Business Planning Guide* (Upstart Publishing, Portsmouth, N.H., 1978).

cial disaster and ruin. We theorize that plans are not prepared for two reasons. First, people feel uneasy looking into the future. Someone has said that the complexity of our society has not only made it difficult to predict what *will* happen, but difficult also to predict what *can* happen. But it can be done. The average American family spends an estimated 100 hours planning its annual vacation and then comes within seventy-five dollars of the projected budget.

As we said earlier, looking into the future involves making assumptions. If the assumptions prove to be incorrect, we must shed any fear that we have about being wrong. Assumptions that prove to be incorrect can be changed. The next time that the plan is prepared, the preparer may make better assumptions.

A second reason plans are not prepared is that the task is too burdensome. This is an excuse for laziness and represents a lack of desire. Anyone using this argument is nothing more than an armchair entrepreneur. If you follow a step-by-step, logical process in the construction of a business plan, the task is not impossible. It will take some work on your part, but most true entrepreneurs see the undertaking as a pleasant experience. Don't cop out and have someone else write the plan for you. The plan is *yours*. It's fine to seek out professionals for aid and counsel (an accountant for the financial section, for example), but, for the document to be significant to your business and your own success, you must prepare it. You will live with it, not the person who prepared it for you.

Many people ask us the underlying reasons for planning. Why plan? Is it necessary? After all, the future is laid out, and there is nothing we can do to change the predestined order. But few successful entrepreneurs that we know are reactive by nature. Entrepreneurs plan ahead. So one reason for planning is that intelligent planning, using information that is correctly assimilated, prevents reactive behavior. Planning involves assembling data and correctly analyzing it. *Planning is the complete and continuous process directed toward improving business operations in the light of existing opportunities.* Now, go back and read that again. Notice the key words: *complete, continuous, improving, opportunities.* Why bother to spend your money and your effort to run your own business with subconscious failure in mind? Why not have fun, plan, and reap the rewards?

A study was done a number of years ago to determine if the planning process had anything to do with success. The population studied included individual Americans, and the measure of success was to be personal net worth (not what we'd define as success, but a useful measure nonetheless). Here is what the study uncovered: (1) The top 3 percent, those who could be called independently wealthy, had life plans that were not only specific but were actually written. (2) The next 10 percent of the group, deemed by the researchers as comfortable, had general goals. (3) The next 60 percent, who, financially, could be called week-to-weekers came closest to planning with their New Year's resolutions. And now comes the sad part. (4) The final 27 percent, those requiring some kind of outside support, be it food stamps or total care, had no plans or goals at all.

A second reason for planning is that it lets the entrepreneur think ahead. One of the critical elements of the plan is the financial section, in which the income and expenses of the firm are projected into future periods using financial statements known as *pro formas* ("before the fact"). If the financial plan shows a maximum cumulative cash deficit of $25,000 occurring in the fifteenth month of operation, the entrepreneur should discuss this with his or her financing source so that the shortfall will be well known in advance and planned for.

Since the plan creates goals (personnel levels, unit sales forecasts, profits) which we constantly strive toward, we could assume that the business plan allows us to work smarter and not just harder. By all the studies the American executive works about fifty hours per week, on the job, and probably many more during home and travel time. At least half of that effort is taken up with such unproductive activities as politicking, game-playing, and protecting one's underside. Much wasted effort is a result of having no workable plan to go by. You, as an entrepreneur, can't afford this loss of time; time management is critical because time is the one element that we all possess equally. With goals in mind, you can judge the effort that is needed to achieve them.

A good plan allows feedback. If the gross sales were expected to be $300,000 over a twelve-month period, and, at the end of six months, they have attained a level of $250,000, then the original plan should be revised to reflect the actual data. The feedback process involves a continuous effort of collecting and analyzing real information to compare with the projections and assumptions in the plan.

Not all plans produce success. The pattern is not automatic. Even very well-constructed plans do not guarantee fulfillment because we are mere mortals. For the plan to fulfill our goals (Pygmalion, again), we must remain committed to the goals that we have set. This means some old-fashioned drive and stick-to-it-iveness as well as a positive attitude.

Others have done it. A friend of ours related a story about two elephants at a circus. He said that he first saw a small baby elephant held fast to a buried telephone pole with a huge steel chain. All during the youngster's waking hours, he tugged and pulled at the chain in a useless attempt to escape. Our friend's heart went out to the poor animal. But then he rounded the edge of the circus tent and saw a magnificent bull elephant standing stock still with its head thrown back. The bull elephant was secured by a thin, frayed rope attached to a flimsy tent pole. The adult elephant had been trained to give up and had come to realize that any effort to break free was useless.

We are all given the opportunity to quit or drop out. Being black, short, too heavy, Polish, female, unattractive, uncoordinated, or old can be a convenient reason not to self-actualize (see Maslow's hierarchy, Chapter 1). If we get it through our heads that each of us is a majority of one, nothing should stand in our way. Age is a criterion that society uses constantly to slow us down. We are told, "Act your age"; "Age before beauty"; "You're too old for that." Classically, we retire at sixty-five and are expected to live out the rest of our days in solitude. There was a radio program called "Life Begins at Forty" which probably really meant that it ended at forty. The hippie era warned us not to trust anyone over thirty. We're supposed to put off childish things at eighteen, the age of majority. Some researchers at Harvard claim they have a test that can determine the success or failure of a child's future life at three. Einstein would have failed that test since he didn't talk until he was four. But the single largest factor in unfulfilled plans is the lack of a strong commitment to personally developed goals.

Goals must be realistic and relevant within the confines of the business enterprise. Many overly optimistic business plans show the venture to be doubling or tripling every year. This is possible, but highly unlikely. Even a 50 percent growth rate in a mature enterprise is difficult to obtain and maintain. Goals should be revised as the plan becomes reality. The plan should reflect tough goals, but they should be honest ones.

Outside influences such as unforeseen happenings, incorrect data, or false perceptions can cause entrepreneurs to react in the wrong direction, at the wrong time, and for the wrong reasons.

In building a business plan, it will probably be necessary for you to consult some number of outside sources. Be careful about accepting advice and counsel from "experts" at face value until you have had an opportunity to verify your information. Some opinions are facts, and some are just opinions. The following interesting little story about the value of expert opinion has been told many times, but it bears repeating.

A young immigrant came to the United States and decided to become an entrepreneur. He opened a hot dog stand and decided to have a very high quality product. He bought nothing but the best meat, rolls, mustard, and relish. He bought a small wagon and selected the time of day to sell when the most people would pass his mobile stand. His prices were fair in relation to the product that he offered. He prospered. After a few years, he traded in the wheeled cart and bought a small permanent stand. Again, he prospered. The business enlarged to such a size that his growing family began to enjoy a fairly comfortable way of life. The hot dog stand grew to a restaurant, he advertised, and people came. They gladly paid the prices because they got what they paid for. The entrepreneur's eldest son finally went away to college and the father had become successful enough to pay for it easily.

After four years, the son returned. The father asked his son what he had learned from his stay at the large university. The son said that there was a recession, and things were pretty tough. People were out of work, money was hard to get at the banks, and many were not buying the more luxurious things of life, including restaurant meals. He advised the father to cut back on his expenditures. The father couldn't quite understand since his business was still booming, but, after all, his son was a college graduate and should know what he was talking about.

So, the father stopped advertising. The next thing that he did was to reduce the portion size of his meals at the restaurant, and he also began serving a weaker drink. Pretty soon, the clientele shrank. The father was forced to go to a small diner to accommodate the smaller trade. Again, he reduced the quality of his basic product, and the number of patrons declined further. Finally, he went back to the pushcart. One evening he spoke to his son. "You know," he said, "there really is a recession."

Business plans are not irrational, inconsistent, immaterial, incompetent, or irrelevant. Plans are also not secret (unwritten), not narrow, not complex, and not just wishful thinking on your part.

Preparation for Writing the Business Plan

The very first step in planning is to define the business as broadly as possible. Be generic. Be sweeping. Encompass everything in your thinking. Then you won't be limited and hampered by "smallthink." One young man who took over his father's business knew how to make broad definitions. When he was a young lad of six or so, he had asked his father what he did. The father replied that his company made trash cans. On the day that the son took over, he stood in his new office (formerly his father's) and looked out over the production line. He concluded that the company did not make trash cans at all but made containers. The firm now produces the detachable containers that ride on the backs of over-the-road trailers and on the decks of sea-going vessels in international trade.

The importance of accurate definition was illustrated when we had the opportunity to visit a friend who owned and ran a small firm. The friend was deeply interested in expanding the operation to take advantage of new business opportunities and wanted some advice. He had a business plan that included his interest in entering such fields as holography, fiber optics, and microprocessors. The conversation went something like this:

AUTHOR. Joe, what business are you in?
JOE. I'm in the electronics business.
AUTHOR. Would you take me through your shop again?
JOE. Sure.
(*Both leave the president's office for the main production floor.*)
AUTHOR. Joe, what's that?
JOE. Oh, that's an industrial television set.
AUTHOR. And that thing over there?

JOE. That's a control unit.

AUTHOR. Did you make the TV set?

JOE. No.

AUTHOR. Did you make the control unit?

JOE. No.

AUTHOR. Where did you get the units?

JOE. I bought them.

AUTHOR. Oh. What are those wires running between the two units?

JOE. They connect the two.

AUTHOR. So that they can operate together?

JOE. Yes.

AUTHOR. Then, you came up with a system to connect the two components for some customer?

JOE. Yes.

(*Both return to the president's office.*)

AUTHOR. Joe, you aren't in the electronics business. You're in the wiring business. Now, before you tell me that you want to get into sophisticated electronics, you'd better concentrate on what you are doing now and forget the fancy stuff until you exploit all the business opportunities available to you. Do that, and do that well, and then you will be ready for the big time.

The first example shows a business definition that was too narrow in its scope; the second, aggrandizing something that wasn't there. The moral is to *define your business well* before beginning the plan.

The first step of the planning process is to define the business. The second step, equally important, is the commitment to plan. In large corporations, this comes from the top. Chief executives have been told that, for the planning process to be complete and continuous, it must start from the top of the organization. In small business, the commitment to planning must come from the entrepreneur—you.

The third step in planning includes taking stock of the environment of the business. The list below includes some items to stimulate your thought:

1. Whom do I serve?
2. Who serves me?
3. What resources do I have at my disposal? Personal skills? Physical assets? Money? People?
4. Is the type of business and product or service that I have chosen a healthy one?
5. What are the risks involved?
6. What limits my business?
7. Why am I doing this particular thing as opposed to available alternatives?
8. What do I want to create in my life?

The fourth preparatory phase in planning has to do with data collection. This is material that may be put to use directly in the written plan or saved and filed for reference, or it may become useless and have to be discarded. Those data may include information on the following:

1. Past financial history of the business
2. Competition, past and future
3. Layout
4. Location
5. Equipment
6. Community life
7. Traffic count
8. Regional economy
9. Professional services
10. Legal forms of the business
11. Future employees
12. Customers
13. Suppliers
14. Potential lenders or investors
15. Products and services
16. Nature of the market
17. Laws and ordinances
18. Transportation
19. Interest rates and down payments
20. Credit terms
21. Insurance
22. Advertising media

and much more. This fourth phase may take a few weeks or a few years.

Writing the Business Plan

The business plan exists for two major purposes, one internal, and the other external. These purposes are equally important to the success of the business:

First, the business plan is a document to raise money. Joseph Mancuso, one of the foremost American authorities on entrepreneurship, has stated that a good business plan raises capital, either debt or equity, and a poor one does not. That's a pretty good delineation. All the well-thought-out cash projections, narratives, and appending data are worthless if the plan does not excite some moneyed source to come up with the necessary financial support for you to begin or continue your venture.

Secondly, and most importantly, the business plan is a document for *you*. It tells you where to go, when certain things are to be accomplished, how these things are going to be done, who will do them, what to expect, why you are even bothering. It gives you milestones with which to check your progress. It lets you plan your cash needs. It gives you something to live by.

The plan, as an agent for you, should represent the complete business picture for a two-year and a five-year period into the future. It should address the four major areas of your business: finance, marketing, operations, and administration. In the following pages, we will lead you through the things that you have to do to fulfill these requirements.

Appendix H contains two business plans that were written to allow their respective authors to become entrepreneurs. These plans have been altered only to correct obvious faults and errors that occurred in their preparation. Therefore, they are not the perfect plans that so often occur in books of this sort. They were created by real people. They can be skimmed or analyzed in detail.

The material that follows outlines some of the items to be included in a business plan. If the terms are unfamiliar, or if you want more explanation, consult the index and turn to the section of the book which deals with the particular subject.

I. Summary Page, Title Page, and Table of Contents

There is some disagreement about whether a *summary* should be a detachable element of the plan. Some say that the summary page should be there to alert the potential investor to what is to come so that he can either toss aside the plan or read further. The decision is really up to you and your own style. Most entrepreneurs do not use a summary page.

If you decide to have one, it should be one page only and should contain the following:

1. The product or service offered, the location of the business and, if applicable, the date of incorporation
2. The market to be served (leisure time, general public, seasonal tourist)
3. The financing required
4. The people involved, by name
5. Sales projections by year for two to five years
6. Anything unique about the business—patents, name, location

The *title page* is the cover sheet for the main document. It should be neatly laid out with the following basic information on it: the name and location of the venture; the preparer(s) of the document; the date prepared; and, somewhere, the words "Business Plan," or "Financing Proposal."

The next item is the *table of contents,* with page numbers, in case the reader wants to go to a particular section first (most do, by the way). The table of contents shown below will also serve as the outline for the business plan that we will describe:

    I. Table of contents
   II. Introduction

    A. The business
    B. Products and services offered
    C. The industry
III. Marketing research
    A. Customers
    B. Market size and trends
    C. Competition—nature and number
    D. Available market
    E. Predictions
IV. Marketing plan
    A. General strategy
    B. Pricing philosophy
    C. Method of sales
    D. Customer service
    E. Advertising
    F. Sales forecasts
V. Operations
    A. Facilities and equipment
    B. Plans for growth and expansion
    C. Overall schedule of events
    D. Risks
VI. Financial plan
    A. Proposal
    B. Use of proceeds
    C. Break-even analysis
    D. Historical statements
    E. Pro forma income statements
    F. Pro forma balance sheets
    G. Pro forma cash flow statements
VII. Management and organization
    A. Organizational structure
    B. Resumes of key personnel and compensation
    C. Supporting professional services
VIII. Appendixes

There is, by the way, nothing sacred about the order above, or even the content. Every plan is slightly different. What we have outlined above is simply one suggested format, not the only correct format.

II. Introduction

If the summary page is not used, the same data can be contained in the *introduction* which prepares the reader for what is to follow. The introduction gives an overall view of the enterprise so that the reader (and you) understand fully what the business is and what it will be in the future.

A. The Business. The opening sentence of this section on the business is crucial. First impressions are important, and whatever you say here is the theme from which all other narratives and evidence flow. Try to be creative and to excite the reader into looking further into the plan. The following is the opening sentence from an actual business plan:

> Sports World will sell every type of sporting good and equipment available.

Not only is this a lackluster beginning, but it's misleading. It implies that someone can go to Sports World and order a tennis racquet, a scuba mask, croquet wickets, hockey pucks, cricket bats, a jai-alai ball, a polo hat, sweat socks, a game of backgammon, golf tees, football cleats, a ski mask, a fishing boat, a catcher's mitt, shotgun shells, and an outdoor bag to put all this stuff into. Contrast the more informative opening of the plan for The Sturbridge Glass Shoppe:

> Glass is a unique substance. There are many ways to work with glass, and each has its own advantages and disadvantages. Some of the ways to work with glass include sagging, laminating, flame-working, enameling, fusing, casting, and glassblowing or free-blown glass. The Sturbridge Glass Shoppe will work in glassblowing and will offer individual pieces for sale as well as demonstrations and instruction in the art.

The opening paragraph of the plan should not only specify the nature and type of business (retailing, wholesaling, manufacturing, services) but its legal form, age of the venture (years in operation), location (address), type of facility (one-story brick, wood frame), and type of occupancy (own or lease). Hours and months of operation are also spelled out.

B. Products and Services Offered. The section on products and services offered is relatively straightforward. There should be sufficient detail provided to give the reader a well-defined description of what it is that the venture does or will do. The following is taken from a business plan for the Twin Dragon Chinese Frozen Food Company:

> The company will manufacture a single line of Chinese frozen food products and will engage in the cutting, cooking, vacuum packaging, marketing, and delivery of products which are economically priced and are made from quality Chinese food according to authentic ethnic recipes: sweet and sour pork, beef and oyster sauce, mushroom chow yock, young pea pods with beef, vegetarian chow mein.

Here is a very simple description:

> Cheshire Trophies will manufacture, distribute, repair, and engrave plaques and trophies.

C. The Industry. The purpose of the section on the industry is to place the particular venture within an appropriate larger category so that the reader can position the business in context. One helpful way to categorize the industry is to use, if appropriate, the United States Government's Standard Industrial Classification (SIC) Code. Rather than describe the market, which is done under the next major head, Marketing Research, give the characteristics of the industry itself here. Consider the following excerpt from the business plan for Well Strung, a venture to service tennis racquets:

> The tennis industry is growing. Many towns are building public tennis facilities. Many club-corporations are being formed to create indoor tennis facilities. There are country clubs, health clubs, and camps offering tennis to beginners, enthusiasts, and professionals. All tennis facilities require the raw materials of the trade: balls, nets, maintenance machinery, racquets, sportswear, courts, and lights. They require the guidance of building specialists and the services of maintenance personnel. There are technical advances made in every sector of the tennis industry. There are new substances and designs for racquets being tested. There are new and improved strings being introduced every year. There is even experimentation with court surface colors for improved vision, both indoor and outdoor. The present supply channels seem to be adequate for current demand. The service and maintenance sectors seem to be inadequate to current needs.

If there are specific, identifiable gaps in the industry that this business seeks to fill, they should be mentioned. One enterprising individual wrote a business plan to create an entirely new marketing approach within the retail liquor business. He sought financing to start an operation like Florist's Telegraph Delivery (FTD) with bottles instead of botany.

III. Marketing Research

It is the entire job of the *marketing research* section to justify what the customer count will be so that the projected financial statements are believable. This is often one of the hardest things for new entrepreneurs to do, but it is not an impossible task. If the business is a going concern, past information from the previous owners is a good start even though the data may not be complete or accurate. If the business depends on highway traffic for its existence, counts of the number of cars per day passing the location can be secured from the state highway department. Often a free map of the entire state is available. Estimates can then be made of the percentage of cars that will stop. For businesses that are located within town or city limits, the population of the buying area can be secured from the United States Bureau of the Census or the local chamber of commerce and that, coupled with the number of local competitors, should yield a reasonable estimate of yearly sales. (See Chapter 6 for further explanation of these techniques.)

A. Customers. It is important for the new entrepreneur to decide upon the type of clientele that will be served. Once that is decided upon, the entire image, including the name, should be focused on the potential customers. Calling a restaurant Chez Henri and serving fish and chips simply don't match. If you choose affluent clientele, then the necessary decor must match that particular image, and any deviation from it can result in disaster.

Customers can be consumers, industry (both durable and nondurable goods that are then sold to consumers or industry, and services), and governmental bodies, and these customers can be located both here and abroad. Your customer group can be potentially very large (the current level of world population: four billion people) or very small (lion farms in the United States: one). The group can be increasing in size (general population), stable (lion farms), or declining (World War II veterans).

The following quotation comes from the business plan for The Olde American Ice Cream Parlour which was to be located in a small college town:

> We expect that most of our customers will be college students, at least from mid-September to mid-May. During this time period, the college is in session, and students from the college will make up the largest single concentration of customers in the area. They are the type who are money-conscious, either unwilling, or, in some cases, unable to pay for something too extravagant.
>
> Spending a little at a time does not worry too many students. They will always be able to afford a soda, if nothing else, and, at the same time, they'll be able to come in, sit down, talk, play backgammon, and just generally relax. During the summer months, the clientele will consist of summer students, townspeople, and tourists.

B. Market Size and Trends. For most small businesses, this section on market size and trends will be brief. The following comes from a business plan for Teddy Bear, a small department store to be located in a resort area:

> There is currently a base trading population of 115,000. That base has been increasing at about 5 percent per year and shows every sign of continuing at its present rate.
>
> The population in the summer increases about tenfold due to the many resorts and camps in the area. The stores in downtown _____ have been doing more business each year.

If the potential market is large (such as all the service stations in California), this should be brought out, as well as any relevant data about whether the market is growing or not. A few phone calls or some library research may be in order. If, for example, you had invented a new kind of bowling ball that looked promising, you should find some of the following information:

1. Total number of active bowlers
2. Number of bowling alleys with a count of the total number of lanes
3. Percentage of bowlers who own their own balls
4. Growth (or decline) of bowling
5. Life of a typical ball

C. Competition—Nature and Number. This section on competition is not always as simple as it looks. The first task, determining who your primary competition is, is relatively easy. Something as fast as a check in the Yellow Pages will get you started on knowing your competitors. But you also need to assess their strengths and weaknesses so that you can shape your venture around them; this usually requires a visit or two and some asking around. Next, you will need to determine their approximate volume of annual business so that you can compute your market share. Every industry and business has a rule of thumb that can be used to estimate annual volume—seats in a restaurant, counter space in a store. You may have significant secondary competition as well. If you run a small taxi company, the bus company, rail line, private vehicle, and even walking habits are competition.

A handy way to do this analysis is to use a tabular form such as Figure 4.1. Later on in the book, we speak about keeping a file on each one of your major competitors so that this important segment of your business is kept up to date.

By the way, do not view your competition as the enemy. View your competitor as a person who happens to be as smart as you are *and* is in the same business. Competitors are simply another source of data for the successful entrepreneur. Visit them. Don't tell them what you're up to at the present time. Simply go and observe. If you can, talk with their patrons or customers. See what they do well and what they do poorly. Capitalize on the best; throw the worst away.

D. Available Market. Later on, in Chapter 5, we will demonstrate a method for calculating the available market as a function of the number of competitors located within a particular trading area. The calculation should be performed so that you will have some idea of what business levels to expect as a function of competition. Your financing source will undoubtedly ask the question anyway. For a business such as a mail order operation begun in your home, this type of analysis is well nigh impossible. On the other hand, if your venture is a retail store located within a community of known size, the calculation is rather easy.

E. Predictions. In this brief section on predictions, we ask the entrepreneur to look beyond his business nose and make a few prognostications as to what the business owner might expect to happen. The following quotation comes from Farmer's Equipment and Supplies, an enterprise which sells and services lawn and garden equipment.

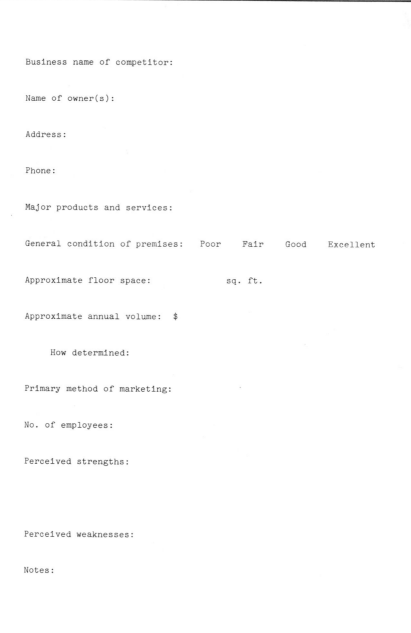

Business name of competitor:

Name of owner(s):

Address:

Phone:

Major products and services:

General condition of premises: Poor   Fair   Good   Excellent

Approximate floor space: sq. ft.

Approximate annual volume: $

    How determined:

Primary method of marketing:

No. of employees:

Perceived strengths:

Perceived weaknesses:

Notes:

Figure 4.1 *Competition Analysis Form*

The growth of business for larger tractors and farm equipment is expected to decline in the short run, but, due to many government programs being adopted to save farms, I feel that it should level off eventually. The future for lawn and garden tractors should have great growth potential. The reason for this is that more and more people that have a small piece of land are starting to grow their own gardens. These people are investing in the eight to sixteen horsepower range of tractors with the Rototiller attachment. After they buy the tractor with the Rototiller, they then wind up buying the lawn mower and snowblower attachments to go with it. As food costs increase, home gardening will continue to grow in importance.

This particular section takes on major significance if your operation is engaged in manufacturing or distributes a luxury type of item.

IV. Marketing Plan

The large companies say that *marketing* should lead the company forward, and they're right. Marketing is the eyes and ears of the firm, looking out and into the future to determine what the market wants and then moving to satisfy those needs. Marketing is the vital link in the delivery system of business, and, as such, must be concerned with satisfying a need expressed by potential customers. Those customers must be willing to pay the price for your wares so that you can succeed. The world no longer beats any paths at all to any doorstep without knowing where it is going. You must make the path-beating easy for them, and this includes using all the systems that large concerns have already discovered.

A. General Strategy. The first section under the marketing plan should address the general strategy involved. You have to reach, nurture, and comfort your available market to reap the maximum benefit from it. If you depend heavily on mail order business, your strategy is different than if you rely on tourist trade. There can be combinations, of course. Brookstone Company, headquartered in Peterborough, New Hampshire, began as an extremely small mail order house and then built a major enterprise on that basis alone. At one stage in its growth, Brookstone opened retail stores in the major cities in the northeast, and this added to their growth and success. The original idea was simply to be a place where craftsmen could find hard-to-get or unique tools. The point is that the marketing strategy obviously has to change to meet not only changing conditions but also the newer desires of the entrepreneur.

The marketing strategy might be rather simple in nature, consisting of doing some preliminary advertising and opening the doors, or it may be far-reaching and complex. One thing that outsiders will look at is whether you have targeted your available market and have a logical plan in mind to blitz the market.

Read the following general strategy for Recycled Records, a retail operation that would sell new, used, and rare records:

> My plan is to attract and gain the attention of the music-oriented community. I will reach them through local publications, various music-related magazines, and newspapers. Signs and posters will be strategically placed in bars, nightclubs, concert halls, and schools. This approach will maximize my exposure to the buying public that I want to reach. I will emphasize quantity as well as quality. My prices will be below those of conventional record stores. Also, my selection will far exceed that of a record store of the standard variety. Even with low prices, my gross margin will be substantially greater than competition due to the variety of product offering.

B. Pricing Philosophy. When you think about pricing, decide whether you are going to shoot for the low end of the market (discount store approach, little or no service, low overhead, items priced to move quickly), the larger, middle segment, or the quality-pricing approach. Too many entrepreneurs adopt the philosophy that they need to enter business with cut-rate prices to gain market share rapidly. They say that, when they have captured their maximum share, they will raise prices to a very profitable level. This seldom happens successfully. They remain as the low-price leader with minimum or no profit margin. Americans have gotten tired of shoddy goods, and many are willing to pay the price for high quality merchandise or service. The Mercedes-Benz automobile costs what it does because the quality is built into the car, and F. Lee Bailey can charge high fees because he performs and delivers.

The following pricing philosophy for Autoword Services Incorporated, is a simple one:

> I will choose a medium-level price for the preparation of typed documents because of the existing competition. Extra prices will be charged for inserting letters into envelopes (stuffing), folding, sealing, postage, and choice of stationery.

More definitive but still brief is the pricing plan for Creative Forms, a printing company:

> Until I can establish a workable cost system based on direct costs and overhead (indirect costs) and profit, my initial pricing philosophy will be a 200 percent markup above the cost of material and labor.

C. Method of Sales. Some consideration ought to be given in the plan to the method of sales to be employed. In most cases, of course, the method of sales will be directly by the entrepreneur himself. This means that the new owner should feel comfortable, even enjoy, meeting and talking with people. If other methods of selling are to be employed, they should be mentioned. Such other methods might include using distributors or agents, exporters, governmental bodies, the mail, factory outlets, or salespersons who operate away from the business itself.

D. Customer Service. Customer service policy is the next area to address under the marketing plan section. This, again, reflects your philosophy about your business. We're certain that almost everyone has been to a restaurant that will return food or drink to the kitchen or bar because of a customer complaint. Most quality dining places operate with the philosophy that the customer is always right. We're just as certain that most of you have had the opposite experience—when you told the waiter or waitress there was a fly in the soup, the response was something like, "I told the cook not to strain it through the flyswatter," and no action was taken.

Entrepreneurs who operate establishments selling the goods of large manufacturers who back their products with warranties are duty bound to honor those warranties. Entrepreneurs who try to fudge their warranty obligations seldom stay in business long. Word gets around.

Expressing your customer service policy in this section is very important. Experienced readers will look at your support and service function to get a general idea of your business ethics and integrity. Both affect the durability of your enterprise.

The following statement by Tim Bruder, Electrical Contractor, is typical of a positive customer service statement:

> I will guarantee my physical labor against defects in workmanship as described in the standard codes that are generally accepted within the industry, and I will perform my work to the satisfaction of the customer within normal limits. I will also guarantee the materials used as far as the manufacturers of them are willing to do so.

E. Advertising. The entire theory behind advertising (or marketing communications) is to get maximum exposure for minimum expense. (Chapter 6 contains a general discussion of advertising and public relations as well as the use of an agency in small business.) It is a good idea to lay out your advertising plan for at least two years. Many entrepreneurs have a prepared time schedule which lists various media (newspapers, magazines, radio, Yellow Pages), the frequency of insertion, and the costs involved. An advertising agency can do most of this in its proposal to you, and you can use the proposal.

F. Sales Forecasts. This section on sales forecasts is optional since the pro forma financial statements will reflect future sales levels in dollars. If your venture manufactures a product line, or if the unit value of your merchandise is extremely high (such as automobiles, machine tools, construction equipment), it is a good idea to forecast unit sales for several years. Figure 4.2 is a sample format for a unit sales forecast.

```
UNIT SALES FORECAST
Product:

                        Units shipped     Unit price      Total sales
First year
      Month 1                                $               $
      Month 2
      Month 3
      Month 4
      Month 5
      Month 6
      Month 7
      Month 8
      Month 9
      Month 10
      Month 11
      Month 12                                             _____
      Total                                                $

Second year
      Quarter 1
      Quarter 2
      Quarter 3
      Quarter 4
      Total                                                $ ‾‾‾‾‾‾‾‾‾‾

Third year                                                 $
Fourth year                                                $
Fifth year                                                 $
```

Figure 4.2 *Unit Sales Forecast*

V. *Operations*

If the business is engaged in manufacturing, the section on *operations* should contain a brief narrative of the various processes. The writer should state the nature, cost, and source of the raw materials necessary to begin the operation. Then each of the major process centers should be briefly described up to and including the final assembly or test operation.

For the nonmanufacturing businesses, the "operational center" concept should be well understood and described so that you and the reader know what happens to turn the product or service into money. The example given below comes from Sportster's Sporting Goods:

> The operation of this business will be that of a proprietorship. I will have an assistant manager who is also knowledgeable in sports and sporting goods.
>
> In addition, three people will aid in the sales efforts to secondary schools and colleges, and one additional person will work in the repair and cleaning service (for sports equipment and uniforms). This business is located centrally in the state of New Hampshire because of a favorable tax situation and because of the proximity to schools and colleges. Shipping and mailing charges will also be minimized. Labor availability is good and the zoning is fair. The physical size was also planned to accommodate a medium-size showroom, a warehouse and stock area, a couple of offices, and a service department. Traffic flow is relatively light, and an interstate highway is nearby.
>
> My general plan will include buying the sporting goods from a wholesale distributor such as —— Products. I will purchase the merchandise on credit. Major yearly inventory will be made up in the slower summer months, and seasonal inventory will be provided when schools are well into their sports programs. During peak periods of ordering just before the various sports seasons, I may hire students on a part-time basis to handle stockroom and inventory needs. As the season passes, the leftover merchandise can either be returned to the supplier or discounted for a sale to the general public. Some equipment can be used by schools for either practice items or nonteam sports. Quality control will be emphasized. My service personnel will be trained in equipment maintenance, repair, and cleaning.

Following is the brief introduction to the operations plan of Smilin' Pete's, a "head" shop stocking paraphernalia of the counter culture, and especially of the drug subculture. (A business plan for a head shop? Certainly, unless the profits are to be as hallucinatory as some of the stock in trade.)

> I will require approximately 900 square feet of space of store capacity along Route —— in ——.
>
> Lockable, glass display-cases are a necessity. All small items, which are easily stolen, will be locked and out of reach of customers at all times: pipes, roach clips, jewelry, tapes, art. Records, posters, and other large items will be

on open display. At some time after the store opens, I will introduce the sale of T-shirts with a wide variety of prints to be placed on the shirts. This will require a special machine and the operation is too risky to undertake at the store's inception.

Inventory will be taken quarterly on the second Sunday of the last month of the quarter. Inventory control will determine which articles move rapidly and which do not. Shoplifting will be discouraged through the use of prominent posters, wide aisles, and closed-circuit television monitors.

I plan to have a major sale every six months. These will be well advertised in advance and will occur one week before Christmas and one week before summer inventory. The majority of my purchasing will be from distributors located on the West Coast since there appears to be no paraphernalia manufacturers in the East.

In the beginning, I will hire two people to work part-time from 9:00 A.M. to 9:00 P.M. on Saturday. The number of employees will be related to the level of business.

A. Facilities and Equipment. A plot plan, which shows the building in relation to other permanent facilities such as roads, and a floor plan or layout area are very handy references for the section on *facilities* and *equipment.* You can draw them or have them prepared by a professional. The plans visualize the establishment and help your own visualization as well. Plans for renovation of existing facilities should be noted.

Equipment should be described and listed. It is important to note how many assets are already owned and how many will be purchased in the future, following financing. Most entrepreneurs list the asset by generic title (steam table, walk-in freezer, hydraulic vise, forklift truck), the manufacturer, the year manufactured, and the approximate value of the equipment. Items under $500 in value, unless unique in their design or operation, need not be listed. For the majority of small businesses, this list will be rather short.

B. Plans for Growth and Expansion. Some preparers of business plans add a section that addresses any future plans for expansion and growth. Obviously, for a manufacturing type of concern, growth would come from additions to the product line. For hospitality operations, this might mean adding additional seating or sleeping space.

The following is taken from The Sturbridge Glass Shoppe:

The way I have set things up, the business will stay approximately the same way for five years. All which is needed for those five years is the bare essentials for glassblowing. Expansion of the business will come well into the future.

After I have been in operation for some time, my work will have been on the market long enough for me to make a name for myself. This is when I will begin to teach the art. I will move into a larger glass studio and conduct classes. After that, I will begin my glass school. It will be located in a rural setting and people will be housed on the grounds and stay for one or two months. The facilities for this place will be extensive and depend upon the financial success of the glass shop.

Good entrepreneurs are visionary.

C. Overall Schedule of Events. Next comes the overall schedule of events. For some businesses, this simply means opening the doors for the customers to come in. For more complex enterprises, this may be a fairly elaborate system of closely timed events; including lining up suppliers, completing renovations, receiving supplies, beginning actual operation, first cash received, hiring of personnel, and training of personnel. Planning this timetable can, in some cases, be extremely critical to the survival of your business.

The following is a schedule from Creative Forms.

1. Incorporate—presently awaiting word from Delaware.
2. Secure office facilities—completed.
3. Contact with customers—in progress.
4. Interview applicants.
    Secretary—January
    Artist—January
5. Order equipment—December 30. Lead time is four weeks.
6. Appointment with bank—January 26.
7. Contact advertising agency—January, with exposure to begin in February.
8. Receipt of first order—received.
9. Delivery of first order—March 1.
10. Receipt of first payment—April 15.

Some people use a chart or a PERT diagram (*see* Figure 5.3, page 85), the latter being the best for visibility.

D. Risks. This last section under operations is one that some people have some trouble with, and rightly so. It has to do with spelling out the risks of the venture. We favor doing so for two reasons, (1) it makes you aware of what might happen, and (2) it shows you are being open and truthful with your financing source. The risk that is of utmost importance is the risk of going out of business. All other risks are subordinate to that one.

This rather lengthy example is presented because of the unique method of financing proposed by the entrepreneur for Towers Marina, Inc.:

1. Losses. The company predicts an operating loss for the first year and one-half with no assurances that the company will operate profitably in the future. However, projections call for a turnaround by the end of the second year.

2. Suppliers. The company purchases all of its supplies from independent distributors. Since a large portion of the retail end of the business will be in marine finishes or fuel and these products are petrochemicals, the availability of oil will influence the availability of these products.

3. Competition. Our immediate competitor is ——— Boatyard, which is about one-half mile above the company's location on ——— Creek. There are two small operations (less than thirty slips) in the ——— area. The rest of the boatyard industry is based primarily in the Annapolis/Eastport area. Though they all offer services similar to the company, there is a waiting list for availability of slips.

4. Control of Company. The company's founders, Messrs. ———, effectively control the company and will continue to do so immediately after this offering.

5. Debentures and Shares Not Registered. The debentures and shares are not being registered under the Securities Act of 1933 (the act). They are being offered by the company in reliance upon the exemption from the registration requirements of the act contained in section 4(2) of the act and rule 145 promulgated thereunder. This memorandum is intended to comply with and furnish the information called for by rule 146, but it does not necessarily contain all the detailed information which would be contained in a prospectus required by the act. The units will be offered only to persons who have, directly or through qualified advisors, the ability to evaluate an investment in the units on the basis of the information contained herein and the ability to assume the financial risk involved in this investment. Each purchaser will be required to make representations to the company confirming his suitability as a prospective investor.

Although the debentures and shares will be registered under the Delaware Securities Act, such registration is not in contemplation of a public offering but merely to satisfy the technical requirements of such act. Such registration will not mean that the Delaware Corporation Commission has in any manner approved or endorsed the shares as an investment, and will not relieve any of the restrictions to which the debentures and shares are subject as a result of the company's reliance on section 4(2) of the act and rule 146.

There will be no market for the debentures at the conclusion of this offering, and it is not anticipated that a market will develop after the two-year holding period required before sales of "restricted securities" can be made.

The applicable limitations of the exemption from registration under the act will require purchasers to hold the debentures and the shares indefinitely until they are registered (or until the shares into which the debentures are convertible are registered) under the act, or until an exemption from registration for a proposed transfer is available and such transfer may be effected without prior registration under the act. The subscription agreement will contain restrictions applicable to subsequent dispositions of the debentures and shares, and certificates will bear a legend referring to such restrictions.

Shares of common stock issued upon any conversion of the debentures will be restricted as to transfer.

The company files reports under the Securities Exchange Act of 1934 (the Exchange Act). Purchasers will be able to make routine sales of common shares under the Securities and Exchange Commission's rule 144 if the requirements of that rule have been satisfied. Routine sales of unregistered securities under rule 144 may be made after such securities have been held for a minimum period of two years. The period the debentures are held before any conversion into common stock may be counted in computing this time period. Other requirements also must be satisfied. The company will provide purchasers with information necessary to enable them to make sales under rule 144.

The units are being offered to only a limited number of persons, including institutional purchasers, who are venture capital investors, and, as such, can evaluate such shares as an investment without the information that registration under the act would provide and who are prepared to assume all of the risks involved in the investment, including the risk of loss of the entire amount invested.

Naturally, the establishment can burn down or be swept away by flood, but these are risks normal to all ventures, large and small.

VI. Financial Plan

The *financial plan* is what most sophisticated investors will read first. A unique idea brought to fruition by talented individuals will go by the boards if it can't be made into a profitable venture. There is no easy way out of the preparation of this section; it has to be done, and that's it. Some businesses are operated successfully without a financial plan, but they are few in number, and the number will decline as time passes. The financial plan begins with the verbal financing proposal and winds up with numbers and projections.

A. Financing Proposal. This can be a very simple statement, such as:

This plan is written to raise $40,000 in debt capital to be obtained at the current commercial rate in the form of a mortgage against the business. It is proposed that this mortgage will be paid off in fifteen (15) years.

Or it can be extremely complex, as is the case with Towers Marina:

1. Terms of the Offering. The units are being offered on a best efforts basis by ———— Securities, Inc. (the agent), East Main Street, ————, as agent for the company. The agent will be paid a commission of 3 percent on all units sold by it and will be reimbursed for out-of-pocket expenses up to $10,000.00. The agent will be paid a minimum fee of $15,000.00 for its efforts which will be a credit against any commission payable on account of the sale of units. The company may offer and place units without the assistance of the agent. No commission will be payable to the agent of those units. The company has indemnified the agent against certain liabilities, including civil liabilities under the act.

The securities offered hereby are to be sold as units. However, in the event any prospective purchaser desires to purchase a constituent part of a unit, the company and the agent reserve the right to effect such sale only if the corresponding or matching constituent part of the same unit can be sold to another purchaser, so that only whole units, whether to more than one purchaser, are sold.

Persons who wish to subscribe for the units may do so by executing two copies of the subscription agreement and delivering both copies to the agent together with a check for the units purchased. Subscription payments delivered to the agent before the closing date, expected to be no later than May 30 19XX, will be held by the agent in escrow until the closing date, unless sooner released in accordance with the terms of the subscription agreement, when (subject to satisfaction of the conditions to closing to be contained in the agency agreement and subscription agreement) the funds held in escrow will be delivered to the company. If for any reason the sale of the units is not consummated, subscription payments will be refunded to the subscriber in full, without interest. Certificates for the debentures and shares will be delivered to each subscriber on or as soon as practicable after the closing date.

If subscriptions for units with an aggregate purchase price of $450,000.00 are not received with the subscription price, the sale of the units offered hereby will not be closed unless the potential purchaser of less than the minimum amount consents.

2. Description of the Debentures. The description of the debentures offered hereby is qualified in its entirety by reference to the debentures. Wherever a defined term is indicated, the definition thereof is contained in the debenture.

GENERAL. The debentures will be limited to $500,000.00 principal amount and will limit the amount of other debt which may be issued by the company. The debentures will be issued in fully registered form, will bear interest from the date of issuance at the rate set forth on the cover page of this memorandum, and will mature on May 30 19XX. Principal and premium, if any, are to be payable at the principal office of the company. The debentures may be transferred or exchanged or converted without any service charge, at the principal office of the company.

Interest on the debentures will be payable semiannually on May 1 and November 1 of each year to registered holders of record on the fifteenth day of the month next preceding such May 1 or November 1. Unless other arrangements are made, interest will be paid by checks mailed to such registered holders.

SUBORDINATION. The debentures are to be subordinated in right of payment to the prior payment in full of all senior debt (as defined in the debenture). No payment on account of principal (or premium, if any) or interest may be made on the debentures unless full payment of senior debt is made when due and no event of default exists with respect to senior debt. Upon dissolution, reorganization, insolvency, or bankruptcy of the company, senior debt shall first be paid in full before any payment is made in respect of the debentures. Senior debt includes all indebtedness of the company now or hereafter created for borrowed money not expressly subordinated, and renewals, extensions, or refunding thereof.

3. *Summary of Financing.*
   Towers Marina, Inc. (50 units)
   $10,000 per unit at
   11% paid semiannually with
   5000 shares of common stock

B. *Use of Proceeds.* This section on the use of proceeds for Towers Marina was:

Land	$ 50,000.00
Land option	5,000.00
Docks	200,000.00
Lift	40,000.00
Lift pier	50,000.00
Tools	10,000.00
Building	50,000.00
	$405,000.00

The balance of $95,000.00 will be used to meet unexpected needs in the future. It also will be used for expansion.

Other entrepreneurs prepare a fully balanced statement which could be called the Source and Application of Funds (Cash) Statement:

Sources	
Personal	$ 25,000
Investor (brother)	15,000
Loan	100,000
Total	$140,000
Applications	
Purchase of business	$ 80,000
Equipment	20,000
Renovations	20,000
Working capital and reserve	20,000
Total	$140,000

C. *Break-Even Analysis.* Please refer to Chapter 7 for discussion of break-even analysis. Most entrepreneurs include the calculations so that the question is answered before it is asked.

D. *Historical Statements.* Historical statements are included only in the case of the purchase of an existing business. Usually, income statement and balance sheets of the last two full years are presented so that the financing source can have a general idea of where the business is coming from. Hopefully, you plan to improve on past performance.

E–G. Pro Forma Income Statements, Balance Sheets, and Cash Flow. These three sets of statements, the pro forma income statements, balance sheets, and cash flow for two to five years, reflect the future profitability, position, and financial structure. Naturally, they won't be totally correct, but they become documents to live and plan by. The cash flow projections are really the future expense budget of the firm balanced against the expected income in cash terms. For the best example, see the business plans in Appendix H.

VII. Management and Organization

A. Organizational Structure. If the venture has any size to it, an organization chart will help an investor or lender to visualize the *management* and *organization* of the business. Sometimes, brief job descriptions are included as well. Once in a great while, we see a section or paragraph on management philosophy, which is usually paraphrased from a textbook on modern management practice. Don't bother with this; it wastes space and reading time.

If there are two or more entrepreneurs involved in the venture, it is a good idea to state who is responsible for what. The resumes in the next section will help to back up the delineation of duties.

B. Resumes of Key Personnel and Compensation. Although many entrepreneurs simply place a copy of their latest resume in this section on resumes of key personnel and compensation, this often fails to impress a potential financial source since the resume was intended for job hunting not running a business. In the first place, the resume (or curriculum vita as some call it) should be in narrative form, not in the stilted prose used for personnel managers. Accomplishments should be stressed, especially those having to do with the role you will play in the new business. They should be limited to one page. (See the sample business plans in Appendix H.)

One good idea is to include the planned compensation level (salary, deferred earnings, stock, benefits, retirement). Investors will ask anyway. What they don't want to see is a disproportionate salary increase following financing. Original equity positions are also a good idea. A partnership agreement, such as the sample document in Appendix H, for B & T Marina, could be included as well.

C. Supporting Professional Services. Such firms and individuals as accountant/CPA, attorney, bank, consultant(s), ad agency, and insurance agent are listed in the following format:

Attorney
   Ernest A. Douhe, Esquire
   Douhe, Cheetham and Howe
   100 East Main Street
   Rutland, Vermont 05341
   (802) 721–4120

VIII. Appendixes

The appendix section is optional, but can be reserved for pertinent material that might help the reader get a better and fuller understanding of the business in total.

What goes in here, if anything, is open to your imagination. Appendixes may contain architect's plans, letters of intent, menus, advertising layout, articles that have been published about the business or its owners, logos, government contracts, floor plans, photographs of the business, foreign orders, uniqueness of the business, or auditor's report. But don't put in items that merely lengthen the business plan; include only items that have a significant bearing on the business.

CHAPTER FIVE

Operations

Businesses are like babies: fun to conceive, but hell to deliver.

Anon.

Some books call operations *production* or even *manufacturing*. This is fine if you're going into the business of converting raw materials into finished goods. But wait a minute—don't all *operations* really do that? The successful small gift-shop buys carefully selected goods, places them tastefully in areas where prospective buyers can find them, possibly uses them as part of a display, and then sells them. The goods are converted by this changing ownership. Therefore, when we talk about *operations,* we will be addressing specific areas of the business that have to do with the *conversion* process.

Location

In the brief discussion of the differences among urban, suburban, and rural locations in Chapter 3, we stated that our preference was the latter. Now we issue a word of warning about the country or small-town location. If you are starting a rural business, take extra caution. Small towns simply don't have the population density that is present in larger areas. Thus your customer base is smaller in the country, unless a large percentage of tourist business is available, or you are not dependent upon the area for providing customers (a mail order business, for example). In any case, you should give very serious thought to whether you want an urban, suburban, or rural location, and, at the same time, you should consider the potential future growth of the kind of business you envision.

The next step in location assessment is to test various sites. Let us assume that you've chosen a town of 20,000 for the location of a possible drugstore, and there are four competitive operations located there now. The first test to be made is whether or not there is room for another drugstore. There is data available from the United States Department of Commerce (in their "Census of Retail Trade" book series) regarding the population that is necessary to support various kinds of businesses; the national figure for drugstores happens to be 3700 people. Thus, our town of 20,000 can theoretically support

$$\frac{20,000}{3,700} = 5.4 \text{ drugstores}$$

If your drugstore would make the fifth in the town, you would have a chance of succeeding unless there was something unique about your competitors (one

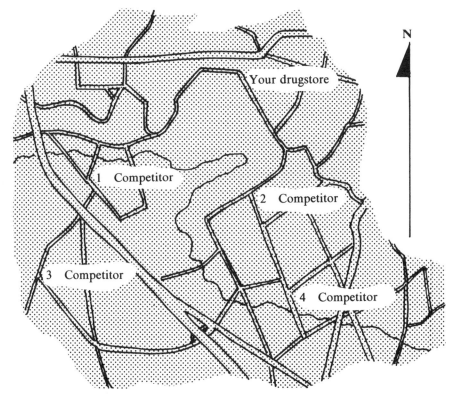

Figure 5.1 *Diagram for Examining the Potential Sales of a New Drugstore*

very large discount outfit that has more than its respective share of business, for example).

Assuming that the competitive drugstores in our example are all of approximately equal size and that the town could handle another operation, we will be ready to examine the potential sales of the new operation.

Consider Figure 5.1 as a possible situation you might encounter. The overall boundaries describe a certain buying area or, in the terms of the Bureau of the Census, a Standard Metropolitan Statistical Area (SMSA), which is a contained area of the population. As we said in Chapter 3, you should visit your local census office to see what information the agents have for you; you'll find them friendly and helpful people. Not only are they delighted to see you, they will tell you lots of interesting things. Their book series, *County Business Patterns,* is of inestimable usefulness. In Figure 5.1, we show you the location of your store in relation to the stores around you. Competitors 1 through 4 are already established, and have, we suspect, thriving and profitable locations. You wish to locate on the north side of town, an area you hope will support a new location.

The next analysis to be performed is a projected sales estimate, as shown in Figure 5.2. Line 1 is the total buying population, which we said was 20,000. Some areas of the country can count on additional tourist business; an estimate can usually be obtained from the local chamber of commerce (line 2). Adding lines 1 and 2 gives the total available market (line 3), some of which will have to be shared with competitors. Line 4 is an estimate of how much of the market you can control, the number of buyers that will come to your operation and yours alone, solely because of location. Line 5 is an estimate of the market that you will share with the other four drugstores. Remember that each of the other stores will have a unique market as your store has its own. In other words, since you can count on 3000 people for yourself and the five of you share 9000, that leaves 10,000 (22,000 − 12,000) reserved for your competitors, or an average of 2500 each. In this example these 10,000 individuals are lost to you totally. Line 6 lists the total number of competitors in the market, the four existing drugstores and yours. Line 7 shows the number of buyers that is the share of each competitor, which gives your total available market (line 8) when added to your exclusive share of the market (line 4). To reach your final result, your ultimate expected annual sales level, you need two research figures: the median annual income in your county or SMSA (line 9), and the national percentage of income spent on or in your type of enterprise (line 10). The expected annual sales is the product of your total available market multiplied by the median income of your area, multiplied by the fraction of income spent:

$$4800 \text{ people} \times \$9817 \times .0032 = \$150,789$$

Several small-business experts have said that the three major considerations concerning retail operations are location, location, and location.

Layout

If you don't think that layout is important to your business, then you don't understand business. We are talking about businesses that are dependent for sales upon the presence within the facility of potential customers. Some people like to spend hours browsing, which requires one kind of layout, whereas others have entered your establishment to find and buy one specific item, which requires another kind of layout. We had a delightful experience recently in a rather large gift shop where similar gift items were placed together in islands. The customer could visit each island, examine competing items, and then move on.

The best rule for effective layout is to put yourself in your customer's place and then decide what would be most effective not only for customer satisfaction, but for sales maximization as well. We like Bob Townsend's man-from-

```
1.  Total resident buying population      20,000

2.  Ten percent tourist business          2,000

3.  Total market (line 1 + line 2)       22,000

4.  Market you control                    3,000

5.  Market you share                      9,000

6.  Number of competitors plus you            5

7.  Line 5 + line 6                       1,800

8.  Your market (line 4 + line 7)         4,800


Following data is to be obtained from the Bureau of Census:


9.  Median annual income in your area    $9,817

10. Income spent on your product           .32%


Final result:


11. Expected annual sales               $150,789
    (line 8 X line 9 X line 10)
```

Figure 5.2 *Projected Sales Estimate for a New Drugstore*

Mars approach. If a man from Mars came into your store to buy something, how would he approach this buying activity? Are things logically laid out by product type, or is everything randomly distributed? How many times have you gone into a specialty store and wanted to buy, for example, shoe polish and shoe laces? You expect them to be together. Not very likely! The shoe polish is with the floor waxes (they both shine things), and the laces are nestled somewhere in with the sewing thread (both are long and stringy).

One nifty way to work out the layout scheme is to get several sheets of graph paper, mark it off to scale, and then paste cutouts of shelf items onto the floor plan. Ask someone for comments. Pretend you are a man from Mars. Does the layout make sense?

When you decide on a particular layout and put it into practice, watch how your customers behave. Ask them how they like it. If enough people say that the beer cooler is hard to find, or that they didn't even know that you had a salad bar, change things around. Your employees, once they are used to the routine, can also help you with suggestions. We have said before that successful entrepreneurs are excellent users of information and feedback. Pay attention.

If yours is a manufacturing operation, you have a different kind of situation. In this case, you want to minimize bottlenecks; no single operation in the conversion process should restrict the flow of goods. A Program Evaluation and Review Technique (PERT) chart can help you.

Figure 5.3 shows a sample PERT chart for a small operation. The numbers shown on each line connecting the various circles are the time to complete each operation in days. The particular product used as an example here is the normal, garden-variety toaster that sits in every American kitchen. We will assume that the firm does not manufacture any of the component parts, but is simply an assembly shop which puts the various pieces together, tests the unit for correct operation, and then ships the toaster to an electrical appliance wholesaler. The various parts to the toaster as they are delivered to the company are as follows:

1. The complete outer case (stamped from chrome-plated steel)
2. The plastic front plate with the name of the manufacturer
3. The dial which selects the darkness of the toast
4. The handle which is used to lower the toast to the heating coils
5. Power cord including the plug
6. Wiring harness that distributes power from the cord to the heating elements
7. The heating coils themselves
8. Plastic legs
9. The bottom plate that keeps little kids from putting their fingers inside (Zap!) and prevents crumbs from going everywhere
10. Guides to keep the toast from falling into the coils
11. The internal switch mechanism which also controls the time of "burn"
12. Screws to hold the whole toaster together

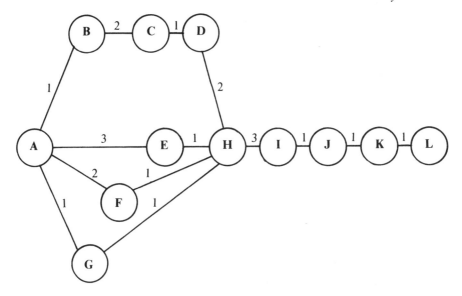

ACTIVITY

A Draw raw materials from stock
B Connect power cord to wiring harness
C Install switch
D Test for electrical continuity
E Mount heating coils and toast guides inside case
F Attach dial to front plate
G Attach legs to bottom plate
H Assemble all subcomponents
I Test toaster for correct operation (with real toast)
J Mount bottom plate with screws
K Attach handle
L Final assembly inspection

Figure 5.3 *PERT Diagram for Assembling a Toaster*

Figure 5.3 is a graphic way to look at the process and determine the bottle-necks that can occur. In our sample, the electrical assembly portion (six weeks) is the governing activity that must take place before the major assembly job can be completed. In all, it takes twelve weeks to assemble the toaster and make it ready to ship.

Later in this chapter, when we talk about Material Resource Planning (MRP), we will bring the toaster back to life for a different kind of discussion.

Layout, in any kind of business, also takes into account various physical and environmental considerations:

Exterior

Would I want to come into my business? Does the physical appearance outside broadcast the kind of establishment which I wish to project? It is true that quaint is cute, but quaintness can go just so far before a majority of people are turned away or turned off by an appearance that doesn't fit. Don't pick or design a location guided strictly from cost. You may want the help of an artist or an architect.

Interior

If you've been successful enough to attract potential customers inside, keep them there! Match your interior design and decor to your business. And pay attention to the total environment. If you sell high quality women's clothing (a true boutique), don't offer loud, raucous modern music; classical music might be nice. Watch the lighting levels. Even though it's right to save energy, keep the place comfortable. Keep the entrance free of obstacles, and keep it clean. Make sure the front door opens easily, and think about an automatic door for the exit (not the same door as the entrance door, please). If you plan to redecorate, get a consultant. You might love puce and violet, but the combination could give your customers a headache. Safety, too, is a consideration. Give close analysis to exposed, sharp corners. Watch the nature of the floor. Can it become slippery when people come in with wet feet? That's lawsuit land! Finally, be careful of a peeling ceiling, and an inferior interior.

General Environment

Watch your neighbors carefully. If your store sells religious articles, you don't want an adult bookstore next to you. Do not, under any circumstances, put any polluting substances into the air, the water, or the soil. You might think it's economical to begin with, but public pressure will get you in the end. Good entrepreneurs are right thinkers. Behave!

Purchasing

In this discussion of purchasing, we're going to be an industrial Robin Hood by robbing from the rich (big) and giving to the poor (small). The large firms have learned some of the secrets of effective purchasing because they do it in tremendous volume each day. In 1958, the Chevrolet Motor Division of General Motors used eighty-eight railroad flat cars of automobile bumpers a day to meet production needs. We have only used up *one* bumper (in an altercation with a very immovable tree). Let's see what guidelines we can borrow from the big operations to apply to ours.

Determine How Much to Buy

This sounds simple at first. Most people say, "I'll buy only what I need." But for how long? Under what terms? Big companies use a technique called the *blanket purchase agreement.* This is an agreement with a supplier to purchase a certain minimum amount of product (in units, gallons, or pounds) over a fixed period of time (usually one year). They arrange with their suppliers to release a certain amount of items each buying period (such as one month). By entering the order for the larger amount, they get a lower unit price which is guaranteed over the period of the purchase agreement. Not only does this hold down the inflationary effect of increasing prices with each order, it also helps the buyer plan items like cost of goods sold and, therefore, cash flow. If the buyer doesn't order all that he contracts for in the beginning, he is charged a higher unit price in the end. The price is charged at the end of the contract period, and, therefore, it will be in "cheaper" dollars (assuming that inflation continues. See the section on discounted cash flow in Chapter 7 for an expanded treatment of the ever-shrinking dollar).

Use Credit

Once you become established in business, you can depend on credit terms from most of your suppliers (this doesn't work with items like liquor). *Credit* is nothing more than a financing tool. You want to delay payment to your suppliers as long as good business sense says you should. Every day that you can make use of unpaid goods is a day you can "use" money. Don't stretch it, though. An angry supplier can begin to hurt your business. (Like a scorned or disappointed lover, they can shut you off.)

If your supplier offers you discount terms, analyze them. You may see on a particular bill the notation "2/10, net 30." This means that, if you pay your invoice within ten days, your supplier will allow you a 2 percent discount on your bill. Two percent may not seem like much, but consider the percentage rate involved. Two percent in ten days amounts to six percent in thirty days $(30 \div 10 \times 2\% = 6\%)$ which is 72 percent $(6\% \times 12 \text{ months})$ per year. Not a bad "investment."

If you get into a cash shortage and can't pay a particular supplier (and this will happen to you), telephone him, explain the situation, notify him when he can expect both partial and full payment, and then live up to your promise. Suppliers are not inhuman ogres bent on your destruction. They are in business just as you are, and they want you to succeed and grow so that they can enjoy more of your business. Use quality suppliers who will treat you equitably and well.

Manage Slow-Moving Stock

Just because you have a fondness for truffles does not mean that your customers share your idiosyncrasy. Possibly, some glib salesperson has talked you into stocking some worthless knickknack that everyone agrees is horrid. Pay particular attention to items that don't turn over well. Your shelf or floor space is valuable. You only have so much of it, and the secret of maximizing profitability is to maximize your use of space. If you notice that some item has an inordinate amount of dust on it, get rid of it, even if you have to give it away or take it to the dump. The chances are that you could use the space more efficiently. At some point in your business, you should know what the turnover rate is for each and every product. Stock that doesn't move amounts to throwing money away; you have paid your supplier for it but have not recovered your investment.

Use Purchase Orders

This may sound pretentious for a small business, but we recommend it. If nothing else, it will impress your supplier. Any good printer will take a standard purchase order (PO) and print your business name on a set of prenumbered forms. Be sure that you use a set of at least three copies; the original and an acknowledgment copy (to be returned to you) will go to your supplier, and one will be retained by you so that, when your order comes in, you can check it against the received goods. The PO becomes positive evidence of just what you ordered, and it gives you a method of rating suppliers, especially on promised delivery.

Material Resource Planning

The material resource planning (MRP) technique may not apply to your business; it is normally reserved for manufacturing organizations. Many large companies consider themselves very lucky for having adopted a sophisticated ordering technique though MRP is nothing more than plain old horse sense.

Let us go back to the example of the toaster, for a moment. There were twelve separate components to the device. Chances are that twelve different suppliers would be used, and that means twelve different delivery schedules. Some items, like the screws, are standard items and are available as stock items. The only time that it takes to receive items like these fasteners is paperwork time, usually a week or less. The stamped case might be an entirely different matter. That particular supplier may have to schedule the run in his plant, set up the various dies and presses, make the run of the required number, inspect each item to specifications, and ship. If the delivery times are all different, it doesn't make much economical sense to order all the parts for, say, 10,000 toasters on one day and then have the components arrive piecemeal. That costs money. MRP allows you to take a look at the item with the longest lead time and then to work backward in ordering items that take less time so that they all (theoretically) arrive on the same day to be put into production. Table 5.1 shows some theoretical lead times for the twelve items in the toaster.

TABLE 5.1

Theoretical Lead Times for Ordering Materials for a Toaster

Item	Lead Time (weeks)
Case	8
Front plate	6
Dial	1
Handle	1
Power cord	3
Harness	4
Heat coils	2
Screws	1
Legs	2
Bottom plate	3
Toast guides	5
Switch	4

The case obviously takes the longest time to receive, so it becomes the governing item from which all others are "backed off" in terms of ordering time. Figure 5.4 shows the ordering schedule for the various parts. The case is ordered on the very first day; two weeks later, the front plate is ordered; a week later than that, the toast guides are ordered, and so on. There is only one hitch—you better have honest suppliers.

Inventory Control: A Technique

A mathematical method that will allow you to minimize inventory costs is the *Economic Order Quantity* (EOQ). It has been used by the big companies for years. We will propose a full development of the method, which is really only intended for mathophiles, but the rest of you can concentrate on the logic and the final result.

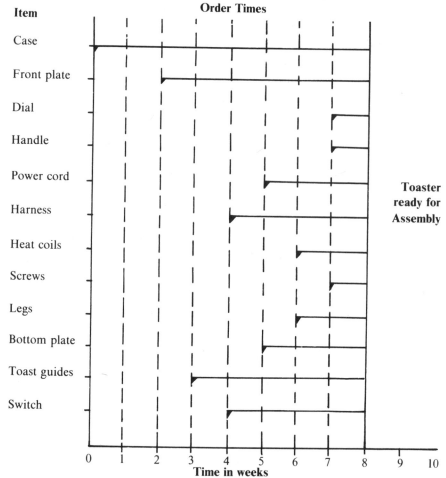

Figure 5.4 *Material Resource Planning (MRP) Schedule for Ordering Materials for a Toaster*

Some assumptions must be made before using EOQ. The major assumption is that inventory is used in a relatively uniform manner over time. The item may be a raw material used in your production process or an item that you purchase for resale.

Both explicit and implicit costs are involved with ordering and stocking particular goods. We are not going to concern ourselves with the price of an item; the EOQ method performs calculations without regard to unit price. It is evident that the process of ordering and inventorying any item has both fixed costs and variable costs.

Fixed Costs

Whether you order one item or 10,000, the fixed costs connected with the order remain about the same. To create the order, you must call the supplier (telephone cost), issue a PO (cost of someone's time), and follow up the delivery process (more telephone, more time).

Variable Costs

Variable costs are a bit more complicated to compute, but estimates can be made nonetheless. The largest segment of this cost is the carrying cost of inventory. That cost has two segments:

> *The Lost Cost of Sale.* The lost cost is a function of the time the item sits in inventory without use or sale. This might be expressed in terms of the original cost. For instance, if your profit margin after tax is 10 percent, a $5000 inventory that is unused or unsold after thirty days has cost you $41.67 ($5000 $\times$ 10% $\div$ 12 months).
>
> *The Use of Floor Space.* If you total all your fixed expenses (rent, taxes, utilities, license fees) and divide by the square feet of total floor space of your facility, you will find the value of any area that you choose to use. This calculation also allows you to examine the opportunity cost of lost space. For example, if your fixed costs are $100,000 per year and you have 20,000 square feet (100' $\times$ 200'), then your annual cost per year per square foot is $5.00, or about a penny and a half per square foot per day.
>
> Other variable costs would include insurance, loss of revenue from stock-out, deterioration, shrinkage (with gasoline and liquor), and theft (now running about 7 percent in a retail establishment).

Before we start the EOQ process, consider Figure 5.5, which depicts a theoretical use of inventory on a uniform basis. The sawtooth line represents a linear depletion of inventory until a level of inventory (r) is reached. At this time (t_0), a reorder of q units of material is made with a supplier whose delivery time is a weeks or days. Therefore, when the order is received (at time t_1), the safety margin of stock has been reached, and the amount of the order (q) is placed into inventory, replenishing stock. Note that the safety margin might be very close to zero. Figure 5.6 graphically depicts the EOQ process. We will find the value for q in Figure 5.5, which will minimize the total cost of ordering and stocking. The total cost (T) is, of course, the sum of the fixed cost (F) plus the variable cost (V), or

$$T = F + V$$

We now need to do some mathematics. Those of you who hate math may skip to the end of this section.

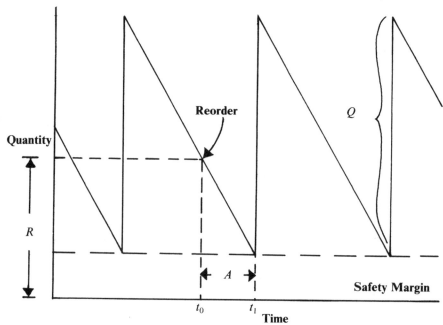

Figure 5.5 *The Changing Level of Inventory with Use*

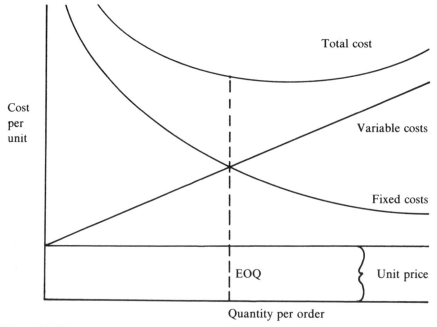

Figure 5.6 *Changes in Cost Levels in the Economic Order Quantity (EOQ) Process*

Consider the fixed cost portion (F) of the equation for a moment. Let us say that we know the number of units that we need in any year (as a function of good planning). This annual requirement or supply we will call s, and it will be expressed in units (cans of peas, number of leather belts, gallons of kerosene). If we are to order q units each time over the space of one year, then we will place s/q orders. Suppose that each time we order, it costs us f dollars to place that order. Then it will cost us $(s/q) \times f$ or $(s \times f)/q$ dollars in total in that year to place s/q orders. The result of this calculation is our fixed cost (F). Therefore

$$F = (s \times f) / q$$

We will now look at the variable cost portion.

Looking at Figure 5.5, and forgetting the safety stock for a moment, we can see that the inventory varies from a high of q to a low of zero. The average inventory over the year, then, is $q/2$, and, if we know that the variable (carrying) cost is c dollars per unit (since we know the amount of floor space each product occupies), then the annual variable cost (V) is

$$V = (q/2) \times c$$

By substituting into the original equation for total cost (T) and differentiating we will solve for q:

$$T = F + V$$
$$T = (sf/q) + (qc/2)$$
$$dT/dq = (-sf/q^2) + (c/2)$$
$$\text{setting} \quad dT/dq = 0 \quad \text{(for minimum cost)}$$
$$(sf/q^2) = (c/2)$$
$$q = \sqrt{(2sf/c)}$$

Let's try an example. A firm buys 10,000 units per year for $2.00 per unit. The inventory cost is 20 percent of the purchase price (rather typical). It costs $20.00 to place an order. How much should the firm order, and when?

$$c = \$2.00 \times 20\% \quad \text{or} \quad \$.40 \text{ per unit per year}$$
$$f = \$20.00 \text{ per order}$$
$$s = 10,000 \text{ units}$$
$$\text{The EOQ is} \quad q = (2sf/c)$$
$$q = \sqrt{(2 \times 20 \times 10,000) / .40}$$
$$q = 1000 \text{ units}$$

Thus, the firm orders 1000 units each time, and the order is placed ten times a year (10,000 ÷ 1000). An order placed ten times per year means an order is entered about every five weeks.

Once these calculations have been done, the entrepreneur can use them even further to his benefit. Possibly a blanket order (resulting in lower unit prices) could be issued to the supplier asking for a drop (partial) shipment every five weeks. No fixed cost!

Utility Cost Control

If you picked up a book written ten years ago on any phase of business, there would be little or no mention about utilities. If there was any at all, there would be a brief mention in the accounting section that you should figure in your costs—electricity, gas, oil, water—as costs of doing business. Now things are different. The cost of utilities will greatly affect your business operation and may be the most rapidly increasing cost of all. The electrical utilities use something called Construction Work In Progress (CWIP). This means that you pay for anything that they decide to build. You can't do much about it, but you ought to be aware of the cost.

The days of cheap, available energy are over. Heat, light, and power are becoming major cost items in some businesses. As a good business manager, you should be aware of the impact that these high costs will have on your income. And, as with any expensive item, it takes attention to minimize costs. Consider the following ways:

Local Building Contractors

Any contractor who knows his business should be able to advise you on steps to take to insulate your physical plant against unwanted exchanges of heat (out in the winter, in, in the summer). Your contractor will be able to demonstrate the savings that you can expect in the future by investing today in energy conservation. We are not going to go into a discussion of things you can do to save money. We'll leave that to the experts.

Tax Savings

It is a certainty that the United States government will expand its present program to reduce the taxes of both individuals and businesses that introduce energy saving devices and methods. Exactly what form the reduction will take from year to year (deduction or credit) and what it will be for (solar energy, wood heat, fiber glass insulation), no one can predict, but, as a good entrepreneur, you should be aware that you will be able to save on your taxes as well as reduce your heating bill. Read the new tax laws each year or have your accountant explain them to you.

Utility Companies

If you ask utility companies the right questions, you might find a few clues to saving money. Be sure that you have your meter checked if you suspect that your rates might be too high. For electricity, look into having the power utility deliver a higher voltage to your facility. Large companies have 13,600 or more volts delivered, and then they step it down themselves. Watch the power factor; matching inductive (motors) and capacitative (fluorescent lights) can help. Again, get expert advice.

Constant Surveys

Take periodic tours of your establishment looking for wasteful power usage. Turn off any lights or appliances that aren't needed. Examine alternate energy methods such as your own generator, a wood stove, a solar panel, a windmill. Think about using timers.

Environmental Considerations

No one likes a bad environmental neighbor. Our breathable air supply is limited to the scant few thousand feet above the earth's surface; we are not creating any new water, either. If you decide to introduce garbage into the air, water, or soil, then you not only become a bad neighbor to those around you, you also can be cited by local, state, or federal authorities. This becomes plain bad business. Regulatory agencies can make you cease operations or, at the minimum, levy a fine.

Most small businesses have little to fear regarding pollution problems, but be careful. Someone, for instance, is worrying about gasoline evaporation from service stations. Even the sanding of wood can produce noxious, flammable wood dust. Check with the appropriate agencies (EPA, ERDA) before you start anything questionable.

Local Laws, Ordinances, and Customs

This brief section does not have as much significance to an entrepreneur buying a going concern as it does to one starting a new enterprise. Certain towns and counties strictly regulate various types of businesses (bars, especially) and may flatly outlaw others (bars again). Zoning laws classifying areas as either residential, commercial, or industrial regulate where various kinds of business may locate. If you wish to start a cottage industry (making products in your home), you should check to see whether or not you might be in violation of zoning laws. If there are such regulations banning business operations in the home, you will want to file a request for a variance with the appropriate municipal authorities, and don't begin any business operation without the variance.

Visit your local chamber of commerce for advice and counsel regarding a new business, and, by all means, check with your lawyer. Don't be like the man we know who decided to begin a logging operation a few years back. He planned to use the river for transportation, then discovered too late that floating logs lost their bark during their stay in the river. This is great for the sawmill or pulp processor, but the tannic acid produced harms fish. The government banned the use of waterways for transporting wood timber shortly after his operation began.

We are not only a nation of laws, we are a nation of customs and habits. If you hold a door open for someone in New York City, he will wonder what kind of a deviate you are. Be courteous to a driver in Boston and you're liable to lose a fender. Down easters (from New Hampshire, Maine, Vermont) can't stand "Flatlanders" (tourists from Connecticut, New York, and New Jersey); Oregonians hate Californians. As Tom Lehrer once said in one of his typically irreverent songs about discrimination, "It's American as apple pie!" We witnessed the opening and the start of business of what appeared to be a potentially successful building supply store in a town of 20,000 people in New Hampshire. There was only one problem—the proprietors were from the Bronx. When they began using the sales tactics so common to the large metropolitan areas, their business failed quickly. People came in only once and never returned.

Not only do you have to be careful of the local laws regarding business operations, you have to pay particular attention to the type of business and the manner in which you plan to operate it.

Maintenance and Repair

An unproductive asset is an unprofitable asset. Nothing will work forever, not even some of the marvelous electronic devices that we are being treated to these days. Ours is a physical world, and everything will eventually wear out and cease its economic life, you included. There are a few simple things that you can do to lessen problems of equipment that does not work on occasion. If you are buying a going concern, an electronics company or a sub shop, inspect all the capital assets. Determine their age and present condition. See if the present owner will furnish you with a maintenance history. Ask if any of the warranties are transferable to you when you take over the business. If any of the items have maintenance contracts, determine what the payments are and what they cover. This also holds true for buying used equipment. You can often find some marvelous bargains at auctions of companies that have gone out of business (machine shops and restaurants, especially) but you have to know what you're buying and getting with the bargain. In the case of new items, first make the salesperson present you with written documentation regarding the warranty, what it covers in terms of repair, the period of the warranty, and what happens once the warranty period is over. (Smith's Law: a new vehicle or machine will have a major breakdown the day after the warranty lapses.) Ask if a maintenance contract is available after the initial guarantee period. Determine who performs the warranty (some manufacturers farm it out) and what is involved (some goods must be returned to the manufacturer's main facility—tough luck if that happens to be Osaka, Japan). Next, ask for the name of a recent customer and visit that customer. Reputable companies will be delighted to furnish you with the names of several customers. If possible, also do some research in the library (*Consumer Reports* is a good source) concerning the item. See if any of the current periodicals have given the items any bad press.

If you decide to buy the item—a lathe, a delivery truck, a meat slicer, or a computer—read the manual thoroughly. If the manufacturer suggests certain preventive maintenance (PM), by all means follow directions. Usually, this is nothing but replacing a filter, cleaning some item, or lubricating a bearing. Schedule your off time to do this. You will be ahead in the long run.

If something in the item is critical and stands a chance of frequent and costly failure, you may want to stock some spare parts. If the item requires repair, know immediately where you can go.

Transportation

This brief discussion of the methods of transportation pertains both to goods being received (which you can specify from your supplier and which you will pay for) and items that you ship (which your customer will pay for). The four general methods of transportation are land, water, air, pipeline. We will not discuss the last item, pipeline, since few small businesses would be concerned with this method.

Land

Mail. Many entrepreneurs engage in mail-order businesses for which the United States Postal Service (USPS) is the shipper. Shipping charges can be readily calculated and billed to your customer. Despite all the jokes, the USPS is one of the most reliable in the world, and doesn't employ people to jump on and throw packages marked Fragile. How many readers have honestly ever lost anything through the mail? If you're a new entrepreneur, visit your local post office and talk with the postmaster about ways to use the United States mail system.

UPS. The United Parcel System (UPS) has evolved into a country-wide service known for efficiency and fair prices. There is little significant data regarding their loss ratio compared to that of other means of transportation, but it must be low. UPS will pick up a package at your facility and deliver it to your customer.

Common Carrier. When you see the tractor-trailers of Consolidated, Holmes, Time-DC, Maislin, and others, you are seeing the common carriers. By law, they must hold themselves out to accept the freight of any reputable shipper (you) and attempt to deliver same to its final destination. Unless you can qualify for a full trailer-load (TL), you will have to pay a significantly higher unit rate based upon a less-than-trailer-load (LTL) and on the particular commodity that you are shipping. Check with the traffic and rate department of the trucking firm before you call it in.

Contract Carrier. Unless your firm makes large items (army tanks, bulldozers, steam turbines), you will only confront contract carriers on the highway or when they are delivering something to you like a 100-ton air conditioner.

Rail. Rail shipping is a method infrequently used by small businesses, and this is just as well. Use it at your peril. We don't know how they manage it, but the railroads have successfully lost whole trains. Where do you hide a train?

Water

As a small business owner, you will only encounter water as a method of transportation in overseas shipments. And even then it will resemble land transportation more than water. Your goods will most likely be placed into some kind of a container and be picked up and delivered by a truck.

Air

Pound for pound, air is the most expensive way to ship, but it's often necessary. Your customer may demand rapid delivery and be willing to pay for it. A shipment can leave New York at nine A.M. (six A.M. Los Angeles time) and be at a customer's facility in California by noon. Probably the best way to go is Federal Express, an airborne UPS. Federal Express also picks up and delivers and has an excellent record. Emery Air Freight and Purolator are also in this field.

In Conclusion

Most books on small businesses devote some discussion to the manufacturing process. We will not specifically do that here since there are many other good references in that area, and each manufacturing operation is unique. The same principles apply to the manufacturing operation that apply to any business operation.

Elimination of Bottlenecks

Examine your proposed or actual operation and determine which of your subprocesses restrict the flow of goods.

Quality Control

The big companies use the following three levels of inspection to assure sufficient quality: incoming (the goods and raw materials that you receive), in process (what happens while items are on your premises), and final (the stage that precedes delivery). Remember that you're allowed a few defects now and then, but keep them to a minimum and keep those in a nondangerous area.

Work Measurement

Forget the stop watch and the clipboard, but do analyze your people and the way they perform their jobs.

Work Planning

Know in advance through good planning when to expect excess demands upon you and your people. Know how to cope with these changes. Much more of this will be covered in Chapter 8.

CHAPTER SIX

Marketing

We are not here to sell a parcel of boilers and vats, but the potentiality of growing rich beyond the dreams of avarice.

Samuel Johnson

If any one segment of any business, large or small, can be deemed the key or pivotal area, that area would be marketing; assuming that a business has goods and services for sale. The large companies realized years ago that the marketing function leads the firm's efforts. It is (or should be) the eyes and ears of the business, looking at and listening to the available and potential market and being ready to meet and satisfy customer needs. The most common definition of *marketing* is the area of the company primarily concerned with providing goods and services that (1) meet consumer demands, and (2) satisfy business goals and objectives at a profit to the company.

Marketing has changed substantially over the last thirty years or so. In the distant past in this country, most companies had only sales departments, and the sales staff were known as drummers. (Hence the phrase "drum up some business.") Salesmen wandered around the countryside with their order pads and display cases trying to sell products that had been developed because someone thought there was a market. Since the buying public was as unsophisticated as the sales methods employed, this method of offering untried and untested products worked reasonably well, but much of the sales approach was pure hard-sell. The job title of salesman began to earn a less-than-respectable status among the American public, and much of this feeling exists today. The bottom of the job heap still appears to be the used-car salesman, and some people still wonder how far the speedometer has been turned back or how much sawdust has been put in the transmission, even though both of these activities are illegal in all states.

Your marketing strategy (and put it in writing, please) reflects your entire approach to your business. It answers some of the questions posed by the six horsemen of any business—the five W's plus H:

Who? Who is the individual within the business with the primary responsibility for initiating, designing, and implementing your marketing strategy? You? Your spouse or lover? Your partner?

What? In the short run, what products and services will you offer to your customers? In the long run, what will you add to your product line to further meet demand and increase profits?

When? When is the appropriate time in a calendar or fiscal year to offer (or remove) various products and services from your total offering? As you expand, when will you add to your product line?

Figure 6.1 *Ivory Tower Manufacturing Company*

Why? Does all this activity have a purpose? Is the profit worth the time and effort? Is there sufficient demand to do what you're doing? What are your real motivations for operating this venture?

Where? In what town, county, or state should the venture be located to maximize business results as a function of the available opportunities? (Notice the similarity to the definition of planning proposed in Chapter 4.)

How? Given a limited amount of funds and time, how should you best apply both of them to maximize profits?

Today, marketing has become a highly intricate and sophisticated operation. In keeping with our theme of using the systems of large organizations, we will address various subsystems of marketing as they apply to the entrepreneur. The major ones are the following:

Marketing research and planning
Product planning
Communications
Credit and collection
Pricing
Personal selling
Sales management

Marketing Research and Planning

The activity within a business that has to do with the collecting and analyzing of data about the marketplace is usually called *marketing research.* In the big companies, the researchers may have their own computer. When the analyzed data is used to chart the future course of the company, it is called *marketing planning.* These two activities are extremely necessary since financial decisions will be made as a function of what has been determined. An actual example may help to clarify this.

A large firm had, as one of its many product lines, fire extinguishing and detection equipment of various types. The company had an active marketing research department. One of the managers in that department, working with and through the national sales manager, had instituted a marketing intelligence system using the sales force. If a salesperson heard, read, or saw anything that might be of concern to the company, he was to report it in his regular call reports. In one week, two sales people reported the same thing: the insurance industry had discovered that a great many restaurant fires had originated at deep-fat fryers or the exhaust hoods above the fryers. It was rumored that the insurance rates for restaurants equipped with these fryers was going to increase substantially in the next year. The company decided to develop and manufacture a low-cost fire extinguishing device that would be mounted under the exhaust hood over the fryers and would quickly extinguish any fire in the fryers or in the hood's filter. When the insurance industry announced the rate increase, the company announced the product and totally scooped the market since the cost of the extinguisher was less than the annual premium increase. Every salesperson had been given a list of all restaurants within his territory that employed deep-fat frying.

If planning stems from marketing research, then this also implies that the entire business strategy for meeting and satisfying customer needs also has its roots here. When you think about that implication, you can see that its effects are far-reaching. If an entrepreneur makes some wrong assumptions in the early stage, they will be multiplied manyfold later on and may spell ultimate disaster for the business.

Market Segmentation

One of the first tasks under the marketing research heading is *market segmentation* and *identification*. All this means is finding out who your market is and then learning as much about it as you can. Doing this wisely should lead you to something the experts call the marketing mix. Table 6.1 is a marketing mix for a hypothetical restaurant.

TABLE 6.1

Marketing Mix for a Hypothetical Restaurant

		Activity		
Customer Type	*Breakfast*	*Lunch*	*Afternoon*	*Dinner*
Blue-collar	3	2	0	1
White-collar	1	3	1	2
Couples	0	1	0	3
Students	0	0	3	0

Key
0 = no customers   1 = minor customer group   2 = average customer group
3 = major customer group

The knowledge contained in Table 6.1 would enable an entrepreneur to tailor the business activity (selling food and beverages) to the major customer types present.

Another benefit provided by market segmentation is that it should keep an entrepreneur from doing too much of everything. There is a strong temptation in your own business to keep adding new products and services, but this has to be controlled and planned for well in advance.

Marketing research should be vitally concerned with the marketing intelligence approach that we introduced in our fire extinguisher example. Use one manila folder for each viable competitor that you have. Anytime you read an

Listed below are some qualities concerning some of the clothing
stores in our town. Please rate each item for each store: a 1
is very good, a 2 is average or so-so, 3 is poor or marginal,
4 is "don't know," and 5 is "never been there."

	Judy's	LaBoutique	Sally's	Sunshine
Location				
Parking				
General appearance				
Sales courtesy				
Quality of merchandise				
Availability of merchandise				
Prices				
Credit policy				
Reputation				

Now, please rank the stores in order from best to worst.

1.

2.

3.

4.

Why did you place one store first?_____

_____

_____

Why did you place one store last?_____

_____

_____

Figure 6.2 *Sample of a Consultant's Questionnaire*

article about a competitor, clip it and place it in the folder. If you hear something, write it down and file it. Review the contents of the folders on a regular basis.

If you have the time and the finances, a brief study of your operation in relation to your competition might be in order. This is especially true if your data on your competitors is sketchy or inaccurate. Figure 6.2 is a reproduction of a consultant's questionnaire actually used in a study of four boutiques in a small city. You can do the study in the evening by telephone (identify yourself as a consultant), or you can use an outside service.

Forecasting

Another area under marketing research and planning has to do with *forecasting*. The forecasting process is also involved with data collection, the making of assumptions, and the projection into the future of various activities, usually sales levels. The good entrepreneur forecasts sales at least three years in advance (monthly for the first year and by quarter for the next two), and then uses assumptions about costs, expenses, liabilities, and assets to construct the pro forma income statements, balance sheets, and cash flow projections. (Refer to the sample business plans in Appendix H.) Forecasting, as vital as it is to business success, can never predict the unpredictable. Another true story will bear this out.

Some years ago, a retired mathematics professor developed what he believed to be an entirely new method of forecasting using formulas so complex that he needed a computer terminal for the analysis. Before he presented his discovery to his colleagues, he decided that he must thoroughly test the model. That meant using a method known as backcasting. Backcasting requires that you go back to some point in the past and then forecast for some future period for which you have the data already. If, for instance, you thought that you had a method that would accurately predict the United States Gross National Product (GNP) two years hence, you would return to some point in the past, say, 1958, and then forecast the data to 1960. Since you know what the GNP was in 1960, you can see if the model was correct or not. Successive tests of the model validate or invalidate the method. The math professor wanted his test to be absolutely conclusive, so he began the search for the oldest successive collection of data in the world. He found it. For nearly 4000 years, at a particular time of the day, someone has gone to a spot on the Nile River and measured the depth of the river. Our academic friend persuaded the Egyptian authorities to let him have the data for analysis. He returned to his computer, began feeding it the information to make the appropriate prediction about the height of the river for the coming day, and then compared the forecast with the actual measured data. The model was astounding in its accuracy, and we suppose that the output looked something like Table 6.2.

TABLE 6.2

Sample Nile River Heights

Date	Predicted Value (ft.)	Actual Value (ft.)	Difference (ft.)
Dec. 4, 1714 BC	12.28	12.31	+0.03
Dec. 5, 1714 BC	8.05	7.97	−0.08
Dec. 6, 1714 BC	11.37	11.15	−0.22
Dec. 7, 1714 BC	9.72	9.93	+0.21

The differences were small indeed until the computer reached modern times. After nearly 1.5 million calculations, the computer said that the model was off by several hundred feet! Someone built the Aswan High Dam. We can't foresee everything.

There are probably more methods of forecasting than any one person would want to contemplate, so we will mention only a few. If any reader wants to pursue the area in detail, he is invited to read any text on business forecasting or attend a seminar on the subject.

The very first step before even beginning any forecasting is to list the assumptions that will underlie the forecast. These assumptions might include such future items as the following:

The level of the GNP, both real and inflated.

Other government projections that might affect business, such as net disposable income, unemployment rate, or the federal fund rate.

Various statistics that pertain specifically to your business. Go to any large library and ask to see the latest edition of *Predicasts*. Then look up your particular product or service.

The suspected moves of competition.

Regional developments (like a highway bypass) that may impact the venture.

The second step in the forecasting process is to assemble every bit of data that will affect future operation. If the business is a going concern, past values of monthly sales and income are the most important data. If the business is a start-up venture, you will have to use a method like that described in Chapter 5 under Location and then make assumptions for later years. If yours is a retail operation, then the resident population plus transient (tourist) potential described in Chapter 5 should work well. If your venture manufactures a product that can be sold in other establishments anywhere, you will need to do some calculations about your total available market (number of potential buyers) and your penetration of that market (percentage that you can capture).

We had the opportunity to view the latter type of operation several years ago, and, therefore, an analysis of it would be appropriate here since the forecasting of the new venture is trickier than that of a going concern. The particular product in question was a plastic, temperature-sensitive strip, about 3 cm. by 20 cm. When exposed to various temperatures (from −40°C to +20°C) it would display the type of wax to be applied to cross-country (X-C) skis. The strip had an adhesive backing, and the manufacturer suggested that the strip be pressed onto the front of one of the two skis. He was interested to know what his expected sales would be. We had only about fifteen minutes to do an initial analysis. Anyone can now go back and check the data and undoubtedly prove us wrong, but we'll challenge anyone to do better under identical circumstances. Here's what we did:

We called a skiing aficionado we know and asked:

Question (Q): How many skiers in the United States?
Answer (A): 16,000,000.
Q: What's the breakdown of X-C versus alpine?
A: Sixty-four percent have tried both at least once.
Q: How many X-C skis sold last year?
A: Approximately 666,000 pairs.
Q: How fast is the X-C ski business growing?
A: Around 12 percent annually.

From the data we obtained, we guessed that there were 2,000,000 active X-C skiers, give or take 500,000. We predicted that the manufacturer might expect market penetrations in the first three years of 2 percent, 5 percent, and 8 percent, respectively. Then we figured the gross sales based on a net price to the manufacturer of $.89 (not the real number) according to Table 6.3.

TABLE 6.3

Sales Projections for Temperature-Sensitive Strip for Skis

Year	Total Market	Share	Buyers	Sales (at $.89 each)
1	2,000,000	2%	40,000	$ 35,600
2	2,240,000	5%	112,000	99,680
3	2,508,800	8%	200,700	178,626

Quantitative Forecasting

Projecting the business levels in a going concern is an easier job than projecting for a start-up since there is an observable, historical pattern. The few techniques that we will talk about are *quantitative forecasting*. A few qualitative methods are available, the most popular of which is the Delphi technique, which was so mysterious that the military classified it as top secret for a number of years. Delphi has very little use in small business today although this may not be the case in the future. Basically, Delphi consists of asking a specific question of a group of experts, tabulating the results, showing the entire set of results to the experts, and then asking for their second (or third or fourth) estimates. Ordinarily, however, the questions have been rather broad and far-reaching, like, "When do you believe nuclear fusion will become a viable source of energy?" or "In what year will man actively colonize another planet?"

But, on to the quantitative methods.

Percent-of-Last-Year. The percent-of-last-year method is, in many ways, a cop-out, but it's better than nothing at all. You simply assume that the business will increase by a certain percentage amount next year, and the year after, and the year after that. Very few people are totally aware of the problem with all this. If you say that your business is going to grow ten percent next year, the immediate question is, what is real and what is inflated? You could raise prices 10 percent and meet the stated objective; you could keep prices uniform, raise volume, and still meet it. If you use the percent-of-last-year method, you should be certain where the growth is coming from. A 10 percent price increase is only inflated growth; you have not pushed any more goods and services out the door. Inflation, outside of some world-wide disaster, will be with us forever, and you will have to raise prices to meet rising costs. Just be certain that you know the difference between real growth and inflated growth. The government does!

Growth rates seem to be difficult for some people, especially when more than one year is involved. The technique is relatively simple if we take it one step at a time. If the appropriate growth rate in dollars is 10 percent, then the growth factor is the number 1 added to the growth rate expressed as a decimal, or in our case, 1.10. This value is then multiplied by the dollar sales in the base year to arrive at the value for the next year. If a small business had sales of $200,000 in the base year and could expect a 10 percent growth next year, the projected value would be $200,000 × 1.10 or $220,000. If the growth of 10 percent could be expected for the second period, the sales in the third year would be $220,000 × 1.10 or $242,000. If we could assume that the 10 percent growth rate would continue for a long period of time (as, say, an average value), then we could project relatively far into the future. Suppose, for example, that we wished to calculate the sales level in our business in the seventh year. We would multiply the base year's sales of $200,000 by 1.10 multiplied by itself seven times (1.10^7). The calculation would look like this:

Seventh year sales level = $200,000×(1.1)×(1.1)×(1.1)×(1.1)×(1.1)×(1.1)×(1.1)
= $200,000×(1.9487)
= $389,743

Therefore, we could say that any future value of sales (s_f) would depend upon the level of sales in the base year (s_b), the annual growth rate expected (r), and the number of years involved (n), or

$$s_f = s_b (1 + r)^n$$

The formula above can also be used to determine what the average annual growth rate has been in the past, given the proper sales levels. Suppose that a business had base year level sales of $200,000 and, six years later, the sales had risen to $500,000. What is the average annual growth rate? We start with the basic formula just described to find the rate (r). We know all the other values.

$$(1 + r)^n = s_f/s_b$$
$$r = \sqrt[n]{(s_f/s_b)} - 1$$

Now, substituting the numbers given for the six year history,

$$r = \sqrt[6]{(500,000/200,000)} - 1$$
$$r = \sqrt[6]{2.5} - 1$$
$$r = 1.165 - 1$$
$$r = .165 \quad \text{or} \quad 16.5\%$$

Most pocket calculators will do the math.

Straight-Line or Linear or Least Squares Regression Method. This approach is relatively simple to use thanks to modern calculators, which will give the numerical answers. The technique must be used along with a graph of the information. (Any good entrepreneur keeps a running graph of sales and profits, anyway.)

This method allows a straight line to represent data that, when plotted, does not result in a straight line. Figure 6.3 shows a group of sample data representing hypothetical monthly sales. The graph of the various points is not linear and thus is impossible to express mathematically. There is a way, however, to place a straight line on the graph so that the sum of the square of the distances from all points to the line itself is a minimum. Figure 6.4 shows the least squares technique, which will minimize the square of d_1 plus the square of d_2 and so on; hence the name *least squares.* The mathematics of the method will analyze the sales information and formulate the equation for the line of best fit. Remembering your high school algebra for a moment, you will recall that the equation for a straight line is

$$y = mx + b$$

In Figure 6.5, b is the y-intercept and m is the slope of the line. Modern calculators will give you both values. Suppose you fed six months of sales information into your pocket calculator using the numbers 1–6 to represent the appropriate

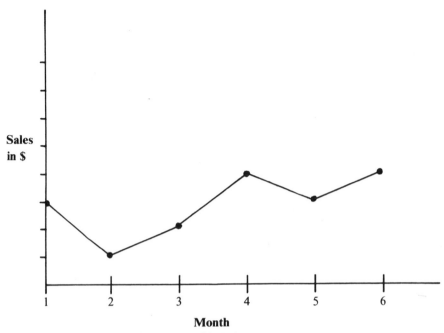

Figure 6.3 *Graph of Hypothetical Monthly Sales*

months, and it displayed 52,500 for *b* and 2500 for *m*. The appropriate equation is:

$$y = 2500x + 52,500$$

and, if sales for month 7 were being estimated

$$y_7 = 2500(7) + 52,500$$
$$= \$70,000$$

It is strongly recommended that the method not be used to project too many periods into the future. Sometimes, to make matters worse, the data is so widely dispersed, that it's impossible to "see" what's really going on, and, if this is so, a straight line approximation is meaningless. Any good statistics book will give you a more detailed explanation of the method.

Moving Average or Smoothing. When the data gets so spiky that it is almost impossible to detect a general trend, then an averaging technique helps to smooth out the peaks and valleys so that the graph is easier to read. A determination can then be made as to whether there is a general increase or a decline in business. It may be true that many entrepreneurs don't forecast because they

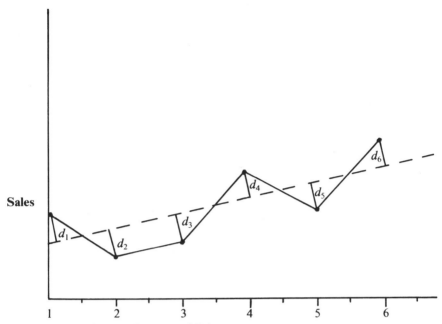

Figure 6.4 *Least Squares Diagram of Sales*

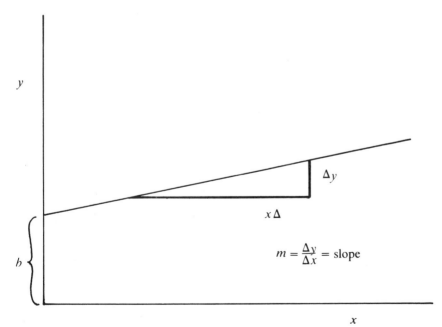

Figure 6.5 *Algebraic Representation of a Straight Line*

don't even know where they've been (except for year-end figures). To demonstrate the technique, take the following twelve months of sales data shown in Table 6.4.

TABLE 6.4

Sales Data for Twelve Months

Months	Sales Data
1	$ 9,000
2	$22,000
3	$32,000
4	$ 7,000
5	$25,000
6	$40,000
7	$ 3,000
8	$17,000
9	$46,000
10	$11,000
11	$27,000
12	$12,000

This pattern is extremely erratic, but we're using it for demonstration purposes only.

The moving average approach simply takes the average of information for any number of months and then continuously moves along through the data until the analysis is complete. If we were using a moving average for two months at a time, the average of months 1 and 2 would be:

$$\frac{9,000 + 22,000}{2} = \$15,500$$

The average would then be taken for months 2 and 3, months 3 and 4, and so on, until eleven pieces of data had been developed as in Table 6.5. Notice that there are only eleven data points instead of twelve; the previous low of $3,000 and high of $46,000 no longer exist. As longer periods of averaging are chosen (three months, four months), the data becomes more uniform, but, at the same time, less data points are achieved.

This method is not really predictive as much as it is useful for determining past trends where normal graphing techniques produce a rather puzzling display. The reader is invited to graph the values in Tables 6.4 and 6.5 and examine the relative differences in what the information shows. There is a method of forecasting known as *exponential* or *weighted smoothing,* but the development of it would take more space and time than we have available here.

TABLE 6.5

Two-Month Moving Average

1. $15,500 ((9,000 + 22,000)/2)
2. $27,000 ((22,000 + 32,000)/2)
3. $19,500 ((32,000 + 7,000)/2)
4. $16,000   etc.
5. $32,500
6. $21,500
7. $10,000
8. $32,500
9. $28,500
10. $19,000
11. $19,500

Deseasonalizing. Deseasonalizing can become a rather useful technique when the levels of monthly sales are seasonally repetitive. A hospitality operation in a tourist area naturally depends upon when tourists are around, summer only or winter only. An extreme example would be a toy store that might experience 50 percent of its annual business during the middle two weeks of December.

To make the analysis meaningful, monthly data for at least two years are necessary. The method makes the basic assumption that the average percentage of annual sales that has occurred in past months will continue to occur in future months. If sales were exactly uniform over the year, each month would have one-twelfth or 8.33 percent of the total annual sales; only in the rarest of cases would this be true, however. Assume, then, for the past three years, that February has accounted for 10 percent of the annual volume and that total sales have been increasing 20 percent every year. If the year just ended produced sales of $400,000, then the sales for the coming February could be expected to be

$$\$400,000 \times 120\% \times 10\% = \$48,000$$

For deseasonalizing to work at all, there must be a repeated pattern of monthly seasonal trends.

Multiple Regression. The mechanics of multiple regression will not be discussed here. This particular breed of forecasting is reserved strictly to the mathematically oriented among you, especially those of you who feel comfortable nestled up close to a computer. The basic theory behind multiple regression is that your business results (sales, usually) are a result and a function of a large number of exogenous (external) variables. Using a computer, it is possible to

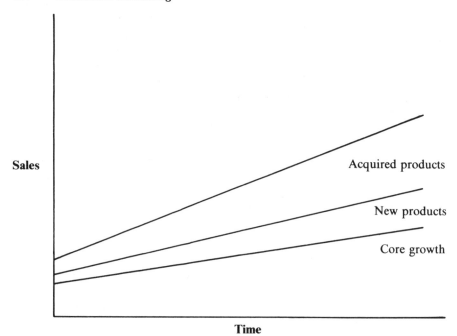

Figure 6.6 *Growth of an Enterprise over Time*

OLD PRODUCTS **(core)** OLD CUSTOMERS	OLD PRODUCTS **(core)** NEW CUSTOMERS
NEW PRODUCTS **(new)** OLD CUSTOMERS	NEW PRODUCTS **(acquired)** NEW CUSTOMERS

Figure 6.7 *Product Grid*

feed in a number of these variables (gross national product, net disposable income, unemployment rate, population growth) and see if, in the past, they correlated with your sales levels. The computer will allow you to juggle different variables for the years in question to see which set fits best. The computer will tell you, mathematically, just how descriptive past data have been. Once an equation has been developed, it can be used with the past information to see how well it would have worked.

There is only one major problem with the technique. Even if a mathematical expression is found that would have worked in the past, its use for future projections is limited by the fact that in order to use the model for, say, next year's sales estimates, you will need to obtain solid predictions for the variables in the equation. As an example, if one of the elements in the equation is the gross national product, one of the most frequently forecast pieces of economic information, you will discover that two authorities can differ by as much as 20 percent in their prognostications.

There are other quantitative methods, some complex and some simple. Until the business becomes well established and a lot of information can be gathered about it, the forecasting methods should be kept as simple as possible, especially when you remember that the most important part of the forecasting, profit forecasting, stems from the sales forecasting.

Product Planning

Many entrepreneurs we know have a difficult time planning ahead to the products and services that they will offer in the future. Either they are afraid to expand, or some slick salesperson gets them to load up on shellfish just as a new wave of red tide is announced off the coast. Our philosophy is one of carefully controlled growth through intelligent and logical *product planning*.

Most large companies look at the growth situation in two major ways. Figure 6.6 shows the thinking of one of the country's large, Fortune 500 companies. The base level of growth is known as *core* growth or, as seen in Figure 6.7, the selling of old (existing) products to both old and new customers. Companies have the opportunity to introduce new products which are usually sold to existing customers (automobiles, for example) and they can acquire products or whole corporations. Figure 6.7 is also helpful as a thinking tool for planning both product and market expansion. A retail business can stock more lines of merchandise (new products) or it can purchase or develop an entirely new operation (acquired products).

Product planning in the majority of small businesses is really not very difficult at all. It means being imaginative about answering the following question, "If I sell (a), can I also sell (b)?" You can probably think of many examples, but suppose (a) is "home heating oil"; then (b) could be—

kerosene
oil burners
wood furnaces
hot-water tanks
space heaters
solar panels
insulation

and so on. The list can be endless.

For entrepreneurs involved in manufacturing, the task becomes a bit more exacting, but doing a good job of marketing research will certainly help. We certainly admire and pity the entrepreneur who needs to get into a manufacturing business but doesn't know what to make. Some of the books dedicated to high technology ventures do a much better job addressing this particular subject than we can do here. If you're working for a big company, keep your eyes out for discarded goodies.

One method of product planning of which we're particularly fond and which can work in many situations is called *morphological analysis*. It's fun, fast, and revealing. Here's how it works.

We tried the morphological technique while teaching an undergraduate marketing course. We used a retractable, pocket ball-point pen. Listed below are the actual results when some thirty students analyzed this writing instrument. Under each major heading, the first entry represents the actual quality of the instrument being held before the class. Students were then asked to suggest different qualities that would fit under each heading.

A. *Basic Shape*
    Round
    Square
    Oval
    Flat
    Hexagonal
    Conical
    Cubical
    Spherical
    Disk
B. *Construction*
    Three-piece, retractable
    One-piece
    Multiple point
    Tipped

C. *Writing Medium*
   Liquid ink
   Graphite
   Charcoal
   Chalk
   Wax
   Blood (really!)
   Invisible ink
   Oil
D. *Material of Barrel*
   Plastic and aluminum
   Steel
   Plastic
   Wood
   Glass
   Rubber
   Gold
   Slate
   Asbestos
E. *Method of Attachment*
   Clip
   Spring
   Magnet
   Chain
   Adhesive
   Velcro
   Mounting hole (like a telephone dial)
F. *Special Features*
   None
   Advertising
   Pictures
   Calculator
   Radio
   Metal detector (same person that selected blood!)
   Thermometer
   Flashlight

The experiment took 8 minutes and resulted in our coming up with

$$9 \times 4 \times 9 \times 9 \times 7 \times 8 = 163,296 \text{ combinations}$$

Somewhere in that group there must be one or two good, saleable ideas.

An even more advanced technique, called *market gap analysis,* allows product planners to examine possible marketing gaps which might exist so that items or services can be developed to fill the gaps. Interested readers are urged to read the description of this method in *The Entrepreneur's Manual* by Richard M. White, Jr. (Radnor, Pa.: Chilton Book Co., 1977).

Communications

By *communications,* we don't mean just advertising although that's probably the most common form of marketing communications. We mean every word, every picture, and every reference to your business, from your phone number in the white pages to your TV advertising campaign. Just as the marketing plan becomes a major part of your business plan, so the communications plan is a contributor to the marketing plan and should be intricately tied into the business development scheme. Since everything said or written about your business will reach someone else, maybe for the first time, maybe for the thousandth, you want that communication to be as positive as possible. Therefore, before we embark on some of the areas within marketing communications, we will touch on something that every entrepreneur who wants to be successful should be vitally aware of—image.

Image

The *image* that you project to your customers should maximize sales. The way you are perceived should not turn people away, or, worse yet, cause the word to spread that yours is not a favorable enterprise. You do not have to conform to what everybody says is in vogue at the present; sometimes the risqué, the bizarre, or the outrageous draw business. Consider the following example:

Some years ago, before the age of sexual enlightenment, we frequented a lounge on Cape Cod. In the ladies' room, there was a full-size, nude, lifelike plastic statue of a man with a fig leaf strategically placed. It was obvious that the fig leaf was hinged. Should some unsuspecting patron lift the fig leaf, her action tripped a switch which started lights blinking and bells ringing. Since this could easily be heard outside the lavatory, there were some evenings when a hapless customer would spend five or ten minutes inside the ladies' room because of embarrassment. When she did emerge, to much cheering and clapping, everyone would gleefully wait for the next unlucky soul to make her investigation. The image that this particular bar wanted to project was one of a place where people could go to have fun.

The image of your business has to be right for your customers and right for you; you must be comfortable with it. Much of this gets down to running an operation that is reputable, honest, and courteous to customers. If you turn off even a small majority, that can have a snowballing effect which may eventually come home to haunt you. A self-fulfilling prophecy will self-fulfill.

Part of the image has to do with being a professional entrepreneur. This usually means becoming involved in your community in one way or another. Joining organizations such as the chamber of commerce and Rotary will get you close to important influences in your city or town. Performing charitable works or donating to deserving organizations is not only tax deductible, but it is, in a way, sharing your good fortune with those less fortunate.

Advertising

Within the framework of communications, *advertising* is probably the largest segment in terms of dollars. Someone once said that running a business without advertising is like winking at girls (or boys) in the dark—you know what you're doing, but they don't.

Advertising and its effectiveness is one of the least understood subjects in small business. If you place an ad in a newspaper or on the radio, who's to say how effective that ad really is? There have been temporary cases in large companies where no advertising was done initially, but business success was achieved nonetheless. Wilkinson Sword Blade, Volkswagen, and Hershey's are three examples, but they all advertised eventually. Many people ask about using an agency and are quite reluctant to approach one, believing that they are all high-priced Madison Avenue organizations. This isn't so. Many agencies have carved themselves viable niches in small business. Let's face it. Agencies are creative, and they understand both media and the reader. Be certain to pick a small agency (less than five principals), check references before you sign anything or engage them to do any work, and get estimates in advance of what any program will cost. Beware of anyone who wants you to embark on an ad campaign and also be very careful of any agency who wants to study you before writing any copy. That's fine for GM, but not for you. You can't afford it (yet). Look for people who will work with you in the early stages. They may be willing to delay sending you a bill for a few months. Once you have mutually decided upon a budget for the upcoming year (and be certain to get a not-to-exceed price), let them do their work uncluttered and alone. You've got your business to run, and they, theirs. If you have confidence in them, let 'em run (not on your bank account, of course).

There are various ways that you and your agency can establish a budget for your communications plan. In your business plan, you should allow funds for this effort. Most marketing textbooks talk about the following four ways to determine an advertising budget:

Funds that are left over
Copying competition
Percent of sales
Goal fulfillment

The first method, using left-over funds, is one unfortunately used by many large and small businesses alike, and assures that most of the expenditure will be thrown away. Copying competition and using a percent of sales are improvements but not large ones. They tend to maintain status quo, and are, therefore, more defensive than anything else; they maintain, rather than seek to improve, market share. Goal fulfillment will let you and your agency set various goals, such as to improve market share by 10 percent, and then determine what must be done to accomplish this objective. If your business plan is a truly useful document, this goal-setting approach should be an integral part of the marketing growth that you've planned for.

Media

The last area to be addressed within advertising and communications is *media,* or where your name and other information about your business will appear. The first and most important item is your brochure. Almost every business needs some kind of document describing what the business does, the address and telephone, the name of the proprietor(s), and perhaps professional photographs. Try to make it clever and appealing so that people will take one. (Many restaurants use their menu.) Don't forget a touch of humor, also.

Your agency should really earn its keep in talking about outside media (other than your own internal documents). Their people have data on newspaper, radio, and TV audience coverage as well as the costs involved. If they're any good, they should have a fair idea of what your customer base is and what combination of media would most effectively reach it for each dollar spent. The nature of your business will determine the media you will use.

Newspapers. Newspapers are probably the most widely used media for small business. Since most small businesses have a local patronage, and since most Americans read newspapers, it makes a lot of sense to advertise in them. It is usually wise to think about continuous advertising, perhaps even on a daily basis. Develop a theme and stay with it. Use your logotype in the ad. Advertise specials. More and more newspapers have front-page advertising. If you are using a local paper regularly and are a good customer, be sure to send out regular press releases. Possibly not every one will be printed, but newspapers are a business, and they understand reciprocity. Also, be sure to check discounts available for increasing space usage.

Radio. Radio, the spoken (or, often, sung) word, makes an excellent accompaniment to the written and visualized word. Remember that the rate for a thirty-second spot will vary significantly from drive time to late evening, just as the number of listeners will change; FM rates are different from AM rates; WNBC in New York will charge more than WARM in Scranton. You might consider sponsoring the weather or the sports news once or twice a week. Keep your message brief, to the point, and understandable. Get opinions from your agency or the station itself.

Television. Use television ads with extreme caution. They are expensive to prepare and expensive to run. Until you get to at least $600,000 a year in sales, fight the urge. And, if you do get to the point where TV might be a viable media, under no circumstances allow your face and voice to appear in the ad. It's unbelievable the number of corpulent, ugly, inarticulate entrepreneurs that feed their inflated egos on the late movie ads. You run your business; we don't need your visage on the idiot box telling us how great you are. It all smacks of political campaigning. Don't discount television; just use it advisedly.

Yellow Pages. The Donnelley people who publish the phone book are right. A very impressive percentage of people (four out of five adults, and each an average of 34 times per year) in the United States use the Yellow Pages for finding all kinds of things, from chiropractors to florists to auto mechanics to health clubs. If your operation is local, give serious thought to at least a 6 cm by 10 cm ad (slightly more than an eighth of a page) with a heavy border. Work with and through the telephone company on this, using their survey data and their layout designs. Most of Ma Bell's service is free, but you will pay for the Yellow Pages space.

Magazines and National Publications. One idea to constantly keep in mind is that, by advertising in magazines and national publications, many businesses which seem local really could be developed into a national or even international business by using the mails for shipping. You'll probably never be ready for *Time* magazine, but a regional issue of the *Wall Street Journal* may not be out of the question. Scrutinize the magazines that cater to your type of business. Be sure you are reaching the audience you want, however. Don't advertise a carburetor rebuilding kit in the *Atlantic Monthly* or a Pucci handbag in *Road and Track.*

Billboards. Use billboards with caution. They're expensive, and, furthermore, some states put severe restrictions on their use, for the good reason that they clutter the landscape with garish, tasteless drivel.

Buses and Taxis. "Car cards" on buses and taxis can be quite effective, but check the costs. Usually such cards cost less than ten dollars per month per vehicle. There are agents who specialize in car-card advertising.

Direct Mail. Using direct mail for advertising is tricky. You can spend thousands of dollars and get absolutely nothing in return except envelopes covered with red fingers pointing to items like *Addressee Unknown,* or *Left No Forward-*

ing Address. Be careful with direct mail. Be especially careful with bulk-rate postage. Until you've built a following that clamors for your next missive, heed the following.

Use a first-class stamp, not a meter.

Put your piece inside an envelope; don't use a self-mailer.

Use an envelope of the white-rag bond variety, with your return address printed (not stamped) in the upper left corner of the front.

Type the address, and address to a real person, not to *Occupant.* (Some people fire envelopes right back marked, *Return to sender. Mr. Occupant no longer lives here.*)

Beware of postage-paid return mail. We have a friend who glues such pieces onto bricks and drops them in the mail.

Consider using Address Correction Requested envelopes to improve your mailing list of addresses of potential customers. The post office will make the correction for you at a charge of twenty-five cents per envelope.

Be certain that your direct mail effort does something. Either it announces a sale and the recipient gets some special deal the general public does not, or it gives the recipient a chance to buy something. In other words, make the reader want to read.

Specialty Items. As with TV ads, be extra cautious of ego trips. Seeing your name on a pen or a book of matches (especially a carton of 10,000) may give you a warm feeling, as if you've finally arrived, but it does little for your business. Probably the best give-away we've seen is the calendar put out every year by the Travelers Insurance Company of Hartford. Each month is displayed with the numbers in large type, and there is a tasteful Currier and Ives print depicting a country scene appropriate to the particular season. Calendars are very nice if well done, and your name is in front of the customer for a year. T-shirts have been popular but may not last. The kids seem to love them. But remember that the message that is on the back of a six-foot two-inch blond surfer from Muscle Beach may also be on the back of a forty-five-year-old unshaven human whale from Hoboken, New Jersey.

Our final note on advertising has to do with measuring its effectiveness. It's difficult at best, but you might try one or all of the following:

In a radio ad, tell your audience that, if they mention where they heard it (Marjorie Talkmuchly's morning show), they will get ten percent off on some item.

In a newspaper ad, include a coupon good for some "two-fer" item.

Advertise one item in one medium only.

Stop using one medium for a period of time and see if sales fall temporarily. If they do, get going again!

Try an all-out blitzkrieg. Hit everything for one week. Count heads the next.

Ask your agency, and tell them you want the truth!

Credit and Collection (C & C)

One thing you will face in your business is *credit and collection* (C & C). If you have one, you will be faced with the other; like Charybdis, it is accompanied by Scylla.

Not giving credit insures that your business has no bad accounts—except for the bad checks you accept. On the other hand, not giving credit could result in lost business to you because your customers patronize a competitor who does extend credit. Somewhere between no credit to anyone and unlimited credit for all, there is a happy medium.

In these days of plastic money, you're practically forced into accepting bank cards: Visa, MasterCard, and others. This will cost you from 1–6 percent of the sale price of each item bought with a card, the percentage depending on the particular bank, but you are virtually guaranteed payment. Many consumers simply won't frequent a business that does not offer them the opportunity to use bank cards, in spite of recent efforts on the part of government and the banks to discourage their use.

If you decide to give credit, keep in mind that you will have both slow-pay and no-pay accounts. These laggards will increase your expenses (bookkeeping, collection, bad debt) and therefore will reduce your profit. There are, however, a few things you can do to reduce uncollectibles.

The very first step in managing your credit system involves screening those people who apply to you for credit terms. Your bank can give you both suggestions and forms for analyzing applicants. Remember that there are credit laws governing your conduct. Key items are that, under no circumstances, can you discriminate on the basis of race, religion, nationality, sex. If you turn someone down for credit, you must be specific in your reasons. You cannot solicit any information about childbearing, either. If you accept a person for credit, you must inform him of the various conditions of the credit agreement and you must tell him the annual interest percentage rate (APR) that they will be paying. Be sure you know how APR is calculated.

Once you have established your credit accounts, the next step in managing the system is to age your accounts receivable. A computer can do this for you automatically. Table 6.6 is a hypothetical aging schedule for the ABC Company, and it tells quite a story. We will address several points regarding credit management using Table 6.6.

First, set credit limits. If you had a $500 limit, then P. Miller has reached it and should not be allowed further credit until some of the past due account is paid up.

Send regular statements. The data for the statements can be gotten directly from the aging schedule. For instance, G. Salzman's statement would read, "Charges this month—$50.00."

Charge interest after thirty days. You might choose to charge 12 percent per year or 1 percent per month on the balance owed after thirty days. The aging schedule is invaluable for this.

Know when to use legal means to collect. If you bring a collection agency in after ninety days, Hegner, Nathan, and Osborn will be receiving nasty letters soon.

TABLE 6.6

A Hypothetical Aging Schedule for Accounts Receivable

Name	Balance	0–30	31–60	61–90	over 90
M. Jones	$ 375	$ 75	$300	—	—
H. Harris	160	60	50	$ 50	—
G. Salzman	50	50	—	—	—
P. Miller	500	300	100	100	—
G. Geipel	50	—	—	50	—
B. Thompson	75	—	75	—	—
H. Strauss	135	100	—	35	—
J. Hegner	125	—	—	—	$125
T. Nathan	400	—	100	100	200
A. Cohen	425	400	25	—	—
G. Young	75	25	50	—	—
J. Osborn	200	100	—	50	50
TOTALS	$2570	$1110	$700	$385	$375
Percent	100	43	27	15	15

Pricing

Some authors include this discussion under a financial section, but we have it under the marketing area since, in large organizations, prices are usually determined and set by the marketing department.

Pricing is really up to you. You can charge exactly what you want. We know of a very well-run restaurant that serves the normal fare of lunches and dinners, but contained in the middle of their menu is the following item:

Two-foot peanut butter and jelly sandwich $55.95 (negotiable)
includes tour of kitchen and insults of chef

Now, of course, this is simply a way to make patrons feel comfortable and to have a laugh when they discover the item. ("Hey, Sally, look at this!") But it does point to the fact that you may charge what you want. If you charge too little, you'll go out of business; too much, and you'll go out of customers. Somewhere there is an optimum mix. Let's look at some of the ways big business sets prices.

"Skimming the Cream"

When skimming the cream, you enter the market first and, therefore, command a very high price. This approach is very difficult in most small businesses. If you have something unique, it might work, but, unless you are Hewlett-Packard, use this method with extreme caution.

Odd Pricing

Odd pricing is tagging something just below an even amount. Unfortunately most businesses assume that all of us will believe that $19.99 is really $19, and not really one penny less than $20. But odd pricing does seem to work, and you should consider using it.

Loss Leaders

Very often, it makes sense to sell some item at or below cost as a loss leader. The reason for this is to get customers to your place of business so that they can buy other items. You have to be careful when using loss leaders. Consumers are getting smarter (they might buy that item only), and the government has regulations about using this method of advertising.

Penetration

Penetration is a method of pricing that will allow for a rapid increase in market share. Basically, you price your product significantly below the competition to attract the market quickly. The major problem with this approach is that it is difficult to raise prices later without driving your customers away; they get used to the low price.

Competition

In some lines of business, competition is keen and you might have to charge the going rate from the outset. We have told many entrepreneurs that it really doesn't cost much more to go first class, but it isn't always possible. If you don't have something special to offer, then you can't charge a special price.

Price Lining

Price lining isn't so much a method of setting a price as it is an entire marketing approach. The theory behind price lining is that you give a customer a choice of quality in any one particular item. For instance, if you carry a line of men's sweaters, you may have a group at $11.99, one at $24.99, and another at $36.99.

Return on Investment (ROI)

Of all the methods of pricing, return on investment (ROI) makes the most sense. It follows the methods used by big companies. When the people at Mobil or IBM look at any investment alternative (and any business opportunity qualifies), they use financial mathematics to analyze the future benefit. (We will do some of this math in Chapter 7.) Using the ROI approach, you decide, in advance, what return or profit you want. Let us assume that you want a 15 percent net profit before taxes and that an item costs you $100. This means that all your costs, when subtracted from the selling price, must yield you a 15 percent return on your investment or your selling price, not your buying price. You must know two other variables, your cost of goods sold (COGS) and your expenses, before you can use the ROI approach. You will remember from your accounting that

$$S - COGS = GM$$
$$GM - E = NP$$

where

$$S = \text{Sales}$$
$$COGS = \text{Cost of Goods Sold}$$
$$GM = \text{Gross Margin}$$
$$E = \text{Expenses}$$
$$NP = \text{Net Profit (before tax)}$$

If we can expect, in this example, that expenses represent 29 percent of our net sales, then

$$GM - E = NP$$
$$GM = NP + E$$
$$GM = 15\% + 29\% = 44\%$$

and

$$S - COGS = GM$$
$$COGS = S - GM$$
$$COGS = 100\% - 44\% = 56\%$$

If the COGS is 56 percent, the sale price (*COGS*) of the $100 item is $178.57 and the GM is $78.57 for a markup of 44 percent ($78.57 ÷ $178.57). Expenses

(*E*) are the 29 percent that we specified ($178.57 $\times$ .29 = $51.78) so that the profit (*NP*) is $26.79, or 15 percent. (If some of this is confusing to you, please consult an accounting text.)

Personal Selling

To be a really successful entrepreneur, you have to be comfortable in a sales role. The only way your business will grow and you will prosper is by increasing your sales and therefore your profit. We are not going to launch into a major treatise on selling, but we suggest that you purchase a basic book on selling techniques for your personal library or attend a seminar or both. Stay away from the How-I-Made-A-Billion-Dollars-In-Beaver-Ranches kind of thing. What you want is a basic text or seminar on some of the ways to handle people without driving them away. Naturally, a pleasant personality and honesty go a long way. So much of the selling process involves logical thinking, something that can't very easily be taught. The following brief, actual example involving sales inventiveness will demonstrate:

Jerry was a very successful and hardworking salesman for a manufacturer of power transmission equipment. He called on companies within his territory to interest them in using his company's devices in their mechanical equipment. One large firm in his area had never bought from Jerry, but only from Jerry's competitor. One day, Jerry was determined to get to see the purchasing agent, a person who heretofore had not granted him an audience. Jerry made such a commotion in the lobby that the receptionist said that he could see the purchasing agent, but only for five minutes, no longer. He was ushered in, introduced, and began his presentation—and a marvelous job it was. He covered everything about his company's products, quality, delivery, and price. As he was nearing the close, the purchasing agent pointed to his watch. Jerry said, "Oh, that's right. My five minutes is up. Well, sir, thank you for your time. I'll check in with you on my next visit in two weeks." Jerry shook the agent's hand and left. The purchasing man had not spoken one word. In two weeks, on the return visit, he was told that he again had only five minutes, but this time Jerry was ready. For exactly five minutes, he did the most descriptive, silent pantomime ever performed concerning an industrial product. For five minutes, the only sound in that office came from the window air conditioner. One week later, Jerry's company had a $50,000 order from a new (but still silent) customer.

The objective of the sales process is to help satisfy buyer need, and this need can be extremely complex, involving wants and desires, utility, and ego satisfaction. There is very little utility in a five-carat diamond ring (outside of glass cutting or the investment possibilities), but there is lots of status fulfillment.

Most books on selling use a little mnemonics to help people remember the four steps in the selling process. It's easy to remember because it's the name of a famous opera by Verdi, AIDA.

Attention: If your customer's mind is elsewhere, your approach will simply be lost. A little demonstration always helps.

Interest: When you hear the phrase, "No, I'm just not interested" a couple of times, don't persist like the door-to-door vacuum cleaner salesman. Back down. You want satisfied, repeat customers. If you force the sale (and this is possible), you may be sacrificing future profits.

Desire: For the sale to be right for everyone, the customer must want whatever it is that you're selling. If you spot his desire emerging, work on it until you achieve the final step.

Action: Believe it or not, this is where even good, trained salespeople fall short. Remember another catch phrase, Ask For The Order (AFTO). One technique is the most direct of all, asking, "Shall I wrap it for you?" Another technique involves choice, asking, "Would Tuesday or Thursday be more convenient?" A third, innocuous and helpful to you, is asking, "Will that be all?" Most sales clerks are taught to ask just that question of patrons. If you have already sold some item to a customer, a suggestion for something additional is not out of line. Ask specifically, "Would you like an after-dinner cordial?" or "Yes sir, two pounds of eight-penny nails. Do you have a good hammer?"

Sales Management

The chances are high that, if you have a small business, you will have employees, maybe one, maybe one hundred. In most cases, these people will be somehow involved in sales and/or customer relations. Although formal training is rarely used, you should tutor your employees in what you expect of them when handling people. Some of your staff will have a natural, pleasant way with customers, and some for deep-seated, unknown reasons, seem to hate their fellow humans and make it a point of demonstrating their grudges. When you're struggling to survive, this is one problem you don't need. (We will discuss personnel management philosophies in a later chapter.) If you can make your venture a fun place to be, this natural attitude will develop as a by-product of the atmosphere and working environment.

You may be using sales agents of one kind or another. These agents can be your own employees, salespersons that represent you exclusively and are paid by you (commission, straight salary, or a combination). Or you might choose to use manufacturer's representatives, who will carry your line of products and possibly five or six complementary but noncompeting lines. They will take orders from customers and send these orders to you to be filled. For this service, they get from 5 percent to 20 percent of the sales price as their commission, and you pay this commission to them monthly, typically by the fifteenth of the month for the previous month's sales. A distributor, on the other hand, is actually your customer. He purchases the goods from you at 20 percent to 60 percent less than your normal retail price, stocks the items, and resells them.

Here are a few pointers about reps and distributors. Before you begin any negotiations, have these people checked out. Call their principals and their customers to determine their reputation and performance. If you use a written contract, have your lawyer go over it for legal implications. Of special interest will be the escape clause (who can get out of the deal). If you get a good agent, treat him like the professional he is. Live up to your part of the bargain. Keep him informed of what you're doing. Invite him to your facility once a year at your expense. Give him a fair commission, and pay it on time.

Government Marketing

Here is one final word on agents. Some people in Washington and elsewhere are known as *five percenters*. They wander through the halls of government agencies looking for contracts for your business. They get 5 percent of any business which they secure for you. Most of them are reputable; some are scalawags. Beware of anyone who is looking for "up front" money. Stay away from them.

Some small businesses cultivate two other sales potentials, the national or state or municipal government and foreign countries. The United States Department of Commerce (field offices listed in Appendix C) can be of help to you in both areas. It has free or minimum-cost documents as well as experts in both areas. One relatively inexpensive activity that the Department of Commerce can accomplish for you is a search for a foreign agent in a particular country using the United States Embassies. There is a fixed fee (less than fifty dollars) for each country. The Department of Commerce and the General Services Administration can help with sales to the government itself. Both sales areas involve a lot of time and paperwork, but can be worth the investment if you have products or services with a broad potential market.

In Conclusion

Of all the functional areas within a small business, or any business for that matter, marketing is the most important. There will undoubtedly be a number of readers who disagree with that statement, and they will correctly argue that, without a product or service to sell, there is no business, by definition. Others will say that the financial control and reporting activity is the most important, since almost all businesses that fail do so because of a lack of capital. All these observations are true, but, if the marketing function is not carried out correctly, the product offered may be the wrong one or the target customer base may not be correct. If marketing assumptions are not made in the right way, then the business is eventually doomed. Another important job of marketing is to determine how the present customer base is accepting the products or services that a business is offering. This is a part of the necessary feedback process. Remember that everything changes, including the tastes of customers. Marketing is that business area that allows an owner to react to the marketplace before the business is in trouble.

Plan to use at least one day a month to take a good look at what it is that you are offering. Listen to what your customers are saying, and keep a sharp eye toward competition. Pay attention to new trends and listen to salespeople who announce new products. You might want to take advantage of them.

Be adaptive.

CHAPTER SEVEN

Finance

There's millions in it.
Mark Twain

This chapter is separated into two sections, *financing* and *finances*. In the first section, we will talk about securing capital for your business venture, and, in the second, we will cover various financial topics that you should be familiar with to run your business.

Financing

Of all the steps necessary in becoming a business owner, *financing* is the most fraught with terror and has the most mystery surrounding it. The two questions that are most often asked are the following:

How will I know how much is enough?
(Answer: Make your business plan.)
Where will I get the money I need?
(Answer: See below.)

The first source of financing is you. Either you have enough money to start or buy the venture, or your don't. It's as simple as that. If you're like most would-be business owners, you don't have sufficient capital and need to look for Other People's Money (OPM). If you have no money and no assets yourself, you had better think about either waiting a while or beginning in your cellar on a limited, part-time basis.

As a beginning step, you should draw up a personal balance sheet. It can be as simple as Figure 7.1.

If you've never made a personal balance sheet before, you may be quite surprised at your net worth. You probably do not want to put your entire net worth to work for you, but you had better be prepared to use most of it. In the first place, if you run your business successfully, it will be the best financial investment you've ever made. Secondly, no secondary money source will feel comfortable extending funds to someone who has not used all of his own funds.

The cash flow section of your business plan should tell you the total amount of funds needed, and that figure subtracted from your available cash should tell you the External Funds Needed (EFN).

Knowing the EFN, are you ready to go scurrying from place to place, hat in hand, trying to raise money to buy or start that dream venture? No, not yet. Your plan to raise capital should be a well-thought-out campaign. If you're

```
        Assets
            Cash                                          $  _____
            Savings                                          _____
            Securities (stocks, bonds, CD's)                 _____
            Equity in real estate                            _____
            Cash surrender value of life insurance           _____
            Other assets that can become cash                _____
                            Total assets                  $  _____

    Liabilities
            Charge accounts                               $  _____
            Debts owed (mortgage, loans, notes)              _____
            Other debts to be discharged (payables)          _____
                            Total liabilities             $  _____

    Net worth
            (Subtract total liabilities from total assets; $ _____
             if this number is negative,
             forget it.  You're insolvent.)
```

Figure 7.1 *Personal Balance Sheet*

totally confident of your own ability to succeed, and if your idea has merit, raising money will not be as difficult as you think.

Before you make your first OPM call, be sure that

> Your business plan is finished and can be left with the person you plan to talk with;
> Your own personal presentation is flawless, or nearly so;
> You not only know how much money you are going to ask for but in what form, debt, equity, or a combination.

Debt

Debt is a loan. It has to be repaid with interest. The cash flow calculations in your business plan show your potential lending source that you have the ability to pay back the loan. We strongly suggest that you invest $50–$150 in a calculator with a built-in feature that calculates monthly payments based on amount borrowed, interest rate, and loan period. Both Hewlett-Packard and Texas Instruments make these devices. As an example, we entered the following into our Hewlett-Packard calculator:

Loan $100,000
Interest 11 percent
Term 20 years

In four seconds, the answer, a monthly payment of $1,032.19 came back. At an interest rate of 12 percent, the payment is $1,101.09, or another $16,535.00 in interest over the life of the loan.

Some loans, especially those involving SBA participation, can be set up with a *no principal payment* for some initial period of the loan, usually one year. Some loans require a *balloon payment,* which means that a large portion of the loan comes due at the end; the final payment is usually refinanced at the then-prevailing interest rate.

Equity

Equity is an investment. It buys ownership. It does not have to be repaid, although it often is at some higher future value. In a partnership, an investor of equity is known as a limited (or silent) partner because he supplies capital but does not work at or for the business. In the corporate form of business, such an investor is known as a stockholder and has a vote. (See Chapter 9 for more discussion about the forms of businesses.)

Equity investors are primarily looking to sell their stock at some future time for more than they paid for it. (We will leave dividends out of this discussion since those are rare in small business.) The equity investor will sell his stock either to someone else, to you, or back to the business at some future date. This investment can be extremely lucrative if things go right. As an example, suppose an investor buys 10,000 shares of your stock for $1.00 per share and is able to sell it for $5.00 per share in 7 years. This is equivalent to an annual return of 25.9 percent. This sure beats a savings account!

Most entrepreneurs make a serious error with equity financing by being too cautious about giving up ownership. This seems to get worse in the case of start-up ventures. Even if you have the idea of the century, that's all you have, an idea with no proven value. Be prepared to give up control if you really want to raise this kind of capital for a new enterprise or forget this kind of capital.

One other word of caution. Every state has what is known as *blue sky* laws. These laws govern what you can and cannot do in offering stock for sale. Although a well done and complete business plan is a good start, be sure to check with your lawyer before you go off peddling blue sky. There are also federal (SEC) regulations to reckon with.

It is often a good idea to put the following warning in the "Risks" section of a business plan:

NO PERSON OR GROUP SHOULD INVEST IN THIS VENTURE UN-
LESS THEY ARE PREPARED TO LOSE ALL OR A SIGNIFICANT POR-
TION OF THEIR INVESTMENT.

Friends and Relatives

Many entrepreneurs feel embarrassed about asking *friends and relatives* for money. Remind yourself that you aren't begging for a few coppers, but offering a sound business investment. Of course, there is risk. If you bury your money in a number-ten can in the backyard, there's a risk that a goat will come along and gobble it up, a dog will rebury it, or an earthquake will relocate it. Banks fail, insurance companies go bankrupt, cities default on debt, and the stock markets lose paper billions in an hour. That's reality. If you're convinced of the soundness of the investment and you know the people you're dealing with, all the better. Be certain to explain the potential risks and the fact that this will be capital placed at high risk.

Private Investors

Many individuals are potential *private investors.* They have capital that they are willing to put at high risk for a high return. The rule here is to be discreet. Don't go knocking on doors like a Fuller Brush salesman. To have a chance at success, you'll need an introduction to these individuals. Use your banker, your stockbroker, your lawyer, your accountant. Most of these professionals will be delighted to help you. Consider contacting groups with high disposable incomes such as physicians, dentists, consultants, executives, and performers.

The Bank

Although there have been many different and creative methods for financing small businesses over the years, the commercial banks of the country (usually the ones with the word *National* in their name) have been and will remain the major source of capital for new and continuing small ventures. Many banks today recognize the contribution of small business to the nation's economy and have programs to expand the bank's role in small business lending as well as to provide support and guidance for entrepreneurs.

Some disgruntled entrepreneurs that we know seem to have bred a great deal of ill feeling about bankers. While it is true that some bankers are unresponsive to the needs of small business owners, they are a minority today. Usually when we trace back to the real reason why an entrepreneur was unhappy about his or her experience with a bank—meaning that their request for a loan was not approved—we can pinpoint one or more of the following:

1. *The basic business idea was unsound or considered too risky.* Certainly the banker's judgment enters into this kind of decision not to approve a loan, but most loan officers have to rely on past performance of other, similar businesses. Many banks are reluctant to loan money for a restaurant; some banks flatly refuse. The failure rate of restaurants is very high and unless you have something unique to demonstrate, as a restaurateur, like successful past performance in another hospitality business, you may be turned down. Any business that has been untried in a particular area will have tough sledding. We know a banker (a liberal one) who approved a loan for a massage parlor, but that's rare.
2. *Insufficient collateral.* While it is true that banks rent money, the rental that is paid being called interest, they want their money secured in some fashion. If your business does not succeed financially, the bank needs assets that it can lay claim to, to satisfy the remaining debt. If you are buying an existing business, you will normally make a down payment of somewhere in the range of 20 to 40 percent of the price, and the bank will loan you the balance you require against a mortgage on the business. If you are starting a business, you must pledge your own assets (home, securities) against a loan, and you must personally guarantee the loan. Don't believe, as some people do, that the corporate form of business organization will protect you from financial liability should the business fail. For any type of loan, try to have assets that are worth about 150 percent of the loan amount and be certain that these assets can be easily converted into cash.
3. *No financial commitment on your part.* Many bankers are reluctant to loan money for business ventures if they feel that the entrepreneur is not fully committed. Although it is true that the bank will have security for its loan, bankers really don't want to have to foreclose or repossess, and then be forced into having to sell assets to collect their money. They want you to make it and to repay the loan, and one measure they may use in assessing the chances that you will do this is how far you have gone yourself in supplying capital.
4. *The use of the funds is unclear.* If you prepare a good business plan, you will spell

out where the funds are going. By the way, don't show a nice fat salary for your-self as soon as you get the funding.

5. *No business plan.* There is absolutely no excuse on your part for this. Many banks now require a written plan.

6. *You.* Sometimes the soundest deals in the world fall through (and, conversely, the wackiest things get funded) because of the people themselves. If you're confident about your idea and can present it with enthusiasm, then you don't need to alibi for anything. The personal factor works both ways, though. Occa-sionally there will be the banker who turns you down strictly because of the way you spell your name, or because his spouse just gave him a bad time and you look like her.

Don't jump with the first bank that you see. Shop around. Discuss interest rates, down payments, collateral required, and the other services of the bank. Understand what the bank wants from you after the loan has been approved.

Finally, one very strong bit of advice about dealing with bankers. If your business plan calls for a loan of $100,000 and that's what you need, don't accept less. That's inviting business disaster.

Venture Capitalists

A *venture capitalist* (or "vulture capitalists" as they are often called) is an individual or organization that invests equity capital in a business to aid that business in its growth and attempts thereby to multiply their own investment. Small Business Investment Corporations (SBICs) are also considered venture capital sources. Many small business books devote much space to venture capi-talists; but we feel they are overrated as sources of financing for small busi-nesses.

In the 1960s venture capitalists were in their heyday. They would invest in start-up ventures, get the business beyond its third year or so, and then sell off some or all of their holdings through a public stock offering. Many venture capital firms were wiped out in the 1969 and 1974 recessions, including subsid-iaries of banks, insurance companies, and corporations (but see Appendix A for a brief account of Exxon Enterprises, Inc., "The Apparent Exception"). SBICs fell to about one-fourth their original number.

Many older venture capital firms are now spending a great deal of time managing their existing portfolio companies, doing management consulting for business turn-around situations, or investing in senior securities. Newer firms have come along; but unless you have the idea of the century, one which can become a multi-million-dollar operation in a few years, you can probably for-get venture capitalists as a source of funds. You'll waste a lot of valuable time courting them.[1]

[1] There are several books available that list active venture capitalists in the country. The most com-plete is *Guide to Venture Capital Sources,* by Stanley M. Rubel. Capital Publishing Corp., Box 348, Wellesley Hills, Mass. 02181.

Job Start Programs

Job start programs are apparently spreading rapidly. Government funds (not SBA) are made available to budding entrepreneurs who cannot raise money through traditional channels. Capital is severely limited, however. In one town we know of, the maximum loan available is $2500. A typical loan went to a man who wanted to go into the firewood business; the money was used to buy a chain saw and to make the down payment on a used pickup truck.

The Small Business Administration (SBA)

The best advice we can give is to visit your local field office and talk with some *SBA* people. Get the loan application forms and fill them out yourself. Stay away from any private individual who claims that he can get you SBA money for a fee. The SBA does make a few direct loans, but prefers to work through a bank and the bank likes the arrangement as well. The bank loans the money and the SBA guarantees up to 90 percent of the loan.

The U.S. Congress raised the SBA's loan limit from $350,000 to $500,000 a few years ago, but this was not without a few government strings attached to it. When the SBA decides to approve a loan for more than the previous limit of $350,000, it must have at least two of the following objectives:

Construction of medical facilities, the need for which has been certified by local authorities.
Conservation or production of energy.
Creation or preservation of jobs.
Performance of a specific government contract.
Stimulation of the economy of a labor surplus area.
Conservation of natural resources.
Improvement of mass transit facilities.
Economic development of depressed urban or rural areas.
Assistance to broadcasting and/or cable TV operations.
Revitalization of SBA-designated neighborhood business areas.
Assistance to businesses for the primary purpose of exporting goods and services.
   At least 50 percent of the loan must be used for direct exporting.

These guidelines are undoubtedly subject to change, so check with the SBA if your loan application is going to be above a certain bottom limit which might also change.

About the best way to solicit SBA help is through your banker. Chances are he or she has personal contacts. If possible, have your banker visit the SBA with you. Work with your banker and the SBA contact.

Farmers Home Administration

The *Farmers Home Administration* is a little-known government agency that works somewhat like the SBA for businesses located in rural areas. If your operation is rural, give them a call.

Your application, which can be to expand, save, or buy a business, will require an FBI background check, an opinion from the Bureau of Labor that your company is not going to be moving in labor from outside your rural location, and an outside feasibility study. The business must be larger than $500,000 in annual sales.

Miscellaneous Sources

Here are just a few other places that might be of interest. The chances of raising money are quite slim, but the following sources may know of other people to contact:

1. Credit unions
2. Insurance companies and corporations
3. Private stock clubs
4. Regional development councils
5. Chambers of commerce
6. Foreign governments or individuals
7. Investment bankers
8. Trade associations

Continuing Financing

We have talked about starting capital and no section on financing would be complete without mentioning *continuing financing*.

Profit

It's surprising how many books fail to mention *profit* as an important source of financing. Unless you have an unlimited slush fund, your business will have to produce a regular, continuing profit after some period of time. For a lucky few, this occurs in the first month of operation. For a high technology venture, the break-even may not take place for years. As your business grows into the profit range, resist the temptation to reward yourself with a higher and higher salary. Use the profit to build the business.

Lines of Credit

Your bank, once you've established yourself and made payments on your loan and sent your banker financial statements, can help you establish a *line of credit*. This is a stated amount of money with a flexible interest rate that you may borrow all or a fraction thereof with a telephone call. The bank may require a compensating balance in your checking account, a certain minimum amount. Review your line of credit annually with your banker.

Trade Credit

Some or all of your suppliers may allow you to deal on open credit terms, giving you *trade credit*. Since you don't have to pay for the goods for a period of time after the ship date (usually thirty days), you have the use of the money. Although most American businesses are taking over sixty days to pay their bills, you should keep current with your suppliers. If things get too bad, they will revert to cash-on-delivery (COD) or even pro forma invoicing (cash before shipment).

Leases

You can lease just about anything today from a typewriter to a supertanker. Most *leases* allow the lessee (you) to purchase the item for a fraction of its original price after four or five years. Even if the manufacturer does not have a lease program, he might be able to suggest a third-party leasing company.

Financing Receivables

Banks are *financing receivables* more and more, taking over from *factors* who, at one time, did this exclusively. Check with your own bank for terms. Once you ship goods on credit to your customers, you create an asset called accounts receivable. This can be financed with the bank, sometimes at the full value of the receivable. You pay the bank when you receive the funds. In some cases, the bank will collect them directly. A factoring firm advances you some percentage of the receivable, usually about 70 percent. Factors usually work with sizable amounts. The James Talcott Company, one of the largest and most reputable in the field, will usually only deal in amounts of $100,000 or more.

Secondary Financing

There may be a time in the life of your venture when *secondary financing* is necessary. Possibly the time is right for a major expansion, or you want to buy out a competitor or open a second facility in a new town. Your bank is one possible source, or you might consider selling stock, if you have not done so previously. If the latter is your preference, check with your lawyer and a reputable investment banking (underwriting) house.

Finances

This section is not intended to be a lesson in accounting, but in how to deal with financial information. If the terms and examples are completely foreign to you, any basic accounting text—especially one with problems to work—is highly recommended.[2] As an entrepreneur, you should have a good working knowledge of the entire financial area. Many accountants are nothing more than bookkeepers; they can't interpret the figures they prepare. The business is yours, and, if it fails, it will take you with it, not your accountant. Many entrepreneurs don't do their own books, but their business decisions are made on the interpretation of timely and well-prepared data, either from an accountant or a computer. We will start with two financial statements similar to those we used in Chapter 3 when we discussed pricing a business. Figures 7.2 and 7.3 present the income statement and balance sheet, respectively, of the XYZ Business. Let's assume that your accountant drops these on your desk early in January of the year 19XX plus one. Now what?

First, here are some basic distinctions. *The income statement* is often referred to as the profit and loss statement or the P and L. Actually, this term is a bit of a misnomer. The income statement does not show P *and* L, it shows P *or* L, hopefully, P. It records accounting income and accounting costs over a period of time—in this case, one year. *The balance sheet* may be called the statement of financial position. It shows what is owned (assets) and what is owed (liabilities and net worth). Assets equal liabilities, hence the title *balance* sheet. It is a still photograph of the firm at a precise point in time—here, midnight, December 31, 19XX.

The income statement tells us what we took in and what we spent. Remember, this is an accounting treatment, not a cash treatment. If we are making loan payments to a bank, only the interest will show as an expense, even though we wrote a check for interest and principal combined.

Net sales usually means net shipments, not necessarily cash received, since a sale on credit shows up here. It is *net* because returns and allowances have been allowed for. The second item is *cost of goods sold,* or what your goods or services actually cost you. The difference between net sales and cost of goods sold is

---

[2] Pyle, White, and Larson. *Fundamental Accounting Principles,* 8th ed. (Homewood, Ill.: Richard D. Irwin, 1978).

gross margin (sometimes called gross profit or operating profit). When the gross margin is divided by the net sales, the result represents the average markup for the firm—65 percent for XYZ. This figure can be compared to averages for the industry. Next come the *expenses* incurred for the year. (*Depreciation* is not a real expense, however. We will cover this subject later.) Gross margin less expenses yields the net profit of $27,300, or 27.3 percent of sales.

If we wanted to make the income statement more reflective of cash transfers, we would take the net profit figure, subtract what the owner took out, subtract any debt principal paid, and add depreciation back in, since it was not actually incurred.

Now to the *balance sheet*. On the left (or sometimes on the top) are the *assets,* and they are usually listed in order of liquidity. The first major category includes the *current assets,* or those expected to turn over within one year or less. The first of these, the most liquid, is *cash.* That can be real money (coins and bills) in the till, checking accounts, and savings accounts. If the business has purchased something like United States Treasury notes, those are classified as *marketable securities* and would appear next on the list. Securities are not cash; they are "near cash." *Accounts receivable* are your credit accounts, those that are owed to you but not yet paid. When they are paid, they become cash. The value assigned to the *inventory* account (which agrees with the December 31st income statement value) is the investment in items that are hanging around but will be sold.

The *fixed assets* are the physical objects that are owned by the business, such as buildings, land, furniture, and equipment. The *depreciation* shown in parentheses represents all accounting depreciation taken to date. Note that the total is $1000 plus $1500, or $2500. The income statement shows an expense in the current year of $1700. Therefore, $800 was taken in previous years showing that XYZ must be a relatively new firm. The value for net fixed assets represents all assets at their original price less all depreciation taken to date. This is known as the *book value* of the assets. If XYZ never buys another fixed asset, the net fixed asset value will eventually fall to zero, and will be fully depreciated.

Some businesses have a third category called, simply, *other assets.* This category might contain the cash surrender value of life insurance owned by the business on the life of the principals, prepaid expenses (like rent), copyrights, patents, or good will (the excess paid by the current owner over the net worth value of the business at the time of sale).

The right side of XYZ's balance sheet contains entries for *liabilities* (debts) and *net worth.* The underlying theory behind this presentation is that, if the business divested itself of all its assets and paid off all its debts, what is left over is the net worth, sometimes called *owner's* or *stockholder's equity.*

Current liabilities are those debts due within one year. *Accounts payable* are your future payments to your suppliers; *notes payable* are usually due to banks, partners, officers, or friends for short-term loans. Other *accruals* can include

```
                    INCOME STATEMENT

                          OF

                     XYZ BUSINESS

          for the year ending December 31, 19XX


Net sales                                       $100,000

    Cost of goods sold
        Inventory January 1      $10,000
        Purchases                 40,000
        Goods available          $50,000
        Inventory December 31     15,000

        Cost of goods sold                        35,000
Gross margin                                    $ 65,000


Expenses

    Interest                     $ 1,000
    Rent                           5,000
    Wages                         17,000
    Supplies                       2,000
    Advertising                    1,000
    Insurance                      1,000
    Delivery cost                  2,000
    Depreciation                   1,700
    Taxes paid                     1,000
    Utilities                      2,000
    Maintenance                    1,000
    Miscellaneous                  3,000

        Total Expenses                          $ 37,700

Net profit                                      $ 27,300
```

Figure 7.2 *Sample Income Statement*

```
                           BALANCE SHEET

                                OF

                           XYZ BUSINESS

                      as of December 31, 19XX

Current assets                      Current liabilities

    Cash                $ 3,000         Accounts payable      $ 1,500
    Accounts receivable   5,700         Notes payable           1,000
    Inventory            15,000         Other accruals          2,000


    Total current assets $23,700        Total current liabilities  $ 4,500

Fixed assets                        Fixed liabilities

    Equipment and fixtures $18,200      Long-term debt        $ 5,000
        Depreciation     (1,000)        Total liabilities     $ 9,500
    Truck                 4,900
        Depreciation     (1,500)


    Total net fixed assets $20,600      Net worth proprietorship  $34,800


Total assets            $44,300     Liability and net worth     $44,300
```

Figure 7.3 *Sample Balance Sheet*

wages accrued but not yet paid, taxes due to the government, the current portion of the long-term debt, or any other short-term liability. The long-term debt is just what the term denotes: the principal amount due on a loan beyond one year's time.

Since, from an accounting standpoint, *assets* minus *liabilities* equals *net worth*, $44,300 minus $9500 equals $34,800.

Ratio Analysis

Various *ratios* can be calculated for analysis of financial data.[3] We will touch on just a few, using the financial statements in Figures 7.2 and 7.3.

Current ratio is one of the liquidity ratios, and your bank will run this one first. It represents how well your current assets cover your current liabilities (debt). For XYZ, this ratio is

$$\frac{\$23,700}{\$4,500} = 5.27$$

or a very healthy margin indeed. Most experts would like to see the ratio between 1 and 2. With a ratio as high as 5.27, XYZ may be operating too conservatively.

Acid test or quick ratio allows us to strip away the inventory value from the current asset value to determine coverage of the current debt more realistically.

$$\frac{\$23,700 - \$15,000}{\$4,500} = 1.93$$

Like the current ratio, this is very healthy, maybe a bit too much so.

Return on total assets ratio shows what the assets earned. For a realistic comparison, we subtract what the owner took for himself from the net profit. If the owner withdrew $18,000, that leaves a profit of $9300. The return on assets, then, is

$$\frac{\$9,300}{\$44,300} = 21\%$$

[3] There are several sources of comparative data for comparing ratios for various kinds of business. Both Dun & Bradstreet and the NCR Corporation have pamphlets available, but the best is the annual report compiled by Robert Morris Associates, called *Annual Statement Studies*. A sample page is shown in Appendix F.

Return on sales (profit margin) ratio is the same as the return on total assets ratio, but the divisor is net sales.

$$\frac{\$9,300}{\$100,000} = 9.3\%$$

Return on investment (ROI) ratio uses net worth as the divisor.

$$\frac{\$9,300}{\$34,800} = 26.7\%$$

This is one of the most important of all the calculations. It compares the earning power of the business with alternate investments, if the owner liquidated the business and invested the proceeds in the best paying instruments available. Certainly 26.7 percent return on the business far exceeds most other investments.

Average collection period. Some businesses collect their bills in a shorter time than some others. To calculate this value the first step is to find the average value of the sales per day:

$$\frac{\$100,000}{365 \text{ days}} = \$274 \text{ per day}$$

and then we divide receivables by the sales per day:

$$\frac{\$5,700}{\$274} = 21 \text{ days (about)}$$

Therefore, XYZ takes an average of 21 days to collect its outstanding bills.

Debt-to-worth ratio shows if your company is too far in debt. Your bank will probably run this computation right after the current ratio. Most people arrive at the debt-to-worth ratio by dividing total debt (liabilities) by net worth (or equity):

$$\frac{\$9,500}{\$34,000} = .28$$

When the ratio reaches .3, your banker reaches for the phone. A .3 means that your total capitalization has too much debt for equity that was invested in the business.

There are literally hundreds of other ratios that may be useful for small business management. After all, any number can be divided by any other number. The advertising expenses divided by the accounts receivable for XYZ is

$$\frac{\$1,000}{\$5,700} = .18$$

but that value may mean something only to a few. In any case, you would need to know the comparable value for a number of other companies in order for the value to be useful knowledge for you.

One analysis that we did not perform involves the sales history of the firm. Everyone has seen the many cartoons showing the sales graph becoming a crack in the wall and falling to the basement, but the time element is really extremely important. We suggest to all entrepreneurs that they graph their sales and profits as an absolute minimum, and keep the graph up to date every month.

Break-Even Analysis

The theory behind the calculation of *break-even analysis* is that some costs, like rent, depreciation, and utilities are fixed; they are paid whether the venture sold anything or not. Other costs, like the cost of goods sold, are variable. Figure 7.4 shows the concept of break-even analysis. The fixed costs remain constant as the volume of business increases, but both the sales level and the variable costs increase by a fixed amount per unit. Below the break-even point, the firm loses money; above that point, there is a profit.

There are two different ways to approach break-even analysis. The first method is used for a business that only has a single product and follows the logic of Figure 7.4. Using this method, we can find the number of units of product that must be sold to cover the fixed and variable costs. The formula is

$$Sn = Vn + F$$
S = sale price of the unit
n = units necessary to break even
V = variable costs per unit
F = total fixed costs of the firm for a period of time

As an example, suppose that the sales price of an item is $300 and the variable cost of the same unit is $100. (Therefore, the gross margin per unit is $200.) If the monthly fixed costs are $40,000, the break-even point is

$$300n = 100n + 40,000$$
$$200n = 40,000$$
$$n = 200 \text{ units}$$

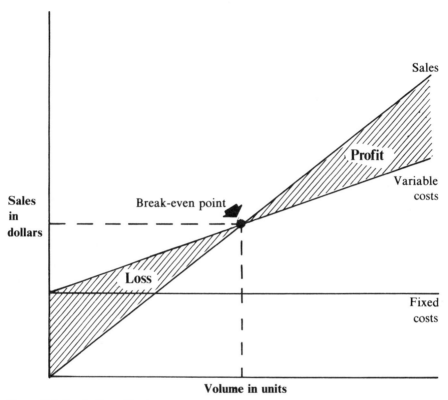

Figure 7.4 *Break-Even Chart*

With 200 units at a sale price of $300, the dollar volume to break even is $60,000. Suppose the firm in question sells 350 units in a month. Then the pre-tax profit is

Sales (350 × $300)	$105,000
Variable costs (350 × $100)	35,000
Gross margin	$ 70,000
Fixed costs	40,000
Net profit	$ 30,000

But very few firms supply only one product. A second method uses information from the income statement or from sales projections. Since fixed costs (F) plus variable costs (V) equal total costs (T),

$$T = F + V$$

If S represents the company's sales in a given period, and if B is the sales level at break-even, we will set the total costs equal to the break-even sales, or

$$B = F + V(B/S) \qquad (B/S = 1 \text{ at break-even})$$

then

$$B - V(B/S) = F$$
$$B(1 - V/S) = F$$

and

$$B = \frac{F}{1 - V/S}$$

Using XYZ's income statement (Figure 7.2), we will assume that the cost of goods sold represents the variable costs and the expenses are the fixed costs. The break-even point for XYZ is

$$B = \frac{37,700}{1 - (35,000/100,000)} = \$58,000 \text{ per year}$$

Depreciation

Depreciation is an accounting treatment of the cost of an asset over some number of years. It has nothing to do with deterioration or obsolescence. One of the basic underlying theories behind depreciation is that the asset has a certain life, and, therefore, the cost of that asset should be spread over that life. The Internal Revenue Service (IRS) can help you select that life through the use of its Asset Depreciation Rate (ADR).[4] You, naturally, would like the life of the asset to be as short as possible.

There are three common ways to calculate depreciation. We will use an asset costing $1000 with an ADR of five years, and will fully depreciate it to zero (i.e., when it has no salvage value).

The first method, and the simplest, is *straight-line* depreciation. The cost of the asset is divided by the ADR.

$$\frac{\$1000}{5 \text{ years}} = \$200 \text{ per year}$$

---

[4] This entire approach will probably change in the years to come. Keep abreast of coming changes in depreciation, or be sure that your accountant informs you of these changes.

The second method is known as *double-declining balance.* To do the calcula-tions, we first need to compute the rate of annual depreciation used under the straight-line method, which is

$$\frac{\$200}{\$1000} = .20$$

We then double that value ($2 \times .20 = .40$) to get the rate to use each year and continuously apply it against the undepreciated balance:

	Depreciation	*Undepreciated Balance*
Year 1	$.40 \times \$1000 = \$400$	$ 600
Year 2	$.40 \times \$600 = \$240$	$ 360
Year 3	$.40 \times \$360 = \$144$	$ 216
Year 4	$.40 \times \$216 = \$86$	$ 130
Year 5	$130	$ 0

Notice that the remaining balance at the end of year 4 is taken in year 5. If this were not done, the calculations would theoretically go on forever.[5]

The third method is known as *sum-of-the-years' digits.* This method, like double-declining balance, is an accelerated method of depreciation. As a pre-paratory step to the actual calculations, we need to find the sum of the digits of all the years of the depreciable life of the asset. For the five-year life,

$$\text{Sum of Digits} = 5 + 4 + 3 + 2 + 1 = 15$$

Note that there is a formula for finding the sum of the digits. If the life is *n* years, then

$$\text{Sum} = \frac{n(n + 1)}{2} = \frac{5(6)}{2} = 15$$

The calculations are shown below:

Year 1	$5/15 \times \$1000 = \$333$
Year 2	$4/15 \times \$1000 = \$267$
Year 3	$3/15 \times \$1000 = \$200$
Year 4	$2/15 \times \$1000 = \$133$
Year 5	$1/15 \times \$1000 = \$ 67$

One important thing to keep in mind is that, although straight-line is the simplest method mathematically, there is a definite financial advantage to using

[5] In actual practice, the business would revert to straight-line depreciation when the straight-line amount in any given year was greater than the corresponding rate for double-declining balance. In our example, this would take place in the third year, since $200 is greater than $144. ADR must be observed, though.

an accelerated method. Inflation will always be with us, and, therefore, the purchasing power of the dollar will continue to decline. If inflation stays constant at, say, 7 percent, a year from now, $1.00 will be worth about $.93.[6]

$$\frac{\$1.00}{1.07} = \$.93$$

In two years, the same dollar will be

$$\frac{\$1.00}{(1.07)^2} = \$.87$$

And further

Year 3 = $.82
Year 4 = $.76
Year 5 = $.71

These numbers just calculated can be called *discounting factors,* and we can compare the effect that using accelerated depreciation has on real cash. With the accelerated methods, a larger deduction for tax purposes occurs in earlier years when the money is worth more in buying power.

Using Table 7.1, we can calculate the net effect on discounted cash, comparing sum-of-the-years'-digits (the more popular of the two) with straight-line.

TABLE 7.1

Comparison of the Sum-of-the-Years'-Digits Method with the Straight-Line Method to Calculate Net Effect on Discounted Cash

1. Year	*2.* Sum-of-Digits	*3.* Straight-Line	*4.* Difference (2 − 3)	*5.* Discount Factor (7%)	*6.* Net Effect (4 × 5)
1	$ 333	$ 200	$ 133	.93	$ 124
2	267	200	67	.87	58
3	200	200	0	.82	0
4	133	200	(67)	.76	(51)
5	67	200	(133)	.71	(94)
TOTALS	$1000	$1000	$ 0		$ 37

[6] If inflation is 15 percent, that same dollar is worth $1.00/1.15 = $.87.

By using sum-of-the-years'-digits, we take smaller deductions in the later years with cheaper dollars. That's why accountants use an accelerated method with the shortest possible life.

One final note on the tax aspects of asset purchases. The IRS has instituted tax credits for the purchase of new assets with a minimum ADR. Since the ground rules change, check with the IRS or your accountant for the current year's ruling.

Valuing Inventories

As most sophisticated entrepreneurs are aware, there are various ways to *value* your *inventories* (and therefore your cost of goods sold as well). If, on January 1, you buy 100 pairs of candlesticks for $18, and if, over the year, you sell 80 pairs, then

Inventory value on December 31 (20 × $18):		$ 360
Cost of goods sold	(80 × $18)	$1440
	100	$1800

That's quite simple, but most businesses buy for inventory a number of times in a year, and, to complicate matters, the prices will most likely fluctuate because of inflation and the purchase of differing quantities.

Let us look at a hypothetical purchasing scheme for a foreign car dealership shown in Table 7.2.

TABLE 7.2

Annual Purchasing Scheme

Month	Units Purchased	Unit Cost	Total Cost
Jan.	10	$ 6000	$ 60,000
Mar.	5	6500	32,500
Jun.	15	7000	105,000
Sep.	10	8000	80,000
Dec.	10	8500	85,000
	50		$362,500

On December 31, we go out to our lot and find twenty-two vehicles: two from January, four from June, eight from September, and eight from December. We call the port of entry and discover that, if we were to take delivery of vehicles today, our cost would be $9000. (The dollar crumbled further.)

We will discuss here five different methods of valuing inventories and the cost of goods sold. The first four methods are legal; the fifth is not, but might be if the American Institute of Certified Public Accountants (AICPA) examines and approves it.

Weighted Average. Weighted average is the simplest method. Units in inventory and the units sold are assigned the same unit value, which value is calculated as a weighted average cost:

$$\frac{\$362,500}{50} = \$7250 \quad \text{per unit}$$

a. Inventory Value

$$22 \times \$7250 = \$159,500$$

b. Cost of Goods Sold

$$28 \times \$7250 = \frac{\$203,000}{\$362,500}$$

Lower of Cost or Market (LCM). Lower of cost or market is another simple method which implies that the firm values the items at the lower of two figures, what the item cost or what the current market value is. Since, in our example, we can assume that the market price will continue to rise, all items will be valued at the costs assigned to them.

a. Inventory value is

$$
\begin{array}{rll}
2 \times \$6000 = & \$\ 12,000 & \text{(the 2 left from Jan.)} \\
4 \times \ 7000 = & 28,000 & \\
8 \times \ 8000 = & 64,000 & \\
\underline{8} \times \ 8500 = & \underline{68,000} & \\
22 & \$172,000 &
\end{array}
$$

b. Cost of goods sold is

$$
\begin{array}{rll}
8 \times \$6000 = & \$\ 48,000 & \text{(the other 8 from Jan.)} \\
5 \times \ 6500 = & 32,500 & \\
11 \times \ 7000 = & 77,000 & \\
2 \times \ 8000 = & 16,000 & \\
\underline{2} \times \ 8500 = & \underline{17,000} & \\
28 & \$190,500 &
\end{array}
$$

Note that, as before, both totals in *a* and *b* add to $362,500.

First-In, First-Out (FIFO). FIFO (pronounced *fife-oh*) states that, in valuing the cost of goods sold (not inventories), the items purchased earliest should be used up until they are totally accounted for. Then the firm switches to the second oldest period, and so on. Therefore, the inventory evaluation would be done in just the opposite manner. Since there are twenty-two units in inventory, we will start with the latest month, December, in which ten units were purchased, and we will use them up at their purchase value. The second latest month is September with another ten units. This means that we need two more units, and we take these from June.

Inventory value is

$$
\begin{array}{rcl}
10 \times \$8500 & = & \$\ 85,000 \\
10 \times \ \ 8000 & = & \ 80,000 \\
\underline{\ \ 2} \times \ \ 7000 & = & \underline{\ \ 14,000} \\
22 & & \$179,000
\end{array}
$$

Cost of goods sold is

$$
\begin{array}{rcl}
10 \times \$6000 & = & \$\ 60,000 \\
\ \ 5 \times \ \ 6500 & = & \ 32,500 \\
\underline{13} \times \ \ 7000 & = & \underline{\ \ 91,000} \\
28 & & \$183,500
\end{array}
$$

Last-In, First-Out (LIFO). LIFO is exactly the opposite of FIFO. LIFO (pronounced *life-oh*) takes the latest units first for the cost of goods sold.

Inventory value is

$$
\begin{array}{rcl}
10 \times \$6000 & = & \$\ 60,000 \\
\ \ 5 \times \ \ 6500 & = & \ 32,500 \\
\underline{\ \ 7} \times \ \ 7000 & = & \underline{\ \ 49,000} \\
22 & & \$141,500
\end{array}
$$

Cost of goods sold is

$$
\begin{array}{rcl}
10 \times \$8500 & = & \$\ 85,000 \\
10 \times \ \ 8000 & = & \ 80,000 \\
\underline{\ \ 8} \times \ \ 7000 & = & \underline{\ \ 56,000} \\
28 & & \$221,000
\end{array}
$$

Next-In, First-Out (NIFO). NIFO (pronounced *knife-oh*) has been kicking around as a concept for years, but it is not, in the words of accountants, a "generally accepted accounting principle." It simply says that the cost of goods sold will be valued at the unit price of the next shipment. That would be 28 × $9000, or $252,000. We'd have to back into the inventory value by subtracting the cost of goods sold ($252,000) from the total purchases of $362,500. Thus, inventory under NIFO would have a value of $110,500.

Table 7.3 shows the results of the calculations starting with the lowest cost of goods sold and increasing in value.

Most corporations use LIFO since it reduces their tax bills by stating the cost of goods sold at the highest rate. Remember that, with LIFO, both assets and profit will be stated at lower values than with other valid methods.

TABLE 7.3

Inventory Valuation Methods

Method	Cost of Goods Sold	Inventory Value
FIFO	$183,500	$179,000
Cost or Market	190,500	172,000
Weighted Average	203,000	159,500
LIFO	221,000	141,500
NIFO	252,000	110,500

Discounted Money

Before we tackle the concepts of *net present value* (NPV) and *internal rate of return* (IRR), we should introduce the reader to the concept of *discounted cash flow* and its somewhat inverse function, *compound interest.* Let's start with the latter, since almost everyone is familiar with savings accounts and the interest that they pay.

When you deposit money in a savings account, you are renting a portion of the total amount of the deposit to the bank. The bank can't use the entire amount, because the Federal Reserve requires that it retain a portion in cash or readily marketable securities, such as United States Treasury notes and bills to meet contingencies, principally withdrawals. Your money on deposit earns more money, called *interest,* the rent paid to you for the bank's use of your funds. The bank then loans out your funds at a higher interest rate to meet its operational expenses and to make a profit.

Our example will be kept simple. Assume that a bank pays 5 percent interest on savings accounts, and that this is compounded (computed) on a yearly basis; i.e., the interest due to you is calculated on the average balance on every anniversary. Suppose that you deposit $1000 in such an account. At the end of the first year, the interest earned and due to you is $50 (.05 × $1000), and the statement will show that you now have $1050 on deposit. The second year passes. Will another $50 be added to the account? No. The interest will be 5 percent of the $1050 that was in the account at the start of the second year, or $52.50, and the account balance at the end of the second year will be $1102.50 ($1050.00 + $52.50). If the money is left for an indefinite period, the interest will compound upon itself at the end of each year. The formula for determining the account balance at the end of any year (*n*) is

$$A = P (1 + r)^n$$

where

A = amount in the account at any time
   following an anniversary.
P = original principal deposited.
r = interest rate in decimal form.

Thus, at the end of the fifth year the account balance would be

$$A = \$1000 \ (1 + .05)^5$$
$$A = \$1000 \ (1.05) \ (1.05) \ (1.05) \ (1.05) \ (1.05)$$
$$A = \$1276.28$$

When many years are involved, the above calculation becomes tedious and cumbersome so that we can use a table like that presented in Appendix D. Suppose that we leave our $1000 in the bank for twenty years. If we follow the 5 percent column down until we find the row corresponding to twenty years, the corresponding factor is .3769. That value is divided into the original principal:

$$\frac{\$1000}{.3769} = \$2653.22$$

Note that we could have converted the factor to the form $(1 + r)^n$ by dividing it into one (1.0):

$$\frac{1.0}{.3769} = 2.653 \quad \text{(to four significant digits)}$$

This is equivalent to $(1.05)^{20}$. By the way, if the Indians that sold Manhattan for $24 (60 guilders) to Peter Minuit in 1625 had found a Dutch savings bank paying 5 percent and had left the money on deposit until 1985, they would have $24(1.05)^{360}$, or $1,019,433,514.

Appendix D can also be used to compute the present value of money. As everyone is painfully aware, the dollar declines in purchasing power because of inflation. When we were in high school, two dollars would fill up a normal gas tank; today, it hardly makes the fuel needle move.

Assume that you agree to loan a friend $5000 at no interest with the understanding that $1000 is to be paid back at the end of each of the five years involved. Although it's true that you will receive the $5000 back, is this a real $5000? Suppose that the average inflation rate over the five years is 8 percent. In today's dollars, using Appendix D, you will receive the following flow of cash related back to current money:

Year	Amount Paid Back	8 Percent Present Value Factor	Today's Dollars
1	$1000	.9259	$ 925.90
2	1000	.8573	857.30
3	1000	.7938	793.80
4	1000	.7350	735.00
5	1000	.6806	680.60
	$5000		$3992.60

You actually lose slightly over $1000 on the deal and would do so on any interest rate less than the 8 percent inflation. Future dollars are cheaper dollars.

There is a third way to use Appendix D. Suppose you need $25,000 for a business expansion that you project will be needed four years hence. Assume further that you can find an investment that will give you an annual return (compounded) of 8.25 percent. How much should you invest today to yield the required $25,000 by the end of the fourth year?

Appendix D shows that, in the fourth year, the 8 percent factor is .7350 and the 9 percent factor is .7084. Therefore, we want the factor that lies one-fourth of the way between the two values, and the computation is as follows:

8% factor	.7350
9% factor	.7084
Difference	.0266

Then $\frac{1}{4}$ of .0266 is .0067 and the factor for 8.25 percent is

$$.7350 - .0067 = .7283$$

And the amount to be deposited today is

$$.7283 \times \$25,000 = \$18,207.50$$

Now we're ready for the advanced course, one of inestimable aid to entrepreneurs.

Net Present Value (NPV) and Internal Rate of Return (IRR)

Calculating *net present value* (NPV) and *internal rate of return* (IRR) is a technique that scares many people, but it shouldn't. Not only is it fairly simple when broken down to its parts, but it is an invaluable technique for analyzing different investment alternatives. The big companies have been using it for years, and now it's time to bring it into small business calculations.

To start everyone off with total terror tactics (TTT), we will make the following statement:

$$NPV = \sum_{t=1}^{n} \frac{R_t}{(1 + r)^t} - C$$

This rather ferocious-looking equation reads as follows: The NPV is equal to the stream of income produced (R_t) in any period ($_t$) discounted at some rate (r) for a maximum number of periods (n) minus the original cost (C).

Now, let's develop it a little bit at a time. If an entrepreneur begins business operations, there will be some initial cost. Business is a device which produces a stream of income consisting of two segments, successive annual profits and the sale price occurring at some future time. Since these incomes will occur at future times, the dollars must be discounted, since, like our depreciation example earlier, these future dollars are cheaper dollars.

NPV, when an appropriate interest rate is chosen, represents an amount of money that is either greater or less than zero (a positive or negative number). NPV has real significance only when you compare two or more investment alternatives. NPV's become bases for decision-making.

Let's use an example. An entrepreneur is considering buying one of the two businesses as shown in Table 7.4.

TABLE 7.4

Comparison of Values of Two Businesses

	Business 1	Business 2
Purchase Price	$ 38,000	$ 50,000
Profits		
Year 1	$ 1,000	$ 1,500
Year 2	3,000	8,000
Year 3	6,000	8,000
Year 4	10,000	15,000
Sale Price, Year 5	$ 43,000	$ 52,000

He would like to find the NPV for each alternative. He must select an interest rate for calculation purposes that represents a rate that he could realize with the best safe alternate investment. We'll use 10 percent for this example.

The formula begins to simplify as

$$NPV = \sum_{t=1}^{5} \frac{R_t}{(1 + .10)^t} - C$$

We will construct a table showing the *discounted cash flow* (DCF). DCF represents the stream of money from Table 7.4 discounted by the 10 percent rate for the specific period (parentheses mean cash paid out).

TABLE 7.5

Discounted Cash Flow (DCF) of Two Businesses

Year (t)	$(1 + .10)^t$	Business 1	Business 2
0	1.00000	$(38,000)	$(50,000)
1	1.10000	909	1,364
2	1.21000	2,479	6,612
3	1.33100	4,508	6,011
4	1.46410	6,830	10,245
5	1.61051	26,700	32,287
NPV		$ 3,426	$ 6,519

Thus, business 2 has a net value at the present time that is nearly twice that of business 1.

We will now calculate the internal rate of return (IRR). This is the return on investment that the business will generate over its life. To find the IRR (r in our equation), we set the NPV equal to zero.

Then

$$C = \sum_{t=1}^{5} \frac{R_t}{(1 + r)^t}$$

or, for business 1,

$$38,000 = \frac{1000}{(1 + r)} + \frac{3000}{(1 + r)^2} + \frac{6000}{(1 + r)^3} + \frac{10,000}{(1 + r)^4} + \frac{43,000}{(1 + r)^5}$$

To find the value for r without a calculator, the trial-and-error method is required. If we try a value for 10 percent we find

$$38,000 \overset{?}{=} 41,416$$

Therefore a larger value for r is required. Try 12 percent.

$$38,000 \overset{?}{=} 38,315$$

Try 12.2 percent.

$$38,000 \overset{?}{=} 38,017$$

Answer: 12.21 percent.

For business 2, the IRR is 13.3 percent, which makes it a better investment. Many modern calculators have the IRR function built in.

Tax Considerations

In Chapter 9, we will list some of the taxes that a business pays. Here, we will touch briefly on the implications of income taxes for businesses and owners. You should check with both your lawyer and your accountant on all of this in advance, since they will know the latest tax rates and laws.

In sole proprietorships and partnerships, profit is taxable to the proprietor(s) or partners. Although small corporations may elect this form of taxation (see Chapter 9), most corporations pay taxes on the net income of the business and individuals pay taxes on incomes received.

Although tax rates change all the time, assume that an entrepreneur can choose to run his business as a proprietorship or a corporation. Suppose the operation has a pretax profit of $60,000 before the owner takes out $25,000. Also assume the following:

Personal tax rates (check latest rates)
    on $25,000, 25%
    on $60,000, 45%
Corporate tax rates
    first $25,000, 22%
    second $25,000, 26%
    all over $50,000, 48%

In the proprietorship form, the entire $60,000 is taxed as personal income regardless of what was withdrawn by the owner. In the corporate form, the entrepreneur pays taxes on $25,000 and the corporation pays on the balance, or $35,000.

Proprietorship Form	*Corporate Form*	
.45 × $60,000 = $27,000	.25 × $25,000 =	$ 6,250
	.22 × 25,000 =	5,500
	.26 × 10,000 =	2,600
		$14,350

This looks very attractive. The IRS, however, has instituted the *improperly retained earnings rule.* If the IRS thinks that you are using the corporate form of business to pay less taxes, it will make you pay dividends to yourself and then tax those. Just be sure to claim that any accumulated funds are necessary for business purposes.

Budgeting

As large corporations do, you should prepare and use budgets. The values for each category should come directly from your business plan. If you want to add real teeth to it, make your plan both a cash-in and cash-out reconciliation. Then you can plan and watch over cash flow. Figure 7.5 shows a cash budget for a hypothetical business for a six-month period. It shows the company reaching a maximum deficit position of $5250 in months two and three and then recovering to a surplus position by month five.

When month one is over, the actual activity in each area should be recorded and then compared with the projected levels. This is called a *budget variance report*. Many people like to see last year's data as well. Figure 7.6 is a sample budget variance report. We have done something that would probably worry an accountant. In the variance column, parentheses are used to show items that are over budget; the standard convention has always been to show underages that way. Using our suggestion, parentheses always mean something bad has happened—a loss, a deficit, or being over budget. Many people add different things to budget variance reports. We could have added a column for Budget, Year-to-Date and another to analyze the actual expenses year-to-date as a percentage of the total year's budget.

Don't get overly concerned if variances occur within your budgeting system. They do in every budget known. Simply know why they occurred and see what can be done for more efficient planning in the future. Until you are skilled at preparing and analyzing budgets, you'll make some sizable errors, usually not in your favor.

Planning for External Funding

Sales growth is accompanied by growth in other areas of the business. It requires *planning for external funding*. It is helpful to understand requirements for both long-term and short-term financing. Long-term financing includes major infusions of capital for significant changes in the business. Short-term financing usually means planning for one year.

Analyzing short-term financing is a relatively simple task as long as we can use the following assumptions for an initial look at the situation: Both current assets and current liabilities will rise at the same rate as the growth in sales; all other assets and liabilities will stay fixed in the short run; the profit margin (percentage-wise) will be the same in the next year.

If sales in the current year are S_1 and sales for the next year are S_2, then the rate of increase in sales is

$$\frac{S_2 - S_1}{S_1} \times 100\%$$

Item	Month					
	1	2	3	4	5	6
Wages and benefits	$ 6,000	$ 6,000	$ 6,500	$ 6,500	$ 6,500	$ 7,000
Travel and entertainment	100	100	100	100	100	100
Gas and oil	200	200	200	200	200	200
Repairs and maintenance	150	200	-	250	-	-
Inventory purchases	5,000	8,000	6,000	8,000	4,000	2,000
Legal and accounting	200	200	400	200	200	300
Rent	900	900	900	900	900	900
Loan repayment	1,100	1,100	1,100	1,100	1,100	1,100
Trash removal and snow plowing	400	300	300	200	200	200
Advertising	1,000	1,000	1,500	1,500	1,500	1,000
Telephone	400	400	400	400	400	500
Electricity	300	300	200	200	100	100
Janitorial service	200	200	200	200	200	200
Supplies	200	200	200	200	200	200
Taxes and licenses	100	100	-	-	100	-
Equipment purchases	200	-	-	1,000	-	2,000
Miscellaneous	200	200	200	200	200	200
Total expenses	$16,650	$19,400	$18,200	$21,150	$15,900	$16,000
Cash in	$14,700	$16,100	$18,200	$23,000	$22,250	$21,100
Surplus (deficit)	$(1,950)	$(3,300)	$ 0	$ 1,850	$ 6,350	$ 5,100
Cumulative surplus (deficit)	$(1,950)	$(5,250)	$(5,250)	$(3,400)	$ 2,950	$ 8,050

Figure 7.5 *Sample Cash Budget*

Item	Budget	Actual	Variance (Over) Under	Actual Year to Date	Last Year to Date
Wages and benefits	$ 6,000	$ 6,200	$(200)	$ 6,200	$5,700
Travel and entertainment	100	60	40	60	90
Gas and oil	200	150	50	150	150
Repairs and maintenance	150	200	(50)	200	150
Inventory purchases	5,000	5,800	(800)	5,800	6,000
Legal and accounting	200	150	50	150	100
Rent	900	900	0	900	900
Loan repayment	1,100	1,100	0	1,100	1,100
Trash removal and snow plowing	400	300	100	300	350
Advertising	1,000	800	200	800	950
Telephone	400	370	30	370	250
Electricity	300	350	(50)	350	200
Janitorial service	200	280	(80)	280	200
Supplies	200	500	(300)	500	200
Taxes and licenses	100	100	0	100	100
Equipment purchases	200	1,000	(800)	1,000	900
Miscellaneous	200	80	120	80	100
Total	$16,650	$18,340	$(1,690)	$18,340	$17,340

Budgeted cash in	$14,700
Actual cash in	16,970
Actual expenses	18,340
Surplus (deficit)	$(1,370)
Budgeted surplus (deficit)	$(1,950)
Improvement (worsening)	$ 580

Figure 7.6 *Sample Budget Variance Report, Month 1*

We will let a represent the current assets in dollars, l the current liabilities, and p the profit in the current year. Outside financing (F), then, is

$$F = \left\{ \left(\frac{S_2 - S_1}{S_1} \right)(a) \right\} - \left\{ \left(\frac{S_2 - S_1}{S_1} \right)(l) \right\} - \left\{ \left(\frac{p}{S_1} \right)S_2 \right\}$$

If sales for the current year are $320,000 with a profit of $2,800, current assets stand at $120,000, current liabilities at $80,000, and sales next year are forecast at $360,000, then the firm will require financing (for the 12.5 percent growth) of

$$F = \left\{ \left(\frac{360{,}000 - 320{,}000}{320{,}000} \right)(120{,}000) \right\} - \left\{ \left(\frac{360{,}000 - 320{,}000}{320{,}000} \right)(80{,}000) \right\}$$
$$- \left\{ \left(\frac{2{,}800}{320{,}000} \right)(360{,}000) \right\}$$

$F = 15{,}000 - 10{,}000 - 3{,}150$

$F = \$1{,}850$

If we do the same analysis for XYZ Business (Figures 7.2 and 7.3) assuming a sales increase of 10 percent to $110,000, then

$$F = \left\{ \left(\frac{110{,}000 - 100{,}000}{100{,}000} \right)(23{,}700) \right\} - \left\{ \left(\frac{110{,}000 - 100{,}000}{100{,}000} \right)(4{,}500) \right\}$$
$$- \left\{ \left(\frac{27{,}300}{100{,}000} \right)(110{,}000) \right\}$$

$F = 2{,}370 - 450 - 30{,}030$

$F = -\$28{,}110$

Notice the minus sign. XYZ would not have to look to outside financing; it can finance its own growth. Therefore, for XYZ, there is an increase in working capital generated by the increase in sales.

Capacity Considerations

Capacity considerations concern major long-term funding. Many entrepreneurs find themselves bursting at the seams at some point in their business history. This usually signals the time that a major business expansion is necessary, and, unless the entrepreneur has been squirrelling cash away somewhere, additional financing will be necessary. It is nearly impossible to tell anyone how large an expansion should be, but it should provide for the next five years as an absolute minimum. About the only way we've found to plan for this major move is to first calculate absolute maximum capacity level and determine how close you are to that capacity, and then to figure your rate of growth in real terms. If your sales increased by 12 percent last year and 7 percent of that was due to price increases, then your real growth was 5 percent.

For instance, if you are growing by 5 percent per year in real terms, you should plan to expand when you have reached about 90 percent of your theoretical capacity. Your expansion should be 20–25 percent of your present facility, consistent with the business's ability to finance that expansion.

One rather simple way to estimate future major financial requirements for expansion comes directly from and should be an integral part of the business plan. Planning for growth from acquisition is much more difficult since you often cannot foresee a competitor's business being for sale, or a similar circumstance. Let us assume that a business is purchased which will gross $300,000 in the base year. For calculation purposes, we will say that sales can be expected to increase at 20 percent per year, one-half of that increase, or 10 percent can be attributed to real growth, and the remaining 10 percent attributed to inflation or price increases. The establishment uses 60 percent of its usable business space. Please note that this does not imply 60 percent of the total available space, since aisles and other unproductive space must be provided if only for satisfying local fire regulations. (Besides, who wants to have customers climb over the loaves of bread to reach the frozen beans or, worse yet, the reverse?) The dollar sales will increase, then, by 20 percent per year, and the space usage by 10 percent as in Table 7.6.

TABLE 7.6

Increases of Dollar Sales and Capacity of a Business

Year	Dollar Sales	Percent Capacity
0	$ 300,000	60
1	360,000	66
2	432,000	73
3	518,400	80
4	622,000	88
5	746,500	97

During the fourth year, the effective capacity of 90 percent will be reached, and expansion time is near at hand. If a 2500-square-foot addition is necessary and the construction cost of such a facility costs forty dollars per square foot, the new wing will cost $100,000. We will use this assumption in the next section.

Controlling the Controllables

This section on *controlling the controllables* is subtitled "Inflation Can Be Your Friend." Everyone worries over, hurls invectives at, and decries rising costs. Oil companies seem to gouge our pocketbooks, steel companies pass on their labor-rate increases, utilities are often viewed as legal monopolies, farmers dump milk into rivers to drive prices up, and even the government, through social security, forces higher payments on us every year. Working people with middle incomes suffer; those on fixed incomes may face effects that go beyond just hardship. Is there no help for the small-business owner? There may be.

As with any workable model, we must make some assumptions. Any reader may either dispute these assumptions entirely or change them to suit his particular situation. Let us go back to our business of the previous section (Table 7.6) for this discussion. We will assume that the sales in years 0–4 and the cost of goods sold (one-half of the sales) will both increase at 20 percent; this means that the gross margin will be a constant one-half of sales and also will increase at 20 percent. The assumption here seems both logical and reasonable. Sales and cost of sales will stay in the same relation to one another.

Expenses (cash expenses, not accounting expenses) consist of items that may be categorized in the following three ways:

Totally variable costs. Totally variable costs will be identical to the items contained in the cost of sales. They will rise with inflation, generally at the same rate.

Semivariable/semifixed costs. In theory, a semivariable cost is different from a semifixed cost, but we will treat them the same way. They are costs that (a) will remain constant over a short span of time, and (b) will increase generally in increments. An example of this would be the hiring of an additional person. It can be said that these types of costs can be controlled in a more efficient way than can the totally variable costs.

Totally fixed costs. The primary example of totally fixed costs is the debt service (principal and interest) of a term loan that has a fixed-interest rate over the term. The monthly payments can be counted on to stay the same, month after month, until the loan is repaid.

If these further assumptions are acceptable to most readers, we can proceed to our example. We will say that in year 0, the business with $300,000 sales (Table 7.6) has a cost-of-goods-sold of $150,000 (half of sales), and variable and semivariable costs of $100,000. This segment of expenses will increase at 15 percent annually rather than the 20 percent increase of the rate of sales and cost of sales. For calculation purposes, we will say that the new owner finances a $200,000 loan at 12 percent interest for twenty years. This requires a monthly principal and interest payment of $2202.17, or annual expenses of $26,400 in round numbers. Therefore, our base year looks as follows:

Sales	$300,000
Cost of sales	150,000
Gross margin	150,000
Variable and semivariable expenses	100,000
Fixed payments (loan)	26,400
Net profit	23,600
Percent profit on sales	7.9

Now, given all the assumptions, look at what will happen in the next four years detailed as follows:

	Year			
	1	*2*	*3*	*4*
Sales	$360,000	$432,000	$518,400	$622,000
Cost of sales	180,000	216,000	259,200	311,000
Gross margin	$180,000	$216,000	$259,200	$311,000
Expenses	115,000	132,300	152,000	175,000
Payments	26,400	26,400	26,400	26,400
Profit	$ 38,600	$ 57,300	$ 80,800	$109,600
Percent Profit	10.7	13.3	15.6	17.6

Sales from the base year have slightly more than doubled, but the profit has gone up over fourfold.

It is an easy matter to convert the model to a mathematical expression to allow for computer analysis and for changing the assumptions. Combining many of the concepts discussed earlier in this chapter, we can calculate that the sales (s_f) in any future year, n, is a function of the sales in the base year (s_b), and the growth factor, r_s as we have defined previously, as follows:

$$s_f = s_b (1 + r_s)^n$$

But the same concept holds true for the cost of sales in both periods (c_b and c_f) and the corresponding expenses (e_b and e_f), both with their proper "growth" rates (r_c and r_e). If the fixed payments are represented as p, then the calculation for cash profit (p_f) in any future time is

$$p_f = s_b (1 + r_s)^n - c_b (1 + r_c)^n - e_b (1 + r_e)^n - p$$

Checking our previous example in the mathematical expression above in the fourth year:

$$p_f = \$300{,}000(1 + .20)^4 - \$150{,}000(1 + .20)^4 - \$100{,}000(1 + .20)^4 - \$26{,}400$$
$$p_f = \$622{,}000 - \$311{,}000 - \$175{,}000 - \$26{,}400$$
$$p_f = \$109{,}600 \quad (17.6\% \text{ of sales})$$

Suppose that we wish to juggle some of the values in the example. Let us say that the cost of sales rises to 55 percent of sales (.55 × $300,000 = $165,000), but only increases at 19 percent per year. We will try an annual average growth in expenses of 17 percent rather than 15 percent.

Then, in the fourth year,

$$p_f = \$300,000(1 + .20)^4 - \$165,000(1 + .19)^4 - \$100,000(1 + .17)^4 - \$26,400$$
$$p_f = \$622,000 - \$330,900 - \$187,400 - \$26,400$$
$$p_f = \$77,300 \quad (12.4\% \text{ of sales})$$

There are, of course, many ways to use the concept, and we will leave that to the interested reader. The point we are stressing is that inflation doesn't have to control the entrepreneur; the reverse can also be true.

In Conclusion

We have now finished what is often the most difficult chapter for many to grasp. It was not our intent in Chapter 7 to spoonfeed technical Pablum to you, but rather to provide some rare beefsteak that may require intellectual chewing. The mental nourishment should be there for those of you who took the time to understand this section. If you understood 70–80 percent of what we said here, the rest is a piece of cake.

CHAPTER EIGHT

Personnel Management

The impression that one gets from a ruler and of his brains
is from seeing the men he has about him.

Niccollo Machiavelli

Your business has physical assets that appear on the balance sheet—cash, inventories, land, building, and equipment. Other assets which can't be easily valued but that still add equity are the name of the business, your enterprise's reputation, and your people. Most experts agree that your people, your employees, are your most valuable asset. Motivated, enthusiastic people, who are treated with respect and dignity, can be a decisive factor in the success of your venture. On the other hand, when people are looked on simply as necessary evils (something akin to paying income tax), productivity falls off. If the situation deteriorates it can result in outright acts of sabotage such as theft, destruction of property, or leaking of competitive secrets. A recent book (and we won't even refer to it by name) has as its major theme that a business owner should take the initiative and screw his employees before he himself is screwed. There's too much of that in big business. No definitive study of people in the work situation has ever demonstrated that the way to get people to work is to constantly jump on them. Of course, you should exercise discipline and control when required. You must manage your people, but you don't have to boss them.

There are many, many articles and books on management. Two useful ones are Peter Drucker's *Managing for Results* and Bob Townsend's *Up the Organization*;[1] they should be a minimum part of your entrepreneurial library. Even though they are both slanted toward the large firm, there's enough meat in them to keep you fed for a lifetime. Even if you read and followed only the chapter called "People" in Townsend's book and the chapter called "The Customer Is the Business" in Drucker's, you would be well ahead of most of your competition in getting the most out of your people and your business.

Most of the body of management theory began in the 1920s at the Hawthorne, Illinois, works of the Western Electric Company. Western Electric's management people, probably the most enlightened (as you will see shortly, we mean this literally) of its day and aware of Frederick Taylor's works on scientific management, decided to make some experiments within the facility to determine what factors, if any, would affect employee productivity. They decided first to increase the lighting intensity within the plant. They did so, and productivity increased. Then they began decreasing the lighting until they reached the point of bright moonlight. Productivity increased again! They were

---

[1] *Up the Organization,* by Robert Townsend (Knopf, New York, 1970). *Managing for Results,* by Peter F. Drucker (Harper and Row, New York, 1964).

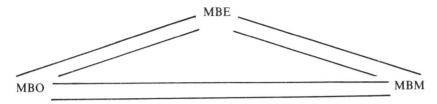

Figure 8.1 *The Management Process*

baffled, and so they called upon Elton Mayo of Harvard for an answer. After an exhaustive study, Mayo concluded the following: When employees are aware that management has taken an interest in them, there is a high probability of increased productivity. However, if management makes demands beyond what employees feel is reasonable, the chance of productivity increase is very small.

Today, we speak of *authoritarian management* (whips) versus *participative management* (carrots). The former rules with an iron hand, totally directing subordinates, whereas the latter allows subordinates to participate in the decision-making process.

A very brief and simple explanation of how the management process should operate is shown in Figure 8.1.

Each three-letter combination stands for one of the *management-by* techniques that have been popular from time to time. About 95 percent of the important management theory and practice can be included in these three simple concepts. Forget for the time being that most textbooks say that managers have a number of responsibilities such as planning, coordinating, staffing, and directing, all overlaid with decision-making. Let's use the three M's to encompass all of it. These principles pertain to you alone, since, as an entrepreneur, you are your own boss. The classic superior-subordinate relationship is established in your position by definition.

Management by Exception (MBE)

If you have good advisors (spouse, banker, supplier, employee, customer), then there is no good reason why you have to involve yourself in every minute detail of the business. You may use the technique of *management by exception* (MBE). We are not suggesting in any way that you should immediately hire yourself a resident manager and then take off to Bimini to become an absentee owner. Although this might be possible in the future, it shouldn't be done until the business is so profitable that it can support you in a manner to which you'd like to become accustomed and until you can pay your resident manager a healthy enough wage to keep his or her hand out of the till when you're gone. MBE has a number of underlying assumptions, but the main theme suggests that you devote as much of your time as possible to the important issues and leave the trivial ones alone. This concept also suggests that your advisors and subordinates only come to you with items that require your attention and that you successfully fight the urge to react negatively to them for doing so. If you have subordinates, don't have them send you weekly reports; leave that to J. Pierpont Freen down at the big mill. He needs ego-building; you need business-building. Don't have weekly staff meetings, but, if you do, turn the temperature down to 15°C (60°F) and have everybody stand, naked. Things will go quickly and, thus, well.

Most readers have heard of the 80-20 rule which originally came out of the marketing area of business—80 percent of a firm's sales are provided by 20 percent of its customers. The rule has implications within the MBE concept: spend 80 percent of your time on the 20 percent of the problems that are truly significant to the business. Follow the advice that Andrew Carnegie once paid a consultant $25,000 for: make a list of all the things you have to do. Put the most important (not the most enjoyable) item at the top, then the second most important, and so on. If you have ten items on your *do list,* the chances are that you should spend 80 percent of your time on the first two and only 20 percent on the next eight.

Management by Objective (MBO)

Big business has beaten *management by objective* (MBO) to such a bloody pulp that it has fallen out of favor in most bureaucracies. Now it's time to bring it to small business. Even if you are the president, sole owner, and only employee, MBO has a definite place, and it, like so many ideas we've discussed, goes hand in hand with the business plan. MBO simply means that you set down in writing certain goals to be accomplished, when you expect to achieve them, and what will tell you when you have attained them. Suppose your three clerks have become so lax about coming in on time that 20 percent of the time two or more of them come in more than fifteen minutes late. The MBO approach would work as follows:

> *Objective:* To reduce tardiness so that two or less employees are no more than five
>   minutes late 10 percent of the time or less
> *Time for Accomplishment:* Three months
> *Measure of Success:* When the objective has been achieved for three consecutive
>   weeks

MBO works equally well in many other situations with employees. One useless invention of big business is the annual employee review or encounter session, a violation of MBE. Using MBO means mutually establishing specific goals and objectives with your people. This way, you avoid the Black Friday of the dreaded annual appraisal. Notice the words *mutually* and *specific*. Saying to one of your people that you expect him to improve his performance doesn't accomplish much, but getting a salesperson to agree that a 10 percent sales increase in six months is possible and desirable is quite something else. When the six months is over, both of you can examine the results and determine whether the goal was met or not. If it was not, you should both determine the reasons, not you alone by reviewing his performance on D-Day.

Management by Motivation (MBM)

There abideth three: MBE, MBO, and MBM but the greatest of these is the third, *management by motivation* (MBM). Most social scientists tell us that true motivation comes from within. You can't motivate your people, but you can go a long, long way toward building the environment which will allow this self-motivation to blossom. There is no magic here whatsoever. Saying "Thanks" or "You did a fine job" costs you nothing, but look what it does for your people.

In Chapter 1, we talked about the self-fulfilling prophecy. People will do what's expected of them. If you expect top performance, chances are that's what you'll get, but it takes work on your part, constantly reinforcing your people until their confidence and motivation is at a sufficiently high level. McGregor was right with his Theory *Y* (see Chapter 1). Most people enjoy working. It's natural. There are very few hermits in the world. Most of the people that win the large lotteries continue right on working. Much of the blame for falling productivity and low morale can be brought right into the executive suite of the corporation. The self-fulfilling prophecy is at work once again, but this time in a negative sense. If it is expected that poor performance will prevail, by golly, it will. When you finally leave your large employer, leave that attitude at the employee exit. Let their profit margins continue to slide while you build yours.

Consider one last thought before we leave MBM. Young infantry lieutenants are taught that, in an offensive attack, the action starts with the command "Follow me!" Don't ever underestimate the wisdom of leadership by example. You can't come into the business Monday morning, walk up to Harry or Sally, say "I sure expect an outstanding performance this week," and retire to your panelled office to wallow in status. If things are busy, you should be out in the trenches with your troops, slugging it out with those 280-pound customers.

Forget fancy offices, administrative assistants, sterling water pitchers, and executive parking spaces. You don't need them; you're having too much fun. If you ever long for them, go to the nearest large company and walk down executive row. Look into the offices and see the prisoners confined to desks cluttered with a welter of waste and trivia. Then go back to your place, hug an employee, and get back to having fun.

Hiring

If people are your most valuable asset, then the *hiring process* is crucial. Everyone develops techniques for selecting employees, and you want to be able to attract and hire the very best there is. But you have a problem that GM doesn't—you are limited in what you can pay someone, sometimes severely. If GM wants someone badly enough, it can bribe him with money and perks, and, when the price gets high enough, the person sells out. Keep this in mind: Money, as high as it is on most people's list, is not the primary motivator in the work situation. Things like achievement recognition and job satisfaction come out on top, and you can provide them—they're free!

The day will arrive when you need a full-time employee to help out in your small business. Now what?

First, if you haven't done so, visit your local IRS office to get your federal identification (ID) number. Your ID is like your business's social security number and will be unique to your operation. Have the IRS explain withholding tax and the forms that go along with it. Never, *Never,* NEVER play any games with taxes and social security that you've withheld from an employee. Send it in when required. The IRS will do some very nasty things to you if you don't.

Next, before you begin your search, you should set down the following specifications:

> Education and training required
> Wages you plan to pay and the benefits you will offer
> What you expect of him
> Personality traits that he should possess

Then begin looking. Before you spend any money, call around to other businesses and see if the managers have any suggestions. They may have had some excellent applicants for which they had no openings. You should also visit or call your local employment security (unemployment) office. Members of the staff will be absolutely delighted to talk with you.

If these two sources fail to turn up anyone, you'll have to use other means. The most common is an ad in the local newspaper. Keep the ad short and descriptive. Run it for a week, including the weekends. Do not state anything about pay rate. Use a blind ad, one with a box number. This hides your identity and prevents annoying phone calls. In the ad, ask for a job and salary history from the applicants. At your leisure, you can screen the data and select those whom you'd like to invite over for a chat. Although it may seem discourteous, you don't have to answer the rejects.

Ideally the respondent to your advertisement or the referral from another source is tailor-made to your requirements. This ideal never occurs, however;

unfortunately, many applicants may stretch their qualifications to meet your specifications in their resumes, transmittal letters, or during the course of their interview. In these cases it is difficult to make proper judgments.

Generally speaking, you are not properly trained to unravel the key points of an individual's make-up. Too often there are gross overstatements by both parties that ultimately break down the relationship between the prospective employer and would-be employee; unfortunately, these errors in judgment or presentation do not become known immediately and can be costly to the operation of the business in the long run.

Interviewing is a skill; so is being interviewed. A successful interview needs planning to accomplish a mutual understanding between parties on the tasks to be performed, the requirements of the position, and the responsibility of both parties to an employment contract.

The work of recruiting competent people for your organization is a "profession." It takes great skill. Furthermore, it is very costly to hire new employees. In a small company, the owner/manager would be hard-pressed to devote valuable marketing or planning time developing advertisements, screening resumes, scheduling interview appointments, and the like. There is an alternative that may be more economical in the long run. The owner/manager may establish a working relationship with one or more qualified recruiting agencies in the community. This agency would invest sufficient time to know your company, your industry, your product or service, and the conditions and/or trends that effect the technology and your marketplace. In addition, they would have a clear and concise definition of each key job position in your organization to help them in their day-to-day recruiting activities, so that spotting qualifying candidates for your company's potential future requirements can be paramount in your minds. These candidates for your organization could then be called upon when and if your needs evolve. This planning stage would avoid the start-up cost of advertising, recruiting, screening, testing, and evaluating that would be incurred if there were unforeseen resignations or rapid growth in your company. Furthermore, the valuable time of you and your key people would not be spent on ancillary efforts that reduce effectiveness and productivity on more important business assignments.

A simple contract can be developed between the company and the recruiting firm with a responsible binder (money). A workable formula for the binder might be developed on the basis of a small percentage of annual payroll and the expected turnover rate of key positions. This advance binder would then be applied to any fees assessed by the agency for successful placement of people.

As you would expect, not all agencies are attuned to this type of philosophy with small-business people. Too often they choose to devote their major efforts to larger firms. You can, however, usually find a dedicated agency that can enhance your recruiting efforts.

When you've selected five or so applicants who seem to fit what you have in mind, call them on the phone and arrange a personal interview for each. Don't interview any of them on the telephone. You can make false assumptions that way.

When you have someone come in for an interview, set a place aside where you can talk in private. Successfully interviewing someone for a job requires enormous skill and patience. When the applicant speaks, listen. Lead the applicant along in a relaxed and comfortable way. Unless you have a Ph.D. in psychology and many years of experience in the field of human communications, don't ask "Did you like your mother better than your father?" Ask the applicant questions about his background, education, hobbies, interests, likes, and dislikes. See if you can discover what really turns him on. Most of all, see if you like him. The president of a major venture capital firm in Boston once said that his final decision whether to invest in a company depended upon whether he liked the entrepreneur or not. If you don't care for the applicant, regardless of whether you think this might change in the future, forget him. First impressions are extremely important, and, if the applicant doesn't come across well, he may be the same with your customers and drive them away.

While the interview is going on, form a mental picture of the applicant in the work situation. Does he fit? See how inquisitive the applicant is about the job and its duties. Does he really seem interested in the position?

Somewhere in the course of the interview, it may be necessary to determine the skill level of the applicant. Stay away from using intelligence tests and personality tests and stick to actual demonstrations of performance. If you're looking for a welder, have him weld something. Ask a secretarial applicant to type a letter, time him and then, later, look it over for any errors.

Once you have made your selection, call that person and make the offer. Be sure to state the pay rate very carefully so that there is no misunderstanding. Also be certain that all questions have been thoroughly resolved. Fix the starting date, and away you go.

You may want to hire the person on a trial basis. Usually, you start a new employee at some nominal pay rate for a fixed period of time, like thirty days. This is a mutual test, and, if at the end of the period it appears to be a good match, you raise the level of pay.

After six months, you'll have a pretty good idea of what you have. If you offer encouragement, training, reward (not only through pay raises but through praise), and guidance you'll lessen the chance that a good person will leave or that you'll have to fire a poor or marginal employee.

Firing

Firing here does not mean laying someone off because there is no work for them to do. It means discharge for cause, for performance consistently below the minimum required for the position, personality conflict, or other reasons ranging from excessive absenteeism to theft.

If you have employees, chances are that you will have to face this most unpleasant task in business. If the person simply isn't right for the job, you must sever the connection. Decide what day you will do it, and then, first thing that morning, get the person alone and explain the situation. Tell him precisely what you are doing. Preserve his dignity as much as you can; the blow will be very ego-deflating. One thing to keep in mind is that, once you have decided on discharge, you must be sure to go through with it. You may have to face tears, pleading, and some really distressing situations. You may have a twenty-three-year-old divorcee that needs the job for pure survival, but don't let that change what has to be done. You're only postponing the inevitable.

Most people who honestly want work can find it, so the person you are terminating will not be out of work very long. Also, the chances are that unemployment benefits will be available. In the final analysis, most people that have been fired have said that it is the *best* thing that ever happened to them.

You may have to face a situation following a firing in which a prospective employer will call you about the very person that you had to discharge. Don't second-guess anything. Be honest, but try to mention some redeeming qualities.

Let's hope that firing people can be kept to an absolute minimum through selective and careful hiring by a supportive employer (you).

Employee Compensation

A word is in order here about *employee compensation.* As we have mentioned before, as a small-business owner, you will be restricted in what you can offer employees in terms of pay and benefits. On the other hand, if you try to buy too cheaply, the best help won't stay. If you have little or no experience establishing wage and salary levels, your local employment security office might be able to give you the prevailing range in your locale. Keep inflation in mind. If you have good people working for you, who are helping you build your business and your profits, it makes personal as well as business sense to reward them financially beyond just keeping them current with inflation. For employees who stay on beyond five to seven years, you might consider giving or selling them part of the business. Check with your lawyer and your accountant on the implications to both parties before you start discussions with your people. There are federal laws, for example, that govern Employee Stock Ownership Plans (ESOP's), and these regulations will change from year to year.

Employees look for more than just money as compensation. Most people expect fringe benefits and, here again, the big companies can beat you handily. Listed below are some typical benefits with some comments.

Holidays

The usual holidays are New Year's Day, Washington's Birthday, Memorial Day, Independence Day, Labor Day, Veteran's Day, Thanksgiving, and Christmas. You might consider adding a floating holiday, such as the employee's birthday.

Vacation

If you have the kind of business that closes for two weeks at some point in the year, that makes scheduling vacations easy. It's up to you whether you have a time-in-grade requirement for paid vacation, such as one paid week after six months and two paid weeks after one year. If your business doesn't actually close and you allow your people to take vacations at their convenience, then the federal government's system of accrual is the simplest. You allow the employee to build vacation time at a fixed rate, say, eight hours per month. You may want to consider longer vacation periods for people who have been with you for a number of years.

Sick Leave

A large percentage of hourly employees receive no sick leave—no work, no pay. The policy is up to you, of course, but the granting of a few days of paid sick leave shouldn't cripple you and might help to boost morale.

Medical Benefits

What many employers do is to pay the medical benefit for the employee and let them pay for the other members of their family themselves. Most of the large insurance companies have gotten into this field but to keep matters simple, Blue Cross and Blue Shield are still your best bet. They aren't the cheapest or the most efficiently run, but the hospitals understand their system. You usually can't qualify for a group rate until you have more than five employees.

Life Insurance

Life insurance is sometimes difficult to justify in a small business, but, when it is done, the face amount of the policy, payable to the beneficiary upon death, is usually a multiple of the employee's annual earnings.

Accidental Death and Dismemberment (AD and D)

Extended coverage for accidental death and dismemberment (AD and D) normally comes as a part of the life insurance package.

Education

It is very rare in a small business, especially a new one, that you would pay for something like a college education. There does appear to be a move afoot for an employer to send people to specialized seminars.

Pensions

Here again, pensions are not often given in smaller businesses. If you are contemplating doing something, be sure to familiarize yourself with the current law regarding the Employee Retirement Income Security Act (ERISA), a series of far-reaching regulations that govern what you can and cannot do regarding pensions. If you do not provide pension coverage, be certain to suggest to your employees that they check with their bank or insurance agent regarding the establishment of an Individual Retirement Account (IRA) which will shelter a portion of their income from taxes if they qualify.

Miscellaneous Benefits

There are dozens of miscellaneous benefits that can be thought up—company picnics, Christmas presents, paid jury duty, employee discounts. These, like any other benefits, are left to your discretion.

Remember that benefits will cost you money.

When you hire someone for $10,000 a year, you will immediately incur about another 10 percent or $1,000 in required benefits, your share of the employee's social security, federal and state unemployment contributions, and workmen's compensation insurance. If you add paid holidays and vacation, five days' paid sick leave, hospitalization, and life insurance, that 10 percent quickly jumps to about 26 percent, the national average.

Be certain that your benefit program and personnel policies are in writing. This isn't a make work project. It is a form of self-protection for your first confrontation with the state labor board regarding some complaint lodged by a disgruntled ex-employee.

Unions

The last subject to be covered in Chapter 8 is *unions.* We are not talking about a business where the employees will be members of a local, such as an electrical contractor's. We mean the situation facing a business owner who has built a business up to a certain point and is now facing the possible unionization of employees.

One sure way to increase the probability of a union election among your employees is to treat them unfairly, both from a personal as well as from a financial standpoint.

If union people are about to descend upon you it may be happening because the union believes that your employees would be a welcome addition to their ranks, and, thus, to their bank account. Union certification is highly doubtful in this situation. Another reason may be that your employees have gone to the union for protection. Union certification in this situation is highly probable.

There's not much point in discussing the latter. If that's happening, you deserve a union. The first case is something else again. If you look out of your office window at quitting time and see some character passing out leaflets to your employees, resist the temptation to go outside and punch him out. Remember, not only has the union planned this entire move, but they've done it all before. You're a babe in the woods, so watch it! Do two things. First, get a copy or two of whatever is being handed out, and then run, do not walk, to a qualified labor attorney. He will tell you what you can and can't do or say. Don't pick fights with the union people or even make things difficult for them. You may be adversaries, but you don't have to be archenemies.

Follow your lawyer's advice. Collect all the union materials and handouts. Keep abreast of the union's activities through employee reports. Keep your mouth shut if you're unsure of something. After the election, you'll either get a union or you won't. If you don't, then you can forget it and go back to running your business.

If you get a union, you'll soon find out that you'll need some training in labor contract negotiation.

David L. Silk, writing in the January 15, 1979, issue of the *Wall Street Journal,* gives us seven basic rules of success if you want to help a union organize your small business:

Rule 1. Don't worry, you are not big enough to be organized.

Rule 2. Owners should not involve themselves with operational details.

Rule 3. Don't worry about communications; if the employee's message is important, you'll hear about it one way or the other.

Rule 4. When in doubt, call in outside experts. Don't try to solve the problem yourself.

Rule 5. Prepare yourself, and react to what the union *may do* instead of what it is *actually* doing.

Rule 6. Follow a prearranged course in your election strategy, and give little heed to what is actually going on at your plant.

Rule 7. Wait until you are into a union election campaign to try to establish management/owner credibility.

There is very little reason to expect a successful union organization attempt if you keep the Golden Rule in mind. By and large, people will not vote a union in as their collective bargaining agent if they feel that they are being treated fairly and are "involved" in the operation of the business. One rather large insurance company successfully fought off a union election on a single major point. The president's letter, written to each employee on the eve of the election (and manually signed by him, often with a brief personal message to each employee), emphasized the fact that, with the union firmly in place, employees would lose their right to talk directly with higher management. In other words, the open door would close forever.

In Conclusion

What many small-business owners and their large organization managerial counterparts fail to realize is that both the superior and the subordinate have somewhat equal goals in the work situation. They want the organization to succeed so that job continuity is possible. Your people will honestly work for the growth and profitability of your enterprise if you give them an even chance. Make them feel a part of what is going on, and they will react in kind. Treat them as human beings, and you and your business will receive most of the benefit.

There will be about 5 percent of the working population that you will never break through to. That seems to be a fact of life. But, if you maintain an attitude that just about everyone wants recognition and a sense of achievement, and if you operate in that fashion, you'll be surprised at how easy it is to have your venture succeed.

The whole idea is to operate on the basis of love and trust.

CHAPTER NINE

Administrative Matters

The first thing we do, let's kill all the lawyers.
Shakespeare (*King Henry VI*)

This chapter and the one following deal with a host of miscellaneous administrative matters that don't fall into specific functional areas such as finance or marketing. These subjects are just as important as those covered in previous chapters.

Administrative matters include the following:

Legal forms of a business
Record-keeping
Risk management
Taxes
Business law
Computers in small business

Legal Forms of a Business

There are a number of *legal forms of businesses* in the United States. The three most common were defined in Chapter 2, the *sole proprietorship,* the *partnership,* and the *corporation.* The form you select will depend a great deal upon your personal desires, the number of other people in the business with you (including your spouse), the type of operation you will be running, the upper limit on the size of the business, the state in which you operate, and the advice of your lawyer and your accountant.

Sole Proprietorship

If your name is Ephraim Henniker and you open Ephraim Henniker's General Store, that might be all you need to do in some states for instant business in the form of a *sole proprietorship.* Check with the secretary of state in your state about the regulations. Usually, if you operate under a name other than your own, you will have to register that name with the secretary. The proprietorship form of business, however, is the easiest to form and to disband. There is no one that you have to share profits with but, on the other hand, you will personally pay income tax on those profits, *not on what you take out as a salary.* The proprietorship ceases to exist as a business entity upon your death, and, since the law regards you and the business as one, you are personally liable for acts committed in the name of or under the general auspices of the business. If someone slips on your newly waxed floor and sues, you may have to reach into your own pocket if your liability insurance is insufficient to cover the judgment. Very few proprietorships reach any significant size. Here's another two-edged sword: you need not consult anyone else when making business decisions, but you don't have anyone else's help, either; most consultants are not only expensive, they are fleeting. Your ability to raise outside capital is restricted to some percentage (say, 70 percent) of your equity in the business and in other real estate. This form of operation is relatively free from paperwork and reports, although the government may end this advantage.

Partnership

The *partnership* form of business is more involved than the proprietorship, but it is still relatively easy to form. A partnership is really nothing more or less than two or more proprietors. In some states, it makes future financial sense for a husband and wife running their own business to form a partnership.

There are two types of partners, general and limited. All general partners participate in the operation of the business, and all are liable for obligations of the firm. Each one is responsible for the actions of the other partners. A limited (or silent) partner contributes capital only and does not enter into the day-to-day conduct of the partnership. Silent partners are limited by the amount of capital that they have supplied.

The partnership has the dual advantage of having more capital available as well as more expertise in operating the venture. Somewhat like the proprietorship, the partnership ceases to exist upon the withdrawal or death of one of the partners. The profits of the partnership are distributed among the partners for tax purposes on a predetermined basis.

Most partners execute a partnership agreement which may, among other things, spell out the following:

The names and addresses of the partners and the partnership.
The nature of business to be conducted.
The duration of the partnership.
The amounts of capital supplied by each partner, their "draws," and their percentage profit distribution.
The duties of the partners and their respective roles, especially if one of the members is to be the managing partner.
The procedure for a partner to withdraw or a new one to be added.
The way the business will be dissolved, including who gets what if a partner dies or is in any other way incapable of functioning as originally intended. This may include buy-out insurance, and will be covered in a later section in this chapter.

A sample partnership agreement is included in Appendix H.

Most partnerships contain the names of the founding general partners

(Begge, Burrow, and Steele) and most are involved in professional services such as engineering, law, accounting, or consulting; but this is changing due to the popularity of professional corporations (PC's).

Corporation

The *corporation* traces its roots back to an ancient English king who decided to give various lords a way to keep themselves personally removed from the actual dealings of business. Thus British corporations still use the designation *Ltd.* for "limited" (limited liability). In France, the terminology is *S.A.,* or the "anonymous society." In the eyes of the law, the corporation is a legal entity or, in effect, a person. It can enter into contracts, it can break the law, it can be sued. Unlike the proprietorship and the partnership, the corporation has a perpetual life.

The two major advantages to the corporate form of existence are (1) the limited personal liability of stockholders and managers, and (2) the flexibility allowed in raising capital. When Chevrolet built the Corvair that collapsed in a slight breeze across its beam, or when Ford released the four-wheel potential crematorium known as the Pinto accused of causing deaths or permanent maiming, no executive was fined or jailed. In a small business, this limited liability might not hold true, but there is some protection nonetheless.

To raise capital, corporations may sell stock. This dilutes ownership but brings in revenue that does not have to be repaid. Corporations can also issue bonds and other debentures, and the interest is tax-deductible.

Before we discuss the problems of a corporation, we should reiterate the points about taxes brought up in Chapter 7 on finance. In a proprietorship or a partnership, the *accounting* profit is taxed by the IRS. If you are the president of your one-person corporation, you will be taxed on your salary, and the corporation on its accounting profit. If you pay yourself dividends, amounts paid out of profits after tax, those amounts are taxable to you and to the corporation. This is the so-called double taxation of the corporation. Also, don't think that you can pay yourself a small salary and then plow all the profit back without paying dividends to yourself in order to create some giant slush fund somewhere, like Scrooge McDuck's three cubic acres of money. Even though the Beagle Boys never seem to get to Scrooge, the IRS will get to you for improperly retained earnings, which we mentioned earlier.

The major problem with the corporate form of business operation is paperwork, and it starts with the formation of the corporation. You must incorporate within a state, and, in some states, this is a major undertaking. It requires time, money, lawyers, petty officials, a trainload of documents, justifications, hearings, and frustration. Some states require that a corporation have a certain minimum number of individuals, each with a certain title; others require that a minimum amount of money be deposited in a bank (called *paid-in capital*) before an application can be considered. All require some kind of written certificate of incorporation (some even require a statement of an intent to incorporate) and a set of bylaws.

To make it simple on yourself, incorporate in Delaware. There is an inexpensive book that will get you through the process with a minimum of fuss, money, and time. Write to Enterprise Publishing Co., 6 Commercial Street, Hicksville, N.Y. 11802, and order Ted Nicholas' book *How to Form Your Own Corporation Without a Lawyer for Under $50.* (Get the paperback version, it's cheaper.) Then do everything you're told to the letter. This is a debatable issue among small-business advisors, whether to use the "quickie-cheapie" approach. The alternatives are filing the forms with the state of incorporation yourself, or using an attorney to do it. There are pros and cons to all methods.

One example (one of the many) of using this method emphasizes why we suggest using Delaware. In most states, when you submit your charter, you must state the nature of the business—retail hardware, restaurant, or electronics manufacturing. In Delaware, the following phrase, inserted under the *nature of the business* section of the charter, is acceptable:

> The purpose of the corporation is to engage in any lawful act or activity for which corporations may be organized under the general Corporation Law of Delaware.

Once you are incorporated in Delaware, you are known as a domestic corporation in Delaware. You will need an agent in Wilmington, but another of Nicholas' companies, the Company Corporation, takes care of that for a nominal annual fee.

The state in which you are operating now regards you as a foreign corporation. (Don't get alarmed. A company from outside the U.S. is known as an "alien" corporation. If we ever have commercially oriented visitors from outer space who set up businesses on earth, their ventures will have to be called "extra-terrestrial corporations.") If you want to do business in your home state, you must register and pay a fee, as you must in any state in which you want to operate.

There may be some actual benefits for you to incorporate in your home state, but don't let your lawyer talk you into it just so he can collect an $800–$1200 fee for having his secretary mail documents to the state capital. Ask for the reasons why you should use your home state.

There are two kinds of corporations which are not standard corporations; they include a little bit of the partnership in them.

The first of these hybrids is known as a *Subchapter S corporation.* This type of organization comes under the rules of the IRS, and the stockholders (less than 15 and all real people) are allowed to take the profits or losses of the corporation on their personal returns. The usual reason for this is to minimize tax consequences. For instance, if the business expects to lose money for the first two years, it would make sense to allow the stockholders to use that loss on their own returns. (Note: This will not allow the corporation to use a tax-loss carry forward.) Then, when the corporation becomes profitable, the stockholders de-elect the Sub S option and let the corporation pay taxes on the (usually) lower corporate tax rate. The board of directors will have to execute IRS Form 2553 to use this option. Be sure to look at prevailing tax rates and present laws before electing or de-electing the Sub S treatment.

The second type, which we mentioned earlier, is the professional corporation (PC). Past law prohibited professional partnerships from forming as corporations except under very special conditions. Today, most states (but not all) permit doctors, lawyers, accountants, and other similar professionals to form a professional corporation. There are some prerequisites which must be met, the most significant one being that all the principals of the firm must be "practitioners in the art" of the firm.

Here is one last note about corporations. There is a tax benefit known as a Section 1244 corporation. As for Sub S, certain conditions must be met, but, basically, the investors in a Section 1244 corporation could take any loss on their equity investment as an ordinary loss instead of a capital loss. This has the effect of doubling the tax write-off since capital losses are computed at a lesser rate than an ordinary loss. Again, check the applicable tax law at time of formation, since this election by the board has to be done early to be allowable, and it has to be in writing.

Record-Keeping

Record-keeping has one basic rule: Keep everything, and keep it forever. Even if you have to rent grandma's barn for storage, it won't cost you much to save every pay stub, invoice, business plan, receipt, tax bill, license fee, letter from your lawyer, cash register tape, cancelled check, accounting statement, architect's rendering, ledger, Visa charge slip, property assessment notice, newspaper article, bank statement, lease agreement, lunch tab, computer printout, and letter of complaint.

This discipline of being a business pack rat starts with the very first day you make the slightest move in the entrepreneurial direction. If on Tuesday, June 27, you decide that working for that person you've been calling boss for the last seven years is really not where it's at and you have to be in your own business, record your thoughts and aspirations. Do your personal balance sheet. Keep the information, even if it's in a folder entitled Thoughts of Me. As you move toward your goal, you still keep everything. You'd better be organized. As everything gets more complex, you will feel as if you're in debt to the local stationery store, but your record-keeping will pay off eventually.

When you start or buy your business, be especially careful about those records. They will become vital when you sell or bequeath the business some day. If the business is a corporation, be sure to put the certificate of incorporation, charter, bylaws, and minutes together in one place.

As your business operates over a period of time, two types of records will be generated, financial and nonfinancial.

Anything to do with the flow of funds in your business should create a financial record of some sort. Actually, several records may be created:

> The bread man delivers a dozen loaves of rye (at $.80 each) for which you sign a receipt acknowledging delivery, and you get a copy.
> An entry is made in accounts payable and in inventory on hand for $9.60.
> You receive an invoice for $9.60.
> You pay the invoice with a check, thus reducing accounts payable and cash.
> In several weeks, you receive the cancelled check.
> The bread company sends you a statement of account acknowledging receipt of the $9.60.

Most of the financial data will be contained in accounting journals (cash receipts, cash disbursements) and ledgers (payroll, accounts receivable), but there should be backup data such as outside statements and cancelled checks.

Nonfinancial records would consist primarily of correspondence (in and out) and articles from books and magazines that you have saved. It's a wise idea to catalog these records by subject headings that make sense to you—legal matters, customer complaints, data on competition. If you write letters to people, keep a copy for yourself.

When your business year is over, bundle up all the appropriate records and buy yourself one of those inexpensive cardboard file drawers. Label the drawer with the year and the contents and stick it in the cellar. Forget about retention guidelines. Just keep it, it can't take up that much room. Then, ten years later, you can spend an amusing evening or two going back and seeing how dumb (or smart) you used to be.

Risk Management

The risks in small business are manifold indeed. Since we know that entrepreneurs will accept a moderate degree of risk without coming apart at the seams, the situation becomes one of managing those risks and/or planning for contingencies through insurance of one kind or another.

Listed below, in no particular order, are some 20 common risks in business and some hints on managing those risks.

1. Lack of sufficient cash.

1. Prepare budgets, use them, prepare variance reports, and attempt to foresee shortages that might occur. Keep an open line of credit for emergencies.

2. Your business burns to the cellar hole.

2. Carry fire and business continuation insurance.

3. The title to the business is faulty.

3. Get title insurance.

4. Your key supplier fails.

4. Use multiple sources of supply.

5. Employees rob you blind.

5. Have employees bonded.

6. A competitor makes some strategic move that can threaten your existence.

6. Keep competitive information files to help you anticipate possible competitive moves.

7. Someone sues you.

7. Get a lawyer whom you can call at home.

8. Your partner dies.

8. Carry two types of insurance, (1) life insurance on your partner with the business as the beneficiary, and (2) buy-sell insurance so that the claims of your partner's estate can be satisfied.

9. The village morons throw a brick through your window.

9. Carry vandalism insurance.

10. Some government agency investigates your business.

10. Keep up on all the governmental regulations that might affect you significantly.

11. Someone slips on your steps and breaks his leg.

11. Carry liability insurance.

12. Your boiler blows up.

12. Carry boiler insurance.

13. The main item you've been selling falls out of favor.

13. Be extremely careful about fad items or services.

14. Someone eats your crabmeat quiche and winds up in the hospital with food poisoning.

14. Carry product liability insurance.

15. Recessions reduce your income.

15. Try to build the business so that it is recession-proof in nature. Building in quality is a good way.

16. Community pressure is brought to bear on you.

16. Stay away from any questionable practices.

17. You receive bad checks.

17. Institute a firm policy on customer checks, and carry fraud insurance.

18. Second-story Sam breaks in and steals.

18. Carry burglary insurance.

19. You are the victim of shoplifting.

19. Any good retailing text can give you a number of hints to reduce this.

20. Your bank calls its note.

20. Work very closely with your banker, and keep him apprised of any forthcoming financial binds.

Hundreds of other things could happen to you, from the local Hell's Angels hanging around to a slaughterhouse constructed next to your vegetarian restaurant. Anticipation of the problem and planning for it in advance will go a long way toward preventing permanent, irreparable damage to your business.

One important step is to get an honest insurance agent (sometimes very hard to find) who can analyze your needs in relation to the size and type of your business. If you're not careful, you can wind up having to write a healthy premium check.

Taxes

We are not concerned in this section with either corporate or personal income taxes, but with other taxes imposed by the federal government, state government, county or town.

The first broad category is *taxes created by employment,* even your own. The two that will affect nearly every wage-earner in the United States are the federal withholding tax and social security, or FICA, tax. With the federal tax, your employee will, in effect, specify how much you, the employer, will deduct from his gross pay by designating the number of dependents he is claiming. The more dependents claimed, the smaller the deduction. It is not your job to worry whether the employee will have too much or too little taken out of his pay to meet his tax obligation for the year; you are simply an unpaid, involuntary, collection agency for the government. Social security deductions are a fixed percentage that both you and the employee must pay up to a maximum level. Unfortunately, either the tax rate or the base amount or both increase each year. Table 9.1 shows a few future periods.

TABLE 9.1

Future Tax Increases

Year	Base	Employee and Employer's Contribution	Self-Employment Rate
1980	$25,900	6.13%	8.10%
1983	33,900	6.70	9.35
1985	38,100	7.05	9.90
1987	42,600	7.15	10.00

A large percentage of states have an income tax as well, and this is withheld from the employee as is the federal tax.

All states are encouraged to have an unemployment contribution system into which employers feed capital based upon a percentage of an employee's wage up to a maximum amount. The percentage rate can be lessened by keeping layoffs and firings low. In addition to the various state taxes, there is a federal unemployment tax. Some credit is allowed for the state tax paid.

The second broad category concerns *taxes that are brought about by the operation and existence of the business.* If the business is being conducted on premises owned by the entrepreneur, the largest of these business taxes will be the property tax. This is paid annually to the city or town.

A great number of states have sales taxes, and, here again, an entrepreneur is turned into a tax collector. Most business owners simply add the appropriate tax to the price. Thus, if an item is selling for $1.00, and the sales tax is 5 percent, the customer pays $1.05 and the $.05 is rung up on the cash register as tax. This makes the accounting and collection fairly simple.

There are as many other kinds of taxes as the mind of bureaucratic man can invent. Some states tax assets used in the business. One state put a tax on year-end inventory until it discovered everyone was having year-end clearance sales to bring the inventory as close to zero as possible by December 31. You might have to pay a business profits tax. If you are a corporation, there will be a stock tax. There are taxes on liquor, vending and pin ball machines, cigarettes, and gasoline.

In addition, you may have to obtain licenses, which are not taxes but might as well be. Licenses are usually renewed annually and may be required to practice medicine, cut hair, or have an elevator.

Business Law

No entrepreneur should try to become his own lawyer, but some knowledge of the basics of *business law* is important if for nothing else than keeping out of harm's way. If you're contemplating some move and are unsure of its legality, check with your attorney.

We trace our legal roots back to the English system of common law, which evolved because enacted or statutory law did not cover all situations, especially those connected with a wrong committed by one individual upon another. In this connection, there are *crimes* (wrongs committed against society) and *torts* (wrongs committed against people). It is possible to commit both a crime and a tort at the same time. If I see you on a street and decide that today is your day for a knuckle sandwich, I have committed a tort (assault and battery) and a crime (public brawling). You will probably never be hauled into court on criminal charges, but, if you're operating a business, chances are nearly 100 percent that you will see the inside of a court room in some equity suit, either as the plaintiff or the defendant.

Contracts

A *contract* is an agreement between two entities (people, businesses) in which each entity gives up a legal right. If you come to work for me, I have given up the temporary right to employ someone else and you will not work for another employer during the same hours you are working for me.

Although experts vary a bit on this, there seem to be five essentials to a valid contract.

Offer
Acceptance
Consideration
Competency
Legality

Notice that there is nothing in the list requiring a written instrument. Except for a few exceptions that come under the so-called statute of fraud (like the sale of real estate), an oral contract is as binding as a written one. Naturally, if you and I are alone when we make an oral contract and later one party reneges, it's difficult to prove the original intent.

Offer. The offer must clearly be an offer that is valid and realizable. If you buy a new sports car and, upon seeing it, I say "Boy, I'd give my left arm for one of those babies!" you can't head for the barn to get the chain saw. Offers made in obvious jest are not enforceable.

Acceptance. Acceptance, too, must be clearly demonstrated. Certainly, the words "I accept" are clear enough, but what about an affirmative nod? It has been held by one court that a nod is indeed an acceptance. A counter-offer is not acceptance. It temporarily reverses the roles of the offeror and offeree. In a dickering situation, this may change back and forth several times:

"My asking price is $2,500." (Offer)
"I'll give you $2,000." (Counter-offer)
"Make it $2,400." (Counter-counter-offer)
"I'll go $2,150." (c.c.c. offer)
"$2,300." (c.c.c.c. offer)
"$2,225." (c.c.c.c.c. offer)
"Done." (Acceptance)

An acceptance can be deemed to have occurred and the contract made valid by performance. If you have a heating and air-conditioning business and I say to you, "I will pay the $2000 for a Fedder's air-conditioning system," and the next day you begin the work, the contract is established.

Consideration. The element of consideration usually means money or tangible goods (called valuable consideration), but it can include something like love and affection (good consideration). Many large corporations require the execution of an invention rights contract, especially by technical personnel, saying that any product or service developed on company time and premises becomes the sole property of the company. Usually, a brand-new dollar bill is given to the employee to seal the contract. The dollar is the consideration.

Competency. There must be competency on the part of the two parties. Insane persons and minors (except in cases of the signing of leases and a few other things) cannot be held to the terms of the contract. Being drunk or stoned usually means an incompetent party, but this can be tricky. If, during an all-night drinking session, you agree to sell me your house, and, the next morning (with a fairly clear, although painful, head), call me to say you didn't mean it, the contract is invalid. If you wait three years, the contract might be enforceable.

Legality. Legality means that the contract must be for a legal purpose. You ask me to rub out Big Tuna (offer) for $5000 now and $5000 upon the untimely demise of said Big Tuna (consideration). I say okay (acceptance). We are of sound mind, over the legal age, and sober (competency). However, nearly every civilized culture makes it a crime to murder anyone, even though Big Tuna might have massacred children. The contract is invalid due to illegality.

Competition and Pricing

The catch phrase in laws on *competition and pricing* here is "in restraint of trade." Basically, you can't get together with your competition to fix prices, nor can you manipulate prices unfairly to threaten competition. The chances that, as a small business, you will ever violate the many federal and state regulations governing trade practices is extremely slim, but you might be on the receiving end from large companies. They can't lower their price to force you to lose money.

You can't discriminate in your pricing by offering different prices to two like customers. There's nothing wrong with quantity discounts, however.

Resale price maintenance or fair trading laws are generally dead. A manufacturer's suggested retail price is fine, but you don't have to stick with it.

Product or Service

When offering a product or service, say what you mean and mean what you say. Years ago, you could get by with all kinds of chicanery in representing your product or service, but now the law has teeth, and you can be severely bitten for failure to follow its spirit and intent. (In fact, it has been said that the consumer protection laws have become so abusive to business that safety pin manufacturers will soon have to affix a label to each pin that says *Close before swallowing.*)

Don't offer anything to the public that is openly dangerous. There may be hazards associated with what you have for sale over which you have no control. The Great Cranberry Scare of the sixties, and rumors that cat food may pass for tuna fish from some canners, are cases in point. There is little you can do to protect yourself from loss of business when a product you sell gets a bad name. Still, though, you can select your product lines with an intelligent concern for user safety. The nice little pistol that fires potato chunks and can put out a child's eye should be banned from your shelves.

You must back up your advertising. If you advertise a going-out-of-business sale, then you had better go out of business. Advertising sales can cause problems if you're not careful. Your ad agency should be able to help you here. If you just got twenty cases of coffee and want to run a loss-leader sale at one dollar per pound just to get people in the store, then adding phrases like "One to a customer, while the supply lasts" will keep you from having to issue a whole slew of rain checks. Don't *ever* advertise something you don't have. The old bait-and-switch routine is now illegal, and there are lots of consumer groups waiting out in the bushes to get you. Besides being illegal, it's just plain wrong.

If you make statements about your products or services like

"Money back if not completely satisfied,"
"Product warrantied for ninety days,"
"Appliance will work on 110 or 220 volts,"
"This device is totally manufactured in the United States," or
"100% wool,"

be certain what you're saying is true. Somewhere there's a little old lady in tennis shoes who will delight in proving you wrong. Don't make false claims. Don't even stretch a point.

If you use contracts or any other legal document in your business, or if you expect to make public statements that *might* be challenged, be certain that your lawyer has looked the documents over carefully, and that you can live up to all terms, written and implied, in your statements.

Patents

Patents may be involved in your business. Unless you've stumbled upon the absolutely foolproof way to change lead into gold, generally forget about patenting what you have. It'll only put money in the pocket of the patent attorney and make you waste a lot of time. Then if your invention is as good as you think it is some big company will spend millions to get around the patent, and they'll probably succeed.

You, as an entrepreneur, however, cannot ignore *others'* patents. If you have something that you regard as unique, you should have a Washington patent-search firm check the files to be sure you are not violating an existing patent. If you are, you might have to consider a royalty agreement with the patent holder or an outright purchase of the patent rights themselves.

Trademarks

Trademarks have no real value in small business, but, if you want one, they're easy to get. A pamphlet available from the federal government for less than a dollar will give you the basics. To qualify, your goods must have been sold in interstate commerce. Copyrights fall into somewhat the same category. Information on copyrights can be had by writing to the Library of Congress. Since most businesses have an office copier or access to one, Congress has even considered doing away with copyrights entirely.

Labor Law

In the previous chapter we touched upon unions and collective bargaining, and their potential impact on a small business. Here, we will briefly talk about *labor law* as it governs any employees.

The federal government can only make regulations that affect firms engaged in interstate (not intrastate) commerce, but most states follow these regulations very closely. The most typical is the federal minimum hourly wage. If you engage in interstate commerce or if your state conforms to the federal level, you will have to pay your employees this minimum rate. A common example of a business that does not conform is a restaurant, where waiters and waitresses receive a somewhat lower minimum wage since the remainder of the remuneration is made up in tips. In 1972, the maitre d'hotel of a major hotel in New York City reported tip income of $125,000. Not everyone reaches that lofty pinnacle, however.

You must pay attention to overtime. In most states, any time worked after eight hours per day or forty hours per week requires extra hourly compensation, usually one and one-half times the base rate. Some states demand that double-time be paid for work on Sundays and holidays.

Employing children (especially under fourteen years of age) is forbidden in all states. With the women's liberation movement, some of the state's regulations regarding the hours and working conditions of women are less restrictive (number of consecutive hours worked, working while close to pregnancy), but you should check your laws nonetheless.

Agency

The law of *agency* defines the relationship between one party, called an *agent*, who may act for another party, called a *principal*. This relationship is contractual in nature. Any person competent to execute a contract may be a principal, but this is not necessarily true in the case of an agent. Minors can be agents, for example. The written document that creates the agency is known as a *power of attorney*.

This subject belongs in a book on small business because it concerns the delineation between employees, agents, and independent contractors. Employees are under the direct supervision and control of their employer. They are hired at a given rate of pay (per hour, per year, per piece) to perform specific duties. They usually cannot legally bind the employer to a third party. An employer has the duty to withhold appropriate taxes from the employee and to pay the employer's portion of taxes. An agent "stands in the place of" [1] the principal and can be directed by the principal to do or not to do certain things within the contractual limits. The agent-principal relationship can be severed as previously agreed upon.

Agents are generally used by small business in the sales area. A manufacturer's representative most often acts as an agent in taking orders that the manufacturer (his or her principal) is obligated to satisfy. An independent contractor is just what the name implies; the principal has little or no control over his performance. If you "hire" someone to paint your building, you can select the paint, and that's about it.

Some business owners choose to hire people not as employees but as consultants in order to avoid the headaches involved with taxes. This can work in operations such as a real estate firm, but it is the exception rather than the rule.

[1] Ronald A. Anderson and Walter A. Kumpf, *Business Law,* 10th ed. (Cincinnati: South-Western, 1976), p. 539.

The Uniform Commercial Code (UCC)

The *Uniform Commercial Code* (UCC) is a set of laws adopted now by all states. It covers nearly every conceivable business situation. The following is a copy of the preamble to the code:

> To be known as the Uniform Commercial Code, Relating to Certain Commercial Transactions in or regarding Personal Property and Contracts and other Documents concerning them, including Sales, Commercial Paper, Bank Deposits and Collections, Letters of Credit, Bulk Transfers, Warehouse Receipts, Bills of Lading, other Documents of Title, Investment Securities, and Secured Transactions, including certain Sales of Accounts, Chattel Paper, and Contract Rights; Providing for Public Notice to Third Parties in Certain Circumstances; Regulating Procedure, Evidence and Damages in Certain Court Actions Involving such Transactions, Contracts or Documents; to Make Uniform the Law with Respect Thereto; and Repealing Inconsistent Legislation.

It is a lengthy document, running well over 100 typewritten pages. We recommend that entrepreneurs obtain a copy of it (with an index) for reference purposes.

Computers in Small Business

A *small computer,* basically defined, is a computer whose central processing unit (CPU) is contained within one integrated circuit.[2] (See Figure 9.1.) These integrated circuits are usually forty pin devices which contain circuitry that, not too many years ago, when the first computer was invented, would have taken up a whole room. The Univac, produced by Remington Rand, invented by J. Presper EcKert and Robert Mauchly, was the first commercial computer and it was not available until 1953.[3] The computer-on-a-chip, as the first microcomputer was called, was the MCS-4 of Intel Corporation in 1971. In less than twenty years, the computer had gone from an enormous mass of cabinets full of equipment to a single chip. The single chip is not the whole computer, however. It is the heart of the computer. Memory and input/output devices are also required. The reasons that the small computer has and will have such an impact on small businesses are its cost and capability. Most small businesses up until now could not afford the expense of owning a computer of their own, leasing one, or paying for a computer service. The cost was just too high. Costs for renting a computer run upwards from $300 per month, while cost of computer

[2] For the complete story, see Brian R. Smith, *The Small Computer in Small Business* (Brattleboro, VT: Stephen Greene Press, 1980).
[3] Theodore H. Nelson, *Computer Lib* (South Bend: The Distributors, 1974), p. 54.

Figure 9.1 *The Data General CS/60 Business Computer System, Designed to Perform a Variety of Commercially-Oriented Applications*

services can range from $200 to $5000 per month. The small computer is also becoming one of the fastest-growing hobbies in America. These small computers can be purchased from many companies and hobby stores in kit form and assembled at home. The home is another place where the computer is becoming popular. Computer stores and electronics retail establishments are the main suppliers of these computers. Computer store sales are projected to grow at a rate of greater than 40 percent per year between now and the next few years.[4]

Home computers was a small business which has now become a large, rapidly growing business. Most of the computers sold presently to homes (70 percent) are used for games, but this will not always be the case as consumers find more and more uses for them. Small businesses are finding new uses, too. Many sales that are made today are made to entrepreneurs who not only want a device to help in their day-to-day operations but also want to experiment and see what they can do with the machine. They purchase the computer with usually an entry device such as a cathode ray tube (CRT) and a printer as well as some software (programs). The programs are usually high level language assemblers which allow a program to be written in so-called macro-languages which closely resemble English. Many of the areas that micros are used in are immediately visible, such as inventory control, accounts receivable, accounts payable, and customer records. As the entrepreneur becomes familiar with computers and their usages, more business benefits are derived from them. The one thing that most small businessmen and companies bring up when talking about computers is, "What about software (the programs) to do all of these things? I would have to hire a full-time programmer, and only he would know what he did. If he quit, where would that leave me?" Today, that is not the case. Many computers are available with pre-written programs to do specific tasks in specific industries. These programs can be purchased with the computer, thereby eliminating the need for a programmer, at least until the business can or should hire one. Many companies never do; they continue to purchase programs as they become available or construct routines themselves, thus eliminating the need for a programmer.

A *canned program* is one which is written to handle a specific task such as payroll. The program is fully written and operational when the business purchases it. The business enters only its own data tables; employee names, pay rate per hour, hours worked, and overtime. The computer will then compute all the payroll requirements and store appropriate withholding information. Other examples of canned programs include those written for inventory control, accounts receivable, accounts payable, receiving, production scheduling, and inventory control. Many others are now available from computer manufacturers and program service companies for a reasonable price.

[4] *EDN Magazine,* May 20, 1977.

Computers have a wide range of applications. They can be used in inventory control to help maintain a stable level of both raw materials and finished goods. This application is one in which most companies see immediate cost savings to the operation, no matter how large or small. The computer is fed the inventory levels of all material and then, as the material is moved from raw material to work-in-process to finished goods, management is immediately able to adjust any area of raw material or finished goods that is too high or too low. This allows for the removal of expensive raw materials that are not used or that are used at a slower-than-anticipated level from inventory, thus freeing up capital. This gives an accurate tracking record of the movement of materials through the factory or retail establishment, and also shows where the most time is consumed—either in waiting or in actual labor. It shows where bottlenecks might be.

Computers also do something which most companies fail to really take into account; it eliminates the need to make fast, expensive purchases to replenish depleted stock in order to meet the material needs. These purchases are often made short-term and in small quantities, both of which make the price more expensive than normal. Finished-goods inventory is the most expensive. Many times, when goods are built or stocked in excess, they become obsolete before they can be sold, thus causing many dollars to be literally thrown away. Finished goods and raw materials also require storage space, and space is expensive. One other major expense of maintaining high levels of inventory is the equipment used to store this inventory and the vehicles to move it.

Most companies are now beginning to realize just how valuable proper utilization of space is. Many businesses are doing away with warehouses because of their expense. Heating costs are soaring at unbelievable rates, and so are electric bills. Taxes are a major item of expense as well. A small company in the Midwest, manufacturing molded plastic parts, was maintaining over $100,000 in raw materials and finished-goods inventory. This company, whose sales were $250,000 for 1975, had a loss of $55,000 for that year. At the end of 1975, this company installed a small computer system to control its inventory, accounts receivable, and accounts payable. The investment for the computer system was $7000 in 1976, a one-time investment. In 1976, the company's sales were $275,000, but, instead of a loss, the company showed a profit of $22,500, a difference of $77,500 on a $25,000 increase in sales.[5] This story and many others like it are being told by smaller companies whose annual sales are in the $200,000 to $2,000,000 range. These small businesses, up until the microcomputer was introduced, could not afford to purchase or rent a computer.

What other uses can a small computer serve? One recent example is that a computer is becoming the friend of a very different business—taxi companies. One of the biggest problems for taxi companies, whether individually owned

[5] "The Coming Boom in Home Computers," *Business Week* (May 16, 1977), p. 24.

units or large city units, is the paperwork required for each trip. This paperwork consumes time which can be better spent carrying paying fares. Now there is a computerized taximeter. Costing less than $1000, this unit is capable of registering as many as six fares simultaneously. It can keep track of the following information: total fares, waiting time, number of trips, total miles, and total paid miles. This unit completely eliminates the need for the costly forms and paperwork for even the smallest of cab companies.[6]

The list of uses for small computers is endless. One example uses computers as industrial controllers replacing the more expensive, larger computers. These controllers can be used for controlling conveyor belt systems, drying ovens, or machine tools. They can be purchased for less than $1000 compared to the $10,000-plus cost of the minicomputer based controllers.[7]

The uses that have been found for the computer since its introduction run from hens to H-Bombs. A farmer who supplies chickens to a fast-food chain found he could save $200 a day by using a computer rather than an electromechanical device to control the assembly line. The computer's capability, both in weighing each chicken and in selecting the proper combination of birds to pack in each box, proved to be much more accurate.[8] A small computer was placed in a canister and buried next to a hydrogen bomb in a western United States desert testing-site. When the bomb went off, the micro proved to be both fast enough to record all the necessary data and rugged enough to survive the blast.[9]

The small computer can be purchased in many forms, and, depending on the application for which it is intended, its purchase price is as varied as its usages.

A small, single-board unit which could be used in varied control operations can be purchased for less than $100. A fully operational development system with terminal and keyboard entry costs less than $1000 compared to larger systems, containing floppy disc and printers, for just over $10,000.

Even the $10,000 cost compared to that of other computers is small by any standard. Some small computers with development capabilities cost in excess of $30,000, but these costs, too, are being cut severely every year. Most manufacturers are cutting prices from 10 percent to 30 percent per year. Hewlett-Packard, according to Robert L. Puette, marketing manager, is cutting its minicomputer prices 25 percent to 30 percent annually and will continue that trend.[10]

Any small business owner who has looked at the small-computer market is probably confused by the number of systems available and the varying costs of

[6] "Taximeter Collects Managerial Data at Touch of a Button," EDN Magazine (March 20, 1977), p. 73.

[7] EDN Magazine (May 20, 1977), p. 84.

[8] "Micro Computers Today," EDN Magazine (Nov. 20, 1975), p. 82.

[9] Ibid.

[10] "The Price Busting Race for Market Share," Business Week (June 6, 1977), p. 360.

such systems. Many new businesses have been formed to help others to determine which computer best fits their needs and applications, both now and for the future. Many articles have been written in business magazines on the subject of selecting the proper computer to fit not only present requirements but future requirements as well.

A toy-manufacturing firm of less than fifty people has purchased a small computer for inventory control, accounts receivable, and accounts payable. This particular firm purchased its machine after one year of investigating its needs and requirements. This system cost approximately $11,000. The company has had the computer less than six months, and it has produced the following results:

Raw materials inventory reduced by more than $5000.
Finished-goods inventory reduced by more than $3000.
Accounts receivable reduced from an average collection period of thirty-six days to thirty-two days.
Accounts payable savings of over $700 because the firm was able to take advantage of discounts.

This firm's management feels that the system paid for itself in six months.

A hardware store installed a computer system solely for the purpose of inventory control. This system is used to help reduce the inventory of slow moving articles and make sure that those items that move the fastest are well-stocked so that the store does not lose sales because it ran out of inventory. The management feels that the computer had a lot to do with not only the increase in profits but also the increases in sales by helping to keep the right inventory on hand. Sales increased by greater than 25 percent, while other stores in the area showed average increased sales of less than 17 percent. The store's profits increased by more than 35 percent.

Computers can relieve the small-business owner of much of the drudgery, cost, and mistakes in accounting and financial reporting. When a transaction occurs, that particular piece of information funnels through the accounting system until it's effect shows up on the income statement or the balance sheet or both.

Suppose that, on January 1, you buy a pickup truck for $9000 cash. The IRS says that the depreciable life is five years or sixty months. You could feed this information to a computer by identifying the various accounts being affected. You would key in the account number for cash, record whether this will be an increase (+) or decrease (−), and the amount. The computer could possibly be programmed to ask you appropriate questions to complete the entry. The entire transaction between you and your computer might go as follows:

Computer is turned on
Computer (C): Program Name? (*Computer asks for program.*)

You (Y): Accounting (*You respond.*)
C: Account to be adjusted?
Y: 1000 (*Cash*)
C: Increased or decreased? I or D?
Y: D.
C: Amount?
Y: $9000.00.
C: What is the offsetting account?
Y: 2020. (*Fixed Assets*)
C: What is depreciable life in years?
Y: Five.
C: Any other entries? Y or N?
Y: N.
C: Program Name?
Y: Bye. (*You sign off.*)

Since you have identified the accounts by numerical code, the computer can make the proper journal entries. If properly programmed, the computer can make the necessary calculations and compute effects upon the financial statements. For the January statements, cash would be reduced $9000, fixed assets increased $9000, and depreciation of $150 ($9000 divided by 60) recorded.

The uses are endless.

If you are contemplating buying a computer, a visit to a retail computer outlet (such as the Computer Store) or a dealer in small systems is in order. Talk with knowledgeable people about the applications that you have in mind and about your budget. They should be able to tailor a system to fit your needs.

Keep one important fact in mind. Computers cannot think.[11] They cannot make business decisions for you, but they can aid in providing data for the decision-making process. Further, if your entry data is incorrect, the results will be also. As the computer freaks are wont to say, "Garbage in, garbage out," or "GIGO."

When you look for a computer and try to assess the qualities of the many that are on the market today, there are a few things to keep in mind. You may not be signing the lease on a multimillion dollar IBM System 370, but you should consider the very same factors that an EDP manager for a large concern does. Here are some items for a computer shopping list when you start looking:

Cost/Performance

Notice that cost and performance are the criteria; we did not specify cost alone. There are inexpensive machines that are truly marvelous considering their size, and there are big, expensive devices that are junk and that, like a ten-year-old used car, spend more time being repaired than they do running.

---

[11] Some computer wags add the word *yet* to that sentence.

For a small business, you will probably be looking at machines that cost from $2000 to $20,000. Get all the manufacturer's specifications, and compare the devices just as you would any other asset. Talk to other business owners that have used the same machine, and get their comments. The ultimate test comes, not from the price tag, but from what the machine can do in relation to what it costs to own and operate. Stay away from bargains and fire sales. Look into a leasing program with an eventual option to purchase. If the manufacturer or the distributor does not want to bother with leasing, find a third party, such as a major bank. Carefully scrutinize the various terms involved.

Machine Supplier

As everyone knows, there is one major supplier of computers in the world—IBM. The initials seem to stand for various things depending on whom you talk with. An employee of the company might say "I've Been Moved," whereas a disgruntled user may quip, "It's Better Manually." Like it or not, IBM has from 60–70 percent of the world market. The company has finally realized that small business is here to stay and has devices designed especially for the entrepreneur. But don't go running to IBM and foreksake all others. Many highly respected computer experts claim that IBM's hardware and software are not the best that can be had for the money. Almost all of IBM's major competitors (Honeywell, NCR, Univac, Digital Equipment Corporation, Data General) have smaller devices. Then there are a host of other good firms, such as Wang Laboratories, that are not as well known in the popular press but that should also be investigated. New firms spring up everyday, and some die by the wayside. Be careful of the new boy on the block without a track record, and be equally leery of toys. The Radio Shack TRS-80, which can be bought for substantially less than $1000 has gotten lots of attention, but it is extremely limited for business applications. The internal memory is small, and it is slow, but it is a fantastic learning tool for the price. It's younger, larger cousin, the TRS-80 II is better.

Software

Software refers to the broad field of programming and the instructions given to a machine to enable it to do its job. Most manufacturers will sell you the machine for a stated price, and that may be all you will get from them. If you want a general ledger program or a routine to do your payroll, that costs extra. Be sure that all this is understood well in advance. Find out how much these packages cost and what they will do for you. Ask how easy it is to have the basic programs changed and how much it will cost. We all know that the tax rates change every year.

Some machines cannot be programmed with ease. A particular program is loaded into the machine never to be changed. This fact is handy for a run but can be a nuisance if revisions have to be made.

Since computers were first developed, there have been thousands of attempts to design languages that can be understood by humans and read by the machines. Since computers operate in a binary fashion (if something is "off" it's a zero, "on" it's a one), you could program a machine that way as well. Just imagine sitting down everyday and writing things like "10011101011111001," and so on. Most people couldn't tell whether you were reciting Macbeth's famous dagger speech or recording a recipe for Peking duck. After three decades of false starts, wasted time, and some unintelligible trash, the industry seems to have decided upon two primary languages, COBOL and BASIC. The first of these, COBOL, is English-looking in its construct and is designed for business types of applications. Large amounts of numbers are read in and printed out with very little mathematical manipulation of the data. The BASIC language is scientific in its notation and is designed to handle only a limited amount of information, although Commercial BASIC (CBASIC) is beginning to look more and more like a business language. BASIC can perform intricate calculations, however.

It is important to know what language the machine in question will use. There are a number of fine self-teaching texts on the market and we will leave that education to those qualified. Just as a comparison, though, if you wanted to add one number, *a,* to a second number, *b,* and store that result in something called *c,* the languages would look as follows:

BASIC: $c = a + b$
COBOL: ADD A TO BE GIVING C.

Service

For service, IBM has won the battle hands down. This has particular significance in rural areas where no one but IBM has the financial power to support a field operation. Get a full understanding of both the cost and the benefit of a service contract. Know who will service the equipment if the manufacturer does not, where the nearest office is located, and the past record of number and severity of breakdowns. If you lease the machine, be certain to ask how easy it will be to upgrade, that is, to go to a larger and more capable machine. Ask questions about the possibility of tacking additional memory onto the device and see if the machine (or possibly its bigger brother) has remote processing capability. There might be a reason for you to operate the computer from your home or other distant facility. Get a fair idea in advance of just what it is that you want the computer to do for you. In this way, you can ask intelligent questions of the supplier even if you don't know all the current lingo.

One of the biggest fears that people have about anything, and about computers in particular, is looking stupid to people that seem to know a lot about a subject that is baffling them. Running and programming a computer can be taught just as bookkeeping or swimming can. The newer machines seem to *want* to teach you how to operate them. Don't rush into the purchase, but don't be intimidated by the technology either. Once you have mastered the techniques involved, be careful. Computers are fascinating, and they have so captivated some individuals that they become slaves to the machine, staying up all night feeding nonsense into the electronic maw of the beast to the detriment of their health, their love life, and their business.

The small computer is nothing more or less than a machine that, properly used, will help both in the day-to-day operation and the long-term planning and analysis function. Small computers are now priced within reach of almost every small business in the country. The *prompts* and other built-in aids help the novice work his way through learning both programming itself and the use of prepared programs. The modern small computer is immensely more reliable than its earlier counterparts. And there are hundreds of programs and applications available now for every conceivable business situation.

But the computer is just a machine. Properly used, it should pay for itself within one year. If improperly used, it may only help to drag your business down, because, if your systems and procedures are confused now, and you choose not to change them to fit a computer, then the machine will only get you fouled up, but at a much faster rate.

CHAPTER TEN

Other Business Matters

"Study to be quiet, and to do your own business."
I Thessalonians 4:11

This chapter is a potpourri of various subjects that don't conveniently fit under our other general headings. These business matters include the following:

Managing the business
The business cycle
The role of government
Business failure
Selling the business
Estate planning
Ethics

Managing the Business

There are probably thousands of books written on *management,* which can be defined as "the art of getting things done by people"—one of whom is you. We will devote only a few pages to the subject as it pertains to small-business owner-managers. Consider the diagram in Figure 10.1.

Entrepreneurs are *goal-setters, planners* and *decision-makers.* We all know what goals are, and have set many ourselves in our lifetime. During our school days, our goals were probably simple, reasonably attainable, and usually immediate. We wanted to make the football team or the cheerleading squad, to get an A in a course, or to have a date with someone we thought was special. As we left school, our goals probably became tougher; they were more complex and the time spans involved were longer. The goal setting and the goal achievement involved the changing of basic life style: to marry a certain person, to live in a certain area of the country, or to work for a particular organization. Paul J. Meyer, president of Success Motivation Institute in Waco, Texas, defines *success* as "the progressive realization of pre-determined, worthwhile, personal *goals.*" Notice that there is nothing in the definition that refers to fame or fortune; as we suggested in Chapter 1, these are usually not goals of successful entrepreneurs, but they can become by-products.

The goals set by the entrepreneur are indeed personal goals, since the entrepreneur is the enterprise and vice versa. When the author was employed by IBM, he received a copy of a book entitled *The Lengthening Shadow,* the biography of Thomas J. Watson, Sr., the man who built the corporate foundation that allowed IBM to grow to become one of the firms in the top ten of the Fortune 500. The title, taken from a statement made by Ralph Waldo Emerson, was particularly apt since IBM, especially in its formative years, reflected

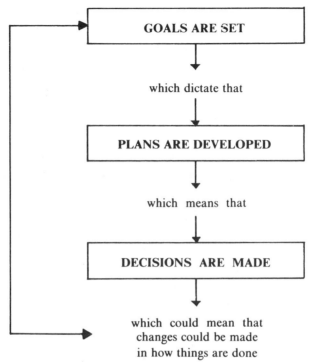

Figure 10.1 *A Plan for Getting Things Done*

the professional and personal beliefs of Watson himself.[1] IBM *was* Watson.

It is axiomatic that, if goals are properly established, the plan of achievement follows. An overused maxim says, "If you have no destination, then any road will take you there." A plan allows the entrepreneur to map out the route of progress that will allow his goal to be met. We believe that, outside of some self-assessment in terms of the entrepreneurial role and its demands, the most important thing that the entrepreneur can do is to prepare his business plan.

Planning is not easy for anyone. Part of the problem is that looking into the future is, admittedly, difficult. But various studies have suggested that both successful companies (as measured by growth) and successful individuals (as measured by net worth—see Chapter 4) plan their respective futures.

The Decision-Making Process

Decision-making is so intertwined with the goal setting and planning processes that it sometimes becomes indistinguishable, because the setting of a goal and the development of a plan require decisions themselves.

---

[1] The Monday-morning song session by the sales force and the super-strict no-drinking rule are two of Watson's routines that are known (and sometimes ridiculed) by many Americans.

Any decent textbook on management has a chapter devoted to the decision-making process. Although everyone differs slightly in his description of the process, most authors stick to the following sequence of events:

The Situation Is Defined. Most people will agree that just defining the situation gets the decision-maker about 90 percent along the way to his goal. An improper or incorrect problem (or opportunity) definition will, obviously, distort the rest of the process.

The Variables Are Set Down and Identified. Internal (controllable) and external (uncontrollable) variables will affect the outcome of any business decision. The entrepreneur can quite obviously control the nature of the business enterprise, but he cannot control the weather, the economy, or impending legislation.

Data and Information Are Assembled and Analyzed. Most successful entrepreneurs are voracious absorbers of data and information. They continuously collect information that would have adverse or positive affects on their venture, such as competitive moves, changes in highways, professional association information, United States government data, and local laws. Entrepreneurs believe that good information makes for good decisions.

The Various Alternatives Are Set Down for Analysis. The choice of alternatives can be as simple as whether to do something or not, or the alternatives can be many, each one highly complex in nature. One easy way to aid this process is to use one piece of paper for each alternative and label each page. Then make two columns for each, one labeled *advantages* and the other *disadvantages.* List as many attributes (debits and credits) as possible; weigh each of them on a scale of one to ten, with one being "of little or no significance" and ten representing "of critical importance." Summing up the various columns and comparing the results should at least begin to narrow down the possibilities. By the way, don't forget what you *want* to do despite all the proper analysis and even despite doubts that something is possible. And don't worry about why you want something.

The Best Alternative Is Chosen. Choosing the best alternative is the critical point because this is when the decision itself is made. It is true that making no decision is, in itself, a decision, but that's usually a cop-out of some sort. The United States Army had a clean and simple theory about decision-making in a combat situation—do *something!* Indecision and inaction could never solve anything because the situation could only deteriorate (the enemy would only get closer). The theory went on to say that doing something would cause action, the action would generate data, and the data could be analyzed. If the wrong decision had been made, then possibly the incoming data would help the decision-maker to change the incorrect decision to the proper one.

The Decision Is Put Into Effect. Once the decision has been put into effect (using a plan, of course), progress is monitored, information is again collected and analyzed, and appropriate action taken. This involves *feedback,* another process that good decision-makers use well. Most people agree that it is much easier to start something than to stop it.

Management, A to Z

The following list includes twenty-six hints that various entrepreneurs we have known have used for periodic review of their businesses and to help them manage more effectively and efficiently. The hints are given in no particular order, except that the first five are probably done on a more regular basis than the later items. A lot of what's contained in the list is a review of many of the things we talk about in this book. Much of this review concerns the business plan. As time passes, events will occur that (1) will have been foreseen, (2) will have been foreseen but miscalculated, and (3) will be totally unforeseen. Continuous review will reduce the number of miscalculated and unforeseen events.

A. Do-List Analysis. Good entrepreneurs keep *do* lists, as we mentioned earlier. You can buy a pad at any good stationery store labeled "Things to do Today," with a place for the date at the top. It doesn't do you or your business any good if you complete the list but then neither follow it nor review it for completion of important items. File old do-lists somewhere.

B. Cash Position and Budgetary Review. A constant analysis of cash (checking accounts, savings accounts, and money in the till) is necessary to keep a sufficient reserve on hand for paying bills and meeting contingencies. The budget variance is usually prepared monthly.

C. Competitive Data. If you're keeping files on your competition and continuously loading information into these files, then they should be pulled frequently and reviewed for possible patterns that might suggest changes.

D. Receivables and Payables Ledgers. We advised in chapter 6 that you age your accounts receivables on a monthly basis as a part of your credit and collection policy. The same approach should be taken with your payables. You don't want to gain the reputation of a slow-pay account with your suppliers. This makes additional credit extremely difficult.

E. Pricing. Nothing on the economic horizon foretells the end of inflation. Apparently, the only way continuously rising prices could be halted would be a worldwide disaster such as World War III. Price increases by your suppliers that are not passed on to your customers will directly decrease your gross margin.

F. Inventory. We watched a small specialty store sink simply because the owner paid no attention to slow-moving stock. It is absolutely imperative that inventory be continuously watched and analyzed. Goods that don't move take up space and cost money.

G. Staying on Track. Any entrepreneur, large or small, is continuously tempted to do all kinds of new and different things. New ideas are great, but they should be well thought-out and well planned. An old maxim goes, "Be not the first by whom the new is tried, nor the last to lay the old aside."

H. Advertising Effectiveness. If you use an agency, it should be working closely with you. You should be keeping data on monthly sales by product grouping and by type of customer response. After a number of months, a pattern should emerge. Keeping the sales information has many benefits in and of itself, not the least of which is determining seasonal patterns of your business.

I. Adequacy of Financial Information. As an absolute minimum, you should receive or prepare the following monthly reports: income statement, balance sheet, budget variance, and cash flow. As you gain experience in reading and analyzing the data, you may find that you need additional information about your business, such as a finer breakdown of items of the income statement or a statement of the source and use of funds. For example, the classification *utilities* may be too broad; you may want to see telephone, electricity, and fuel oil separated out.

J. Change in the Legal Form. Many an entrepreneur begins his operation as a sole proprietorship because this legal form is simple and needs fewer formal records. The business grows, and so does the personal tax liability. But there is usually a time in the life of the venture when it's wise to review the possibility of a change in the legal form, usually to a corporation.

K. Employee Progress. You will want your key people to grow with their job and to enjoy themselves in the process. As you learn more about the strengths and weaknesses of your employees, you will want to capitalize on the former and work with them on the latter. Giving them more responsibility not only increases their own satisfaction but also relieves you of some of your work. Many entrepreneurs work one or two key people into a position where they can be trusted to run the business so that vacations can be freely taken. MBO (chapter 8) is an excellent technique for tracking employee progress.

L. Self-Improvement. The world changes at a ferocious pace, and the changes in small business are probably occurring even faster. Entrepreneurs today, just like doctors and lawyers, must keep up with developments in their field. Classes and seminars are in order. Books on small business (like this one!) should be purchased for reading and reference. Conventions and other appropriate meetings should be attended. General knowledge of business operations should be expanded.

M. Retirement. As an entrepreneur, unlike your counterpart in big business, you must provide for your retirement years yourself. Along with your Keough (H.R. 10) individual retirement plan, you should be planning other investments for the future. Your business is going to be your major investment, since it will increase in value over the years and your loans will decrease resulting in an equity increase. Each year you should prepare a personal balance sheet and compare it with the previous year.

N. Economic Outlook. You should subscribe to the Wall Street Journal and make it a part of your required reading. Each Monday, there is a column called "The Outlook" which discusses the opinions of experts regarding the economic future. Recessions and booms are a way of life. Some businesses are not highly affected by the shifts in economic conditions; others feel them severely. Pity the entrepreneur who purchased or started a car agency specializing in large automobiles prior to the increases in gasoline prices.

O. Insurance Coverage. When you begin, your initial insurance coverage will most likely be minimal, limited to absolute musts. As you grow, two things will happen: (1) you will need additional kinds of insurance (chapter 9), and (2) you will need broader coverage in policies already in effect. Even though selling more insurance often appears to be a ploy by insurance companies, the value of your business will increase and so should your coverage.

P. Review of Legal Documents. Documents such as contracts and leases should be reviewed at least annually. It's very probable that, at some stage in your business's existence, you will be leasing a piece of equipment with an option to buy, and the time may come when the purchase makes more economic sense than a continued rental plan.

Q. Expansion. As the business grows, there is increasing pressure on its physical size. Pretty soon, everything is bursting at the seams, and it's time to either make more efficient use of existing space (affecting layout), to move (affecting location), or to expand the existing facility. The latter may involve decisions regarding new assets and certainly would have a financial impact on the operation. The entrepreneur has to decide whether to self-finance or go to the bank. Our rule of thumb is that, if your operation earns more (percentagewise) than the going loan rate at the bank, you should use the bank's money.

R. Location. If you are occupying leased space and renewal time is coming, it's a good idea to take a hard look at your present location. Have you heard any complaints that you're hard to find, that there's insufficient parking, or that people confuse the kind of store you are because of the ones around you?

S. Personnel Policies. As you grow, the chances are that you can be more liberal in terms of pay, benefits, and policies. Possibly it's time to add paid hospitalization to the benefit package, or maybe it's time to take Jill off hourly and put her onto salary. Policies and benefits should be reviewed annually at a minimum.

T. Supplier Performance. Once you have established yourself with your various suppliers you run the show. Be very certain that you don't tie yourself into a single source if at all possible; have alternative suppliers ready to go. If you experience poor performance on the part of a vendor—inordinate price increases, late deliveries, inferior quality—inform him of the fact in writing; if he doesn't improve, drop him.

U. Sales Trends. It's a good idea to review a graph of your sales over a period of time. If your dollar sales have been increasing at, say, 5 percent per year, then you're not even keeping pace with inflation and are losing ground. The other pattern that you should be looking for is any seasonality that might be taking place.

V. Government Regulations. Unless some miracle worker comes along and somehow reverses the trend, government will encroach more and more into small-business concerns. You won't like it, but there's little you can do. Just be glad you aren't a big business. Several years ago, Exxon submitted one required report to one of the federal energy offices. The length was 445,000 pages. The SBA can give you some help regarding federal requirements, and, just by reading the newspaper, you should be able to keep pace with state and local developments.

W. Theft. If theft levels are increasing, you've got trouble and should do something about it. If the thieves are primarily employees, it's not only time to change the staff, but also to discover why they're doing it. If it's shoplifting, begin a positive campaign to bring it under control. Train your people to spot it, prosecute offenders, post prominent signs, and use mirrors, one-way glass, and even TV monitors.

X. Sales Methods. At least annually you should review the way you sell your product or service. If you use agents (reps), maybe it's time to hire your own salespeople. Possibly it's time to begin a mail-order business.

Y. Maintenance and Repair. If you have assets that require simple preventive maintenance, it's a good idea to check them periodically. This could mean cleaning out exhaust hoods, oiling bearings, or replacing worn fan belts.

Z. Utilities. Keep records of the rate of usage and cost of electricity, gas, oil, and telephone. There might be lights turned on all day that could be turned off, or the wattage could be lessened. Possibly wood or solar heat could replace oil. The one black desk phone might have been fine when you started; now, you might need several instruments with intercom capability. Be very careful with the phone company, because you'll be paying business rates. Telephone company salesmen love to show you all kinds of fancy gadgets and then insist on advance payments to keep your service.

The Business Cycle

The *business cycle* (sometimes called the product cycle) is the large historical pattern of general business prosperity and distress, expansion and contraction, over time! Your business is part of it.

Figure 10.2 shows the cycle of a business if nothing significant is done to change the nature and character of that business. We have depicted four phases in the cycle. Phase I is start-up. It is characterized by an agonizingly slow start until the business is known. In phase II, the survival stage, which can last years, solid growth takes place if the business is succeeding; if not, a high rate of failure occurs. Any business should make it through phase I, if for no other reason than that the owner's capital keeps it alive. Phase II is the real test of the staying power of the business. In phase III, maturity and market saturation take place and growth slows or stops altogether. Phase IV, like phase II, is critical. Three things can happen. With case A, the world around the business changes but the business does not. Since the entrepreneur is oblivious to the changes (everything from demand drying up to a highway bypass), the business decays and dies. In case B, the market stays saturated and the business no longer grows in a real sense. Smart entrepreneurs operate like case C; they know when they reach phase III, and begin planning some new strategy to combat phase IV's eventualities. Establishing the same business in a neighboring town would be an example.

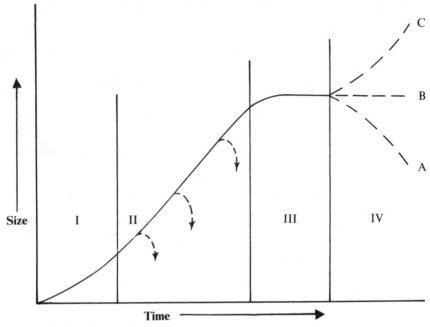

Figure 10.2 *The Business Cycle*

The Role of Government

This section will be brief since we have previously mentioned the *role of government* taken by various federal agencies (SBA, Department of the Census, Department of Commerce). Outside of the SBA and the Postal Service, your most frequent communication will be with the Internal Revenue Service (IRS). Smith's Law number 26 says, "Taxes are like hangovers; they may be postponed but never forgiven." Another sage once said, "File your tax, don't chisel on it." We strongly advise you to compute your tax, report every item of income, take every allowable deduction. It's that simple. Although the temptation is great, and you can probably get away with it, don't "skim." For one thing, unreported income is just that. It doesn't show up on your income statement as income (and, hence, profit) or on your balance sheet as cash; thus, it lowers the value of your business.

The IRS is probably the most powerful of all government agencies. Its agents have supraconstitutional powers and can deprive you of things like your house and car without the due process of law that is usually guaranteed all citizens. They once seized all the funds of a company, keeping them locked up for months and eventually throwing sixty people out of work, because of a clerical error that the IRS, not the business, had made. The IRS admitted the error but did nothing to help the entrepreneur get the venture going again. Moral: Don't do anything to bring the IRS to your door. If you are audited, pray you have good records and can validate all your claims. Practice tax avoidance, not tax evasion.

Another powerful agency is named for the Occupational Safety and Hazard Act of 1970 and is known as OSHA (pronounced *oh-shuh*). The original intent of the act was to protect workers from grossly unsafe conditions such as moving machinery, falling objects, unguarded machine tools, dust, heat, or chemicals. What actually happened was that many companies were cited and fined for petty violations: one concern, for having its fire extinguishers 2 inches below the required height; another, for having a coffee cup on the window sill. These practices are being brought under control, but you may be required to install devices or procedures that you could clearly never afford.

The Equal Employment Opportunity Commission (EEOC) is also an agency you must contend with. Instead of assuring that everyone got an equal break when it came to jobs, EEOC agents required employers to hire unskilled, unqualified people strictly on a racial or ethnic basis, a practice which can also be discriminatory. Simply treat everyone as human beings. Hire and fire on qualifications or the lack of them, and leave race, sex and religion out of it.

If you are dirtying the air around you or dumping some horrid waste into a stream, you might be visited by the Environmental Protection Agency (EPA) or its state equivalent. Be a good neighbor and they won't bother you.

There are many other groups that businesses must deal with, usually as a function of the nature of the individual operation. If you have a charter air service, you will have dealings with the Federal Aviation Administration (FAA); a radio station, the Federal Communications Commission (FCC); an interstate trucking service, the Interstate Commerce Commission (ICC).

Business Failure

If you start, rather than buy, a business, the odds are heavily weighted against your success. Like it or not, those are the facts. Buying a going concern lessens the failure possibilities, but even if you do everything this book tells you, there will still be a reasonably high probability of failure.

The death of a business can be quick and merciful, as from an uninsured fire, or it can be prolonged, long and agonizing, with little breaths of optimism, until the inevitable finally occurs. One thing to keep in mind is that, if your business fails, all your creditors can take from you is physical assets. They can't sell your children or imprison you. Many good entrepreneurs fail before succeeding. Our advice for owners of a failed business comes right from a well-known song: "Pick yourself up, dust yourself off, and start all over again."

Business failure happens because of money—not enough of it. Failure is usually preceded by some basic flaw in business practice, such as poor inventory control or lack of a market. Eventually, there is not enough cash to pay the bills and the loans. This condition is known as *insolvency* or *illiquidity*. The next series of events that will occur are heart-rending:

Unpaid suppliers shut you off.
The bank calls the loans.
Employees quit.
Rumors spread.
Competitors laugh.
The phone, if not disconnected, rings off the hook, and few of the callers are pleasant.
Your landlord starts showing the location to new tenants.
Your kids whine that there's no money.

One stopgap measure is known in the trade as "going into chapter eleven." This refers to chapter eleven of the Federal Bankruptcy Act, which now contains fifteen chapters. The first seven chapters deal with straightforward personal bankruptcy; chapter eight, farmers and railroads; chapter nine, municipalities; chapters ten and eleven, businesses; chapter twelve, real estate; chapter thirteen, wage-earner plans; chapter fourteen, maritime deals; chapter fifteen, railroad cases.

For the small-business owner seeking protection from creditors, chapter eleven is the main issue; chapter ten really only comes into play for large businesses that have publicly traded stock.

In the pre-1978 law, there was both a voluntary and an involuntary bankruptcy proceeding. This distinction is no longer available. While it is still true that three creditors can get together and apply pressure on a small business to approach the courts, they cannot force the issue as they once could.

The small business that is insolvent, along with its attorney, petitions the United States District Court for protection. From then on, the company (the debtor) provides reports to the court, and a creditors' committee is formed which represents the claims of all the creditors. The company's legal name changes from "The ABC Business" to "The ABC Business, Debtor in Possession," and is, in actuality, a new venture in many respects. The business may resurrect itself like the *phoenix* from its own ashes; or sink like the Titanic, belly-up.

The most important consideration in all these proceedings is to have a qualified attorney handling the case, an attorney who has had experience in bankruptcy cases.

When the court declares you bankrupt, all your business assets are sold and the proceeds used to satisfy creditors. Legal fees, unpaid wages, and taxes are paid before secured creditors, unsecured creditors, and investors. Even if you used the corporate form of business, you probably had to personally guarantee any loans. This may mean personal bankruptcy as well, but, in most states, you can keep your house and personal belongings. You may have to remortgage your house, however.

So now we find you on the corner of Main and Elm, collar pulled up to your ears and your pockets inside out. Penniless. Friendless. Alone in the world. Maybe divorced as well. That's what it'll seem like, but it doesn't have to be that way for long. They may have gobbled up your cash, but not your brains and guts. And just think of what you've learned. It's been an expensive education, but, right now, you know as much about small-business management as anyone in the world. It's important for you to realize what went wrong rather than to blame yourself for the failure.

What do you do? You hustle around to get enough money to get back into the game. This might even mean getting a job. Or it might show you that you were not cut out to be an entrepreneur, and you really belong back in the executive suite. Or maybe you should go into consulting for small business, or teaching, or writing.

Chances are, though, you've got the entrepreneurial bug. See you back soon.

Selling the Business

There may come a day when you decide to sell your money machine.[2] The reasons are as varied as a desire for retirement, wanting a new business, regaining your health (we hope not), keeping it out of the hands of lazy, incompetent progeny, or realizing a fat capital gain. If you're selling because the venture is a dog, most buyers will find this out. Occasionally, a new buyer can turn a business around, but don't count on it.

Assuming, then, that you have a viable, profitable enterprise, there are several things you must do before you put an ad in the paper or look for a business broker to work with.

Although there's controversy on the subject, we believe that you should tell your employees that you plan to sell. Some entrepreneurs keep everything in the dark, and then, one bright morning, spring the new owner on everyone. This is unfair to the good people who may have come to work because of you and not the business. And, if you tell your employees, you might be surprised. One of your own people might have the money and desire to buy the operation. Some employees may quit; others may take a wait-and-see attitude to be sure that the next owner doesn't make Simon Legree look like Santa Claus.

A concurrent activity is to put all the financial records in shape. No prospec-

[2] For a very thorough treatment of this subject, see Richard Buskirk and Percy Vaughn Jr., *Managing New Enterprises* (Minnesota: West Publishing, 1976), pp. 431–470.

tive buyer will go very far with you without a very close look at the financial statements. Some buyers will spend weeks doing this because they've gained experience with big business.

Setting the Selling Price

The most difficult task is *setting the price* (see Chapter 3). Chances are you will have a sticker, or asking, price. This price is quoted to keep the unqualified buyer away, but it generally is not the final price unless you say something like "$295,000 firm." You should get an appraisal of the business. Be certain that the appraiser is well-qualified in both business and real estate appraisal. Good appraisers, like good bankers and good lawyers, are rare, but they're around.

A primary factor to remember in selling a business is the profit that the business can generate for the new owner. The starting point is the present profit in dollars; future levels are computed in the financial section of the business plan. Most sophisticated people who are considering the purchase of a going concern go beyond (1) the fun of the venture itself, and (2) its capability of providing a financial livelihood. In the final analysis, they look on the business as an investment, a vehicle to provide a desirable return on their invested funds. This means cash, not the acountant's figures on profit as shown on the standard income statement. Among many entrepreneurs and business brokers, you will hear the term *capitalization* (or *cap*) *rates*. This refers to a very simple calculation by which profit (or assets or owner's equity) is converted to a larger number by dividing the profit by a rate that represents a return on investment. Thus, if a business can be expected to provide an average cash profit of $50,000 and the desired return is 10 percent, the cash price should be $50,000 ÷ .10 or $500,000. (Note: this is the same as a *times earnings* approach, since it gives the same result.) Discounted cash flow should be worked into calculations as well. (See Chapter 7.)

Just as a quick review, suppose that you wanted to sell your business for $400,000 and that a buyer could purchase the business with 30 percent down, the remainder to be bank-financed. This means that the potential buyer would have to invest $120,000 of his or her own money. That same money could be invested in alternate sources of revenue production—savings account; life insurance; certificates of deposit; land; the stock market; municipal bonds (tax free interest); United States Treasury notes, bills, and bonds; mutual funds of all kinds; tax shelters such as oil rigs, freight cars and cattle; real estate investment trusts; annuities; money market certificates; the commodities market; precious substances like gold, silver, platinum, or diamonds; art treasures; antiques; stamps and coins; famous signatures; beer cans, especially rare ones; Superman funny books; and worm farms, to name a few. But this $120,000 is going to be invested in a business. If the best return on investment could be expected to yield an investor 15 percent on his capital, consistent with prudent risk, then the business should earn an annual cash profit, after all real expenses (including debt service), of $18,000.

The real value of any business is its *market value*. Formulas, appraisals, and earnings projections are only means of approximating an estimate of market value. As with any other commodity, both price and market value are functions of supply and demand; as supply decreases or increases, the price goes down or up; as demand decreases or increases, price responds accordingly.

Market value is affected by every similar property available in the market-place. In the final analysis, the market value is determined in precisely the same way as the market value of food, used cars, gold, money, houses, medicine. The only exceptions are where a free market does not exist. There are literally hundreds of factors which affect the market value or selling price of a business. Here are some of them (the list is long to make the point that the price of a business may be determined by a host of matters, tangible and intangible).

Profitability
Value of tangible assets
Competitive posture
Value of good will
Quality of management
Availability of labor, if needed
Economy of country
Economy of region
Economy of town
Aesthetic considerations
Size of initial investment
Trend in consumer taste
Flexibility of expansion
Availability of parking, if needed
Repairs required to property
State, local, and federal regulations
Educational facilities nearby
Demands upon time of owner
Ease of resale
Liquidation value
Value of inventory (original cost, current cost, retail value)
Quality of inventory (slow- or fast-moving, obsolete or current, margins)
Rate of turnover of inventory
Capital intensive or not?
Quality of demand—solid or soft?
Training required?
Availability of living quarters
Availability of mortgage funds
Price of mortgage funds (interest and points)
Availability of owner financing

Nature of any leases
Availability of credit from suppliers
"Clean" or "dirty" business (Junk yards usually sell for less than marinas with equal earnings.)
Indoor or outdoor work
Cooperation of local authorities
Cash and cash equivalents included
Tax audit coming up? Just completed?
Adverting costs, co-op opportunities
Government regulated business or important supplies allocated?
Amount and age of payables and receivables
Demand for businesses in region
Quality of environment in area
Deferred maintenance or repairs
Special factors affecting future expenses or growth (for example, new pollution control laws in works)
Ease of management by unskilled person
Stability of market (is this a fad?)
Cost of expansion (new land or buildings required?)
Quality of suppliers
Variety of suppliers
Financial records available
Discrepancy between financial records and IRS returns
Affluence of community
Crime rate in area
Climate
Fire and municipal services
Size of town
Stability of earnings
Cyclical character of business
Amount of tax shelter available
Nature of purchase (stock vs. assets)
Vulnerability to depreciation recapture
Quality of equipment
Tax loss carry forwards and backwards
Tax credits available
Past tax payments (available toward purchase of tax loss?)
Years in business
Growth pattern of business
Quality of title to real estate
Amount of land available
Urban renewal plans in region or area
Effect of OSHA requirements and state codes
Quality of CPA firm or accountant
Personal references of sellers
Business based on basic needs or dispensable needs?

Cash or accrual accounting method?

Key employees needed to stay?

Danger of competition from seller

Are patents involved? How long to run? How strong?

If manufacturing, job work or proprietary lines or combination?

Deed restrictions on property

Records on past customers, good and bad

Where pertinent, bearing loads of roads, other highway matters

Cost of fuel in area, and its availability

Allocation of assets among real estate, improvements, personal property, fixtures, inventory, good will, convenants not to compete, patents

Tax effects of above on both seller and buyer

Outright purchase, lease with option to purchase, contract for sale, tax-free exchange, lease, and tax effect on both buyer and seller of method

Need for buyer to invest quickly for tax purposes, need for seller to sell quickly for tax purposes

Experience of buyer in field

Permits required (liquor, food, health, building, environmental)

Trust among buyer, seller, broker, attorneys

Special talents required?

Any government contracts? Political connections required?

Method of depreciation (straight line, accelerated)

Status of position of owner

Hours required to do work

Opportunity for vacation, days off

Availability of substitute management in case of emergency

Sellers' plans (will they be around?)

Other buyers interested?

How long for sale?

Reason for sale?

Proportion of business in service, goods, processing, manufacturing

Shelf life of goods

Good consulting help available

Airline, train, truck service

Delivery delays from suppliers?

Health of seller if his help will be required?

Valuation of business by various methods, various appraisers, accountants, lawyers, mothers-in-law

Health considerations of buyer

Special assessments coming up

Stability of business

Reputation of business

Fringe benefits of business

Friends or relatives in area

Availability of water

Gut feeling

Using a Broker

The next subject regards the use of business brokers. Reluctance is natural. "If I can sell my business for $400,000, why should I pay $40,000 for selling my business when I can do it myself?" This is a natural question and requires a very solid answer. The answer, however, becomes a series of questions. How many businesses have you sold? How well do you know the potential buying market? Can you answer all the technical financial questions of a potential buyer about tax-loss carry forward, investment credits taken, or job incentive credit? Could you successfully handle the final negotiations that have to do with price *and* terms? [3] If your banker reneges on the deal, do you know at least three others that you could go to? We favor the use of brokers in the same way we would recommend a real estate agent to sell a house, an accountant to do bookkeeping, and a lawyer to approach the bench. A good broker can easily earn his fee by:

> Getting to know your business as well as you do.
> Recommending things you should do before the sale.
> Comparing your asking price to any other business of the same kind.
> Designing the most favorable terms.
> Bringing only fully qualified and interested buyers to the operation.
> Helping to negotiate price and terms.
> Assisting at the closing.

Believe us, good brokers earn their commissions.

Once the business is sold and the new owner(s) in control, you, as past owner, will probably stay on for a period of time to aid in the transition. The new owners will come up against dozens of problems that to you were routine. In almost all cases, this time is not free; you are to be paid a consulting fee (sometimes $25,000 or more) which is made a part of the purchase price.

Estate Planning

There are three important people in your life when it comes to your estate. These are your insurance agent, your banker, and your lawyer. The main task of your attorney is to be certain that your will reflects your exact wishes, to be carried out upon your demise. Under no circumstances should a small business owner die intestate (no will). This is as much a part of your business planning as pricing. The will should be reviewed with your lawyer every two years or so.

---

[3] Most people forget that a deal contains both price and terms. The story is told about two people dickering over the sale price of a dilapidated business. Since agreement couldn't be reached, the parties decided that the owner could state the price, and the buyer, the terms. The owner then quoted the price at $1,000,000. The buyer said that was acceptable and the terms of payment were to be one dollar per year for 1,000,000 years, interest free.

As you get older, it becomes even more important to listen to legal advice about your estate. For example, if you are seventy-two and decide to sell your million-dollar restaurant to your eldest son for $10,000, and next week the Lord calls you home, the IRS will claim that the sale was "in contemplation of death," and no tax advantage will accrue.

Earlier, we suggested that, when you select a bank, you use its full services. This holds true with your estate. You should have a bank trust officer to work with. Rather than being concerned so much with estate legalities, the trust officer is concerned with money. Maybe junior is relatively irresponsible as a teenager, but you feel (since he's yours) that he might settle down by the time he's twenty-one. You and your bank can design a trust fund that will only allow him to begin drawing amounts from it when he reaches that age. The most important party to this planning, by far, is your insurance agent. Be sure that he or she is a Certified Life Underwriter (CLU). This means that he has passed certain uniform tests and is qualified to help you plan your estate.

For entrepreneurs, the biggest single reason for estate planning is not to minimize death taxes, although that is often a valuable secondary by-product. The major reason is to head off the possible chaos that might occur.

Assume that you are male, married, and forty-five years of age. Ten years ago you got fed up with your career at Mammoth Industries, Inc., in Manhattan, and decided to sell your over-inflated house in Greenwich to someone more foolish than you and move to Vermont. You buy a hardware store in a delightful town and build it into a fine, profitable business. You have a son in college and a daughter in the local high school. Outside of helping with the annual inventory, your wife has pursued a career of her own. One bright winter morning, you choke on a chicken bone and die. Now what? Your kids are still in school and your wife doesn't know the business from a truck. Assume that no will has been written (so there are no appointed executors). The situation becomes one not only of sorrow, but of utter panic for your survivors. In these circumstances your business may have to suspend operations. Even if the suspension is temporary, it will drastically reduce the value of the business, and hence the value of the estate you expected to pass on.

One last hint. Many entrepreneurs squirrel things away, usually money. If you've got $5000 in a coffee can or numbered bank account, put the location of the can or the account number on a piece of paper, seal it in an envelope, write *To Be Opened Only in the Event of My Death* on the envelope, and give it to your trust officer.

Ethics

No book on the entrepreneur would be totally complete without some mention of *ethics* and its impact on small business management. The classic (and largely incorrect) image of the entrepreneur has been one of a conniver, a schemer, a plotter, a scalawag, and a rogue. The suspiciously fictitious story of Abraham Lincoln slogging miles through a raging storm to return ten cents to a woman who was given the incorrect change at the general store in which he was a clerk probably received its century-long fame because of the unique adherence to ethics involved.

Ethics is not related to law except in the case where law demands conformity to statutes resulting from public outcry that certain businesses be enjoined to act ethically. Many of the consumer protection laws that have been enacted recently are really ethically based.

Some years ago, the author was a young, married second lieutenant stationed in Washington, D.C. These were the days when both military and civilian government employees were paid just slightly less than survival pay. (We used to call our paycheck the "government's monthly insult.") The base pay for a second lieutenant at that time was $222.30 a month, which would have been fine if one was stationed in the Faeroe Islands, but was not princely in the Nation's Capital.

My duties required only a nine-to-five day five days a week, which afforded me the opportunity for a badly-needed part-time job. One day I read in the Washington *Post* the following want ad:

TEACHERS, MILITARY PERSONNEL: Our firm, which specializes in the sale of a highly technical, rapidly-selling, revolutionary product for the home, has openings on our professional staff for two qualified public relations directors to assist our marketing staff. Hours are flexible.

A telephone number was given in the ad, and my call resulted in a Saturday-morning interview.

During the interview, the following facts came to light: The company was involved in the sale (to be euphemistic) of a built-in vacuum-cleaning system. It consisted of a collecting tank and suction motor combined in one unit, which was normally mounted in the cellar. From the tank, PVC pipe was run to a series of baseboard-mounted outlets, each outlet covered by a spring-loaded cover which, when raised, activated the suction motor. The outlets were made to accept a lock connector at the end of a vacuuming wand. On the opposite end of the flexible wand was the suction head (the business end of a vacuum cleaner). The company would guarantee that sufficient outlets would be installed so that every area of the house could be reached.

Sound great? Read on.

The company employed three telephone sales operators who sat at phones with the Washington DC/suburban Mayland/suburban Virginia White Pages and called one number after another with a canned pitch about a "marvelous and revolutionary product no home should be without." They would try to arrange a home sales-visit by one of the salespeople of the company and were forbidden to divulge either the product in question or the price. Most sane people on hearing a pitch like that would simply hurl obscenities at the operator and hang up, but, since every city contains its share of gulls, about one out of forty calls would result in the desired appointment.

Once the salesperson got into the house, he or she was either going to walk out with a signed order or would leave the premises feet first. There was no middle road. The sales pitch was totally memorized, including voice inflections. Claims about the equipment, although not false, were vastly exaggerated. One salesperson stated that no one in the house would ever catch cold because the vacuum system would remove germ-laden dust particles that a regular bag or canister machine would simply blow back through the exhaust. Another peddler told a couple that the company would install outlets on the outside of the house because the system could be used to vacuum up the leaves in the fall (neither happened). The Professor Harold Hill Award for Creativity, Horn Swoggling, and Bamboozling goes to the unsung salesperson who told an elderly homeowner that if he opened all the outlets in the house, the system would suck flies out of the air.

The price to the consumer for the installed system was $895.00, cash. Most everyone, however, decided upon the "easy monthly payment of only $32.81 for only three years." Who could refuse a dollar a day? Today, many people could refuse when they found out that the effective annual percentage rate on that loan is 19 percent! The three-year note was sold by the company for immediate cash to an outfit in New Jersey that made the Mafia look like a minor Sicilian disturbance. The sales contract was to be signed right then and there. No let-me-think-it-over was to be allowed.

At the time, Sears came out with a nearly identical unit for $188.88 plus installation. Fly-by-Night Vacuum Cleaner's income statement per machine looked something like this:

Net sales revenue		$895.00
Cost of goods sold		145.00
(direct from manufacturer)		
Gross margin		$750.00
Expenses		
Salesperson	$100.00	
Installer	50.00	
Public relations director	10.00	
Freight	20.00	
Company overhead	80.00	
Total expenses		$260.00
Net profit		$490.00

Not bad!

The job of the public relations director (me!) was simple. The new owner was told by the salesperson to expect a visit from the company's public relations department two or three days after the installation to be certain that everything was as it should be. The PR visit consisted of two stages. The first stage involved asking twelve yes-or-no questions regarding such inconsequential items as the courtesy of the installer (whom they most likely never saw). The second stage was a bit trickier, but had to be done if the PR Director was to collect his ten dollars. The owner was asked to sign the questionnaire.

Just as music soothes the savage beast and soft words turneth away wrath, so a glib tongue, a smile, and a seeming betrayal of a confidence can cause misgivings to be forgotten. When asked to sign the questionnaire, most people were somewhat skeptical, but the following typical conversation did the trick:

> Owner (O) (conversationally but somewhat firm): I don't see why I should sign this.
>
> Public Relations Director (PR): Well, the primary purpose is to be sure you're totally satisfied.
>
> O: I am, but why the signature?
>
> PR: So that my boss can be sure I'm doing my job.
>
> O: But you could just sign it yourself and turn it in. Your boss would never know.
>
> PR: Sir (or madam), you don't know my boss. He's a stickler for detail and fair practice. He will compare your signature on this document to the one on the sales contract. You know how bosses can be (with big, toothy smile, appropriate chuckles, and eyebrow-raising).
>
> O (chuckling and reaching for the proffered pen): Yeah, I sure do. (Signs document and PR beats a hasty retreat for the next sucker's house.)

The kicker, of course, was in the fine print hidden in an obscure corner of the form. The text of the statement was worded in legal language, but, when translated into plain English, it absolved the company from every stated or implied promise *including the warranty.*

The saga of Fly-by-Night Vacuum Cleaners is included as an object lesson. Fly-by-Night broke every rule of ethics in the book. Note that their many transgressions boil down to one chief sin: Lying. Fly-by-Night deceived the buyer in advance of the sale, hoodwinked him on the credit terms of the sale, and evaded their warranty obligations after the sale. Most of these practices would be outlawed today, but the point of the story is not law, but ethics. By the way, the company left its office in northern Virginia with the door unlocked and the empty drawers of the file cabinets wide open, never to be seen again.

Most successful entrepreneurs are in business for the long haul, not a hit-and-run operation. This means continuing attention to business and personal ethics. One question that we do get asked is just how far ethical and moral conduct should go. We have to leave that up to each individual, his standards of behavior, and, of course, his personal conscience.

CHAPTER ELEVEN

Women as Entrepreneurs

"I suspect that Woman will be the last thing civilized by Man."
George Meredith, 1859

At the present time, a substantial body of knowledge is being assembled regarding women and small business. Several books have been written. There is no doubt at all that a larger percentage of future entrepreneurs will be women, and there is some early evidence that they may be more successful than their male counterparts.

The Department of Commerce estimated that, in 1972, there were only 400,000 women-owned businesses in the United States. By 1976, this figure had more than doubled to 978,000. It is likely that this figure will grow during the coming years.

A recent survey conducted for the President's Task Force on Women Business Owners, which is directed by Anne Wexler, showed that "half of the interview participants were in the service industry and a third in retail, wholesale, finance, insurance and real estate," with a smaller number in manufacturing and construction. The report also concluded that "similarities between male and female entrepreneurs are great. Significant differences do exist in the nature and magnitude of the barriers encountered, however." The report stated that the success of the women-owned businesses surveyed was "nothing less than remarkable," with more than half having realized profits within two years of their operation.

Thus, there is no question but that women are able to own and manage practically any small business—if they have access to appropriate financing and education, and if their own, as well as male attitudes, continue to mature.

Nancy Becker, who with her husband now owns and manages a large inn in New Hampshire, but who previously worked for the General Electric Corporation, said in an interview, "I would never work for a big corporation again. Too many people there are trying to make decisions. Corporate management is a clique-y bunch trying to look good, but what they do is not always good for the company. They kept making surveys of personnel morale, but we never saw the results of the surveys. In corporate life, everybody has got to match the image of the others. If you speak your mind, you are considered disloyal. People are better in corporations if they are not leaders and don't like making decisions. It's just like the Army. At least here I feel I have some control. If I don't like the meat supplier, I get rid of him."

Another woman, who was the personnel manager for a branch of a large chain store, said that she was ordered to hire only women as clerks because "men could never live on such low pay." The woman also said that a campaign was launched asking for suggestions from the women employees, whose best suggestions were then preempted by the male manager. He took credit for the ideas when passing them on to his superiors in the corporation.

Small business offers an attractive opportunity to many women because small businesses are more egalitarian socially and economically than most corporations. A large proportion of past small-business owners comes from a working class background, but this is changing because of the new interest in owning small businesses as demonstrated by middle-management corporate executives. Further, corporations not only prefer men as managers, they also tend to favor executives who have college degrees, and who come from distinguished social backgrounds.

Women have long been conscious of such discrimination against them in big business, but curiously, few have considered the alternative of owning their own businesses until recently.

Need to Dream

According to Susan Braude, a psychological therapist associated with a county mental health agency, "The idea of a woman going into business for herself is at the far end of the scale, a kind of epitome of what women think they can strive for. It simply does not occur to most women. The only women I can think of who consider it are artists, who are entrepreneurs in a sense. But women artists do not think of themselves as businesswomen."

Ms. Braude added

> People have to fantasize themselves in a role before they consider taking on that role. Owning a business requires women to allow themselves to fantasize being "in control." But more often women fantasize themselves as *being* controlled. They are more likely to imagine being carried off by a knight on a white horse.

The fantasies of both men and women are partly molded by cultural stereotypes, such as models in ads, and heroes and heroines in movies, books, and television shows. Few women in real life are as physically perfect as the heroines depicted in the media, a daunting realization for any young woman of average appearance. Few of the women in magazine advertisements seem to have more on their minds than making themselves look even better so as to "catch a man" who promises economic security as well as love. A woman pictured sitting at an office desk in an ad is more likely to be quoted as worrying about breaking her fingernails on the typewriter than about planning an expansion of her own business.

These cultural standards have a very powerful effect upon the subconscious minds of men and women. According to Dr. Roy Abney, a psychiatrist on the staff of the Brattleboro Retreat, a private mental hospital in Vermont, "Children are still being raised in the same way today," which means that the traditional sexual stereotyping is still being inculcated in the subconscious of both men and women. As these stereotypes come under the increasing disapproval of society, a great deal of stress can result. When either men or women deviate from the standards instilled in their subconscious, they can become victims of an anxiety that can wreak havoc with their ambitions and achievements. Some theorize that young girls are inordinately influenced by their fathers to adopt feminine stereotypes rather than to fantasize careers that are traditionally reserved for men. "Fathers of all classes, trades, and professions who could, theoretically, be excellent role models or mentors for their daughters simply aren't." [1]

Conversely, the American Management Association's survey of women business-owners indicates that parental support was an important element in their aspirations and ultimate success. The women business-owners, "while close to both parents, appear to have a strong bonding to the male parental role," according to the report. Monique Fisher, the owner of a successful interior decorating and retail firm in Vermont, concurred with the theory. "My father was in the Air Force, and always said that I should learn to fly too," she said.

Many authorities have pointed out that some women "fear success." They seek subconsciously to fail if success threatens to contradict their self-image or the stereotyped role that they have been raised to play. Women students of adequate or superior intelligence have been known to flunk college courses for fear of incurring the disapproval of male students, and to protect their own self-image as a passive, feminine woman. In business, women may often affect meekness when assertiveness would be the more appropriate, businesslike behavior. But such behavior might contradict the standards of femininity she (and her male colleagues) still uphold.

"The subconscious can be changed," Dr. Abney said, "but it is difficult, and there is a great deal of human suffering as a result."

Money and Other Motives

Another problem for women in the business world is the peculiar psychological connotations surrounding money. For writing a book, painting a picture, knitting a sweater, or washing a dish, money as a standard of success is unfamiliar to many women. Women are raised to "feel the same way about sex as they do about money. Traditionally, women are not supposed to say they want to make money or to make sex. Women are supposed to marry for money and/or financial and social security, but they are not supposed to say so. They must

[1] *Women, Money & Power*, by Phyllis Chesler and Emily Jane Goodman (Morrow, New York, 1979), p. 73.

say—and believe—that they marry for love, for children and for God. Psychologically, female financial ambition or the female need for economic self-sufficiency is completely at odds with the female need to either be or to be seen as a Lady." [2]

Another author suggests that "Money is what all business is about, and therefore it retains all the power of the central mystery of a religious cult. Most people will tell you anything about themselves except what they earn, and most corporations approach the task of deciding upon salary increases in an atmosphere of secrecy, intrigue and conspiracy suitable to a CIA plot." [3]

According to a recent survey of women conducted by *Ms.* magazine, most women are extraordinarily conservative in their use of money. Although women certainly enjoy having a good deal of money as much as men enjoy it, it is apparent that fewer women measure their own accomplishments in terms of money, which is natural considering the historical pattern of women's incomes.

Rather than for money, many women (and men) who own businesses do so for self-satisfaction and other nonmaterial rewards. Mary Lou Schmidt, who owned a toy business in Pennsylvania, that she modeled after Tupperware parties, said, "Women don't have the same ego problems as men. They have ego problems—but they are not the same. If a woman chooses a career, she wants it to be meaningful. If the money comes, that's fine. But men want success."

Small-business ownership is almost never an appropriate field for either men or women who seek power or the luxuries associated with power and success, such as expensive cars, paneled offices, and elegant houses. Such image-building accoutrements are so expensive that small-business owners risk imperiling their firms if they invest in such indulgences.

The successful women business-owners who were surveyed by the American Management Association indicated that their primary reason for entering business was rather simple: "They had an idea for a product." Other motivations included a need for financial security coupled with a desire for independence, a lack of adequate opportunity to earn a good salary at a job, and the desire to use a talent or skill.

Risks and Independence

Women who contemplate owning their own business are, almost ipso facto, nonconformists (which is also true for men who own small businesses).

An ex-nun whose yearning for independence caused her to leave the convent and start two small businesses (vinyl repair and chimney-sweeping), said, "I always considered myself to be on the fringes of society. I could never adjust to

[2] *Ibid.*, pp. 9–11.
[3] *Power! How to Get It, How to Use It,* by Michael Korda (Random House, New York, 1975).

reporting to an office every morning, wearing the right clothes, and living with those conventions. I could never work for anyone else."

A former teacher who owned an inn in New Hampshire said, "Educational psychologists say that people either feel dependent or independent. If you feel dependent, you need a structure already set up for you, such as the company where you hold a job. But independent people would rather create their own structure, such as their own business." The innkeeper concluded that she was the dependent sort, and sold out.

Women have classically made a distinction between their work or careers and their home life, whereas, for men, the division has not always been so clear-cut. For women to be successful in their own businesses, they must make a commitment to it that they may not have been prepared to make. For business owners, a work-as-play attitude needs to be developed and fostered.

Although women in general are not acculturated to be risk-takers, business ownership requires an ability to take reasonable risks, and, often, a willingness to post one's entire personal equity as collateral. Most small-business owners are not the sort to expect their businesses to grow into giant enterprises, such as the Xerox Corporation or the Ford Motor Company. Some owners of comparatively humble small businesses, such as restaurants, are entrepreneurs in the sense that they build up one business, sell it at a profit, buy another, and so on. But the majority of small businesses are mom-and-pop stores, gas stations, hardware stores, and small service businesses that are not expected to grow spectacularly. Thus, their owners are not required to be more flamboyant promoters.

However, the vast majority of successful women business-owners surveyed by the American Management Association started their businesses from scratch; only 6.2 percent bought their businesses from others. Because it is much more difficult to start a new business and build it to success than to buy an ongoing business, this certainly indicates that some women are willing to take major risks.

There are many theories about the personality requirements for people contemplating owning their own small businesses. Although an independent-minded person is likely to prefer self-employment to job-holding, small-business owners also tend to "suffer fools gladly," as a Southern woman innkeeper expressed it. A clothing-store owner said, "To be successful in doing something with the public, you have to share the values of most of the people. Basically, I don't. Some mornings, I feel that if anybody came into the store, I simply could not deal with them, so I call up Iris and ask her to take over the store. But, on other days, I feel outgoing and sparkling, full of enthusiasm. That's what sells things—enthusiasm." Sue Burton Tanner, who owns a garden-supply shop in Bennington, Vermont, emphasized that women business-owners should also "become known" by being active in community affairs. The need for an affinity with people is very important, she said. "Retailing is quite fascinating. You know who you can joke with, and who you can leave alone."

Women have already demonstrated sales ability, a fact that has long been recognized by retail stores that hire women as salesclerks. This should hold true for women who happen to own the stores as well.

Intuition and Markets

According to another authority on entrepreneurship, James Howard, "Anyone can learn the basics of business. It takes time and application, but the basics tend to be logical and sensible. Only the application of time and effort is required. Being really successful requires a great deal of instinct, and a willingness to believe in one's instincts. The best businessmen combine a strong reliance on instinct with procedural controls over their instincts to avoid falling into traps. Perhaps it is easier to start with the instincts and create a discipline over them than it is to start with the discipline and cultivate the instincts."

Psychiatrist Abney expressed a generally held belief: "Women have more intuition than men." Women are raised to be less coldly "objective," detached, and analytical than men. While this may mean that women, on the whole, are less talented in mathematics and engineering, it is a good portent of their other business talents. Women business-owners readily admit that they use their intuition and instincts, as well as their traditional training in home-making.

Barbara Robinson, who started and now manages her own successful clothing store, asked sixty women friends what sort of store their town needed. She concluded from these conversations that a store selling unusually elegant clothes would be especially welcomed. She stocked the store "with extensions of my personal taste," she said. Curiously, none of her original sixty friends patronize the store: "It was the right idea for the wrong reasons." (The resistance of her friends probably reflects other problems, such as the implied embarrassment of being waited on by a friend and social peer.)

Another woman business-owner said, "It doesn't matter what you sell, so long as you believe in it." A nurse who sought to own her own business chose an obvious product, natural foods, and her training in nutrition became a major selling asset. Women who now hold jobs of various kinds will no doubt find ways to turn their skills into services or products suitable for their own businesses.

There are indications that women who instinctively and successfully analyze a market can find new ways to serve that market. Instinct or intuition is a form of judgment on which decisions are based, but the judgment's validity cannot be proved or disproved until tested. Although there are scientific methods of analyzing a market, there remains a great deal of room for chance. This intuition serves well when there is a lack of hard data that would guide a business owner's decisions in promotion, product development, purchasing, and other aspects of business that require "a sharp instinct, attention to nuances and subtleties as opposed to the obvious and demonstrable," according to Howard.

The use of instinct and intuition, which already borders on the metaphysical, can be carried too far by some women. According to the Center for Venture Management in Milwaukee, Wisconsin, women entrepreneurs differed in only one respect from their male counterparts: "The women displayed a strong interest in astrology."

Women business-owners are also likely to be acutely aware of the appearance of their stores, and to utilize their homemaking abilities and experience to keep the environments of their businesses attractive.

Ms. Fisher remarked that she was surprised that more women did not consider entering her field, interior decorating. "It is strange that men come here to sell ruffled curtains to me. You would think that more women would be doing this kind of business," she said.

Because a large share of customers of small retail outlets are women, women owners of such businesses would logically understand their market and the potential for new products. Mary Meyer of Townshend, Vermont, and her husband founded and built a lively manufacturing industry based on her talents for creating stuffed animals. Toys seem to be a field in which women are particularly adept in designing and selling. Kitchen utensils, food, furniture, and other household items would seem to be equally appropriate for women to merchandise.

Barriers to Success

During the next twenty-five years, women may be the most successful new owners of small businesses in this country.

The major reasons for this are that women are exhibiting intense new interest in business careers, and they are discovering that small-business ownership is particularly suited to them. At the same time, traditional barriers against businesswomen are rapidly falling, including financial, educational, and cultural impediments.

These barriers are already less formidable in the small business world than in the world of big business. Small businesses are community-based, are involved with such activities as retailing, personal services, entertainment, and the hospitality industry. Big corporations, however, dominate economic sectors—the extraction of resources, manufacturing, utilities, and transportation—that may be less amenable, for cultural reasons, to female leadership. A woman who is the owner of a small business immediately escapes much of the sexist discrimination that may hamper the career of a woman in corporate management, while entering an environment that is likely to be congenial with her background and experience.

Yet there remain some discouragements to women who might otherwise attempt careers as small business owners. None of these obstacles is insurmountable if private and public institutions address the need to remove them.

Finances

Whereas few women now have the capital necessary to invest in small businesses, new sources of equity and debt capital are needed. Traditional sources could be encouraged to aid women entrepreneurs more extensively.

Education

Less education is available about the management of small business than is needed, for either men or women. However, private firms as well as the traditional education system are accelerating their efforts to close this gap.

Discrimination

Cultural barriers—the assumption among both men and women that business is an inappropriate career for women—are becoming obsolete as the equality of women in overall skills becomes more widely acknowledged. There are still formidable psychological and cultural obstacles to women, but they are disappearing almost as rapidly as they are understood.

In Conclusion

If it is true that women will become the proprietors of a much larger portion of this nation's small businesses, the social and economic ramifications may be profound. Women's talents, often discouraged in the past, may alter many traditional business practices, introduce now-unimagined products and services, and contribute to the nation's productivity in new ways.

As more women own businesses, the general economic status of women will be improved. With the improvement of their economic status, their political influence is also likely to increase, particularly on local and state levels.

CHAPTER TWELVE

Husbands and Wives as Entrepreneurs

A light wife doth make a heavy husband.
Shakespeare (*The Merchant of Venice*)

No definite count has been made, as far as we can tell, of business enterprises in the country that are owned and operated by husband and wife teams, but the number must be substantial indeed. Usually, these businesses are the traditional mom-and-pop variety, but some grow to significant dollar volume. Unfortunately, little has been written on the specific subject, since many couples entering business for the first time not only have many questions about business operation, but also about what this new arrangement will do for or to the marriage bond.

We first became interested in this specific field several years ago. When we searched the appropriate literature, we found nothing of any help. We then contacted practicing psychologists and professional marriage counselors and, to a person, they offered no assistance. One was even horrified, and suggested that joint business ownership was much too great a burden to place on a couple considering the already fragile situation of the marriage contract. We were surprised by the statement since a great number of businesses are run that way now.

Many married couples ponder over or even ask what will happen to the marriage bond after they accept the entrepreneurial role. We don't pretend to be marriage counselors, and we have absolutely no experience in this area, but we will propose this general theory: Entrepreneurship will probably strengthen a strong marriage bond, and will probably destroy a weak one—and the business with it. Notice the word *probably* was used twice. By "a strong marriage," we mean the usual definition, a marriage with love, mutual respect, cooperation, and good communication. By "weak," we do not necessarily mean "a marriage with conflict," however. Many experts have told us that, if there is conflict in the marriage, then there will be conflict in the business, and both, then, are doomed. But this isn't always true. Some years ago, management specialists came to the realization that the elimination of conflict in the work environment not only was impossible, it was not desirable; therefore, they began studying ways to manage it. The issue seems to come down to this: in the strong marriage, the couple has evolved a successful method for introducing and resolving conflict.

Four Interviews

Rather than discuss theory, we'd like to give the results of four interviews with husband-wife teams operating their own businesses.

CASE I: A Country Store

Married twelve years before going into business together
Two children
Business in second year

The first preventative step of any problem, this couple said, is to make sure there's adequate capitalization when buying the business. Money is already a sticky enough issue in marriage.

"The two of you gotta be good friends," they said. In fact, one of the main reasons they began to work together was precisely because they wanted to be together more.

They were asked, "How do you continue to smile at the same face over the cash register that you said good-night to?" She pointed out something very interesting: Rather than constant companionship being a problem, it helped them get along better. Simply because the situation demands more awareness of each other's personal needs, each is more careful and "pays more attention to tolerance."

The problem was periodically getting away from the store, rather than from each other. The husband did need to "get out with the boys" every so often, however. Just in case privacy might be a problem, however, they suggested separate vacations might be a good idea. He was about to take his first, while she had had a few independent buying trips. "But as far as I'm concerned," she said, "I can't get enough of his company."

The husband pointed out that they had already been married for a long time before they started the business. Their relationship was proven to be a strong one. "There can't be any surprises," he said. "You've got to know each other well." The problems such as who will do what in the store, who will be in charge of what, and so on fell into place fairly naturally as a result of their knowledge of each other's personalities. In retrospect, they said that they should have been a bit more explicit in the beginning when delegating responsibilities in "those gray areas."

Also, and very importantly, the proven success of their marriage meant they each felt secure enough of the other's love so that business arguments were not taken to mean "I don't love you." Blame-finding is poison. Business arguments, on the other hand, are a different matter. But each person must be able to recognize when a business disagreement is just that, a business problem, and not a marital problem.

This couple felt they managed to make this distinction for themselves quite well, but they did have to make it clear to the children that "just because Mom and Dad are raising their voices doesn't mean they don't still love each other." In general, they try to shut off business talk at meals for the sake of the children.

An important feature of their marriage, they felt, one crucial to the success of both the business and the marriage, was that they already had "open communication lines," as he put it. They already knew how to air gripes, speak up when one disagreed, as well as "give credit where credit is due." Even from a business point of view, this ease of communication is necessary, they pointed out. You can't hold back for fear of hurting your spouse's feelings, from resentment, or whatever.

They characterized their interrelationship as one of "equality." They said that the issue rested on the question, "Is just one or the other making the decisions?" Also, "Are both pulling their share of the load?" If one person handles most of the decisions, they felt that there would probably be problems of resentment, although they qualified this by saying perhaps some people worked well this way. "If something comes up where we both have to agree on a decision, and we can't reach some form of accord, we simply don't make a decision." A wife who has never had to make decisions before, even in the business of running a household or balancing the family's finances, is possibly being put into too challenging a position when entering into a business.

Balanced against the issue of decision-making is the division of labor. For this couple, this meant a complementarity of skills. Each is a specialist in certain arenas of the business. That is, each is in charge of the policies, decisions, responsibilities, and efficient functioning of those arenas. "It simply makes good business sense," he said. "It makes for consistency—you can't have one person say 'yes' to a salesman who returns the next day only to get a 'no' from the other." Even though the country store is a small business, its operation is sufficiently complicated and bulky to require a division of labor.

Specialization, however, does not preclude flexibility. "Besides," they said, "we simply know each other well enough to know how the other thinks." That is, neither has to constantly check with the other to find out if a decision made independently is okay.

In addition to their complementarity of skills, this couple pointed out a very interesting complementarity of personalities that "worked well businesswise." She characterized herself as the more "confident in the success of the business" of the two. While she is always anxious to expand, he is much more cautious. Both attitudes are necessary; she supplies the enthusiasm, while he applies the necessary brakes.

A sense of humor works well as a distancing device. Many a rough spot is smoothed over with the proper perspective. She gave the example of the community resistance to the idea of her being an equal member of the business partnership. By letting it get to her, she said, she'd waste too much energy.

Realistic expectations of actually how much work the business will take are needed ahead of time.

"*Everything* gets sacrificed for the store," they said. "Everything. The point is, it's all worth it."

Slow periods, such as periods after the big holidays, are bound to come up. They are necessary as breathing periods, but there is the problem of getting sidetracked. Each person has to be careful of how he or she gets the other back on the track without nagging.

Although they hadn't felt the need for it personally, they suggested that perhaps an advance evaluation of individual strengths and weaknesses would be useful. They had put their resumes together, however, and were amazed to find how well their skills fitted together. Personal weaknesses that an individual might have, weaknesses that could be a problem in the business, might well be compensated for by a division of labor.

CASE II: An Inn

Married eight years before going into business together
Two children
Business in second year

The greatest problem this couple saw in the business-marriage arrangement was the conflict over priorities. The two major areas of priorities are the business and the family, with the priorities of the individual making a third. Trouble is inevitable when one person sees the priorities differently than the other.

They called their expectations of how well they would be able to juggle the demands on their time in each of these areas as "idealistic." They had thought they would both be able to work full-time. Since very young children are involved, they had planned to hire a sitter while she worked. But the demands proved to be too great, so they decided that she would become a full-time mother all day until her evening hostess responsibilities.

The priorities of the individual are difficult to manage. In other words, with time being so precious, is the individual going to take his or her free time away from the business hours or the family hours?

She, especially, felt the strain of never being able to get off by herself away from the business and the children, especially since she didn't like the idea of having sitters bring up the children. A major characteristic of the inn/ restaurant business is that one's whole life is public. "You just can't let loose in public," she said. "There *is* no privacy."

The issue of not being able to "let loose" publicly led to that of conflict resolution. They said that the couple must make it clear to themselves when a conflict is a business one. But the problem is that, because the two owners are married, they are much more prone to take such conflicts personally. "Familiarity makes you less tactful, since you're not afraid of losing your spouse." This works the other way around as well; the conflict between married partners can increase because they're talking dollars and cents. Some way must be evolved, they said, for setting up rules that resolve these conflicts.

This couple saw the division of labor as a good solution to power struggles. Each of them has a defined area of responsibility. It is a good idea, they said, to set down on paper exactly whose responsibilities are whose in both the business and the family. If these areas are not defined, there is the possibility of one person becoming dominant, which leads to the resentment of the other. Unless the boundaries have been mapped out, the sphere of one person's dominance can spread and take over the others.

As he saw it, there are three sets of relationships involved: husband/wife; husband as employer in his specialty/wife as employee; and wife as employer in her specialty/husband as employee. "There must be some way of insulating these roles from the others," he said.

An understanding of the risks ahead is crucial before going into the business. They felt it was preferable to start out pessimistically. The couple must be realistic and ask of themselves, "Are we willing to accept X, Y, or Z failing?" But the greater the risks, the greater the rewards.

Most people feel that it is much easier to save face as someone who has been divorced than as someone who has failed in business.

They mentioned the issue of the inevitable metamorphosis of a so-called normal lifestyle. In a business/marriage setup, one can't expect to cling to a normal way of life. The couple must be adaptable both as individuals and as a married unit. This can be difficult, especially given people's usual resistance to change of any sort, he pointed out. Just as a business must be flexible enough to adapt to changing consumer demands, so the marriage must be flexible.

"It's expected as natural that one have a high degree of adaptability in business," he said, "but people are much less willing to be so in marriage." In business, outsiders immediately put pressure on a business person to change when needed. But, in marriage, there is no outsider to apply the required pressure. "No one teaches us how to adapt in marriage—which means, how to be married. But there are always plenty of experts in business." Marriage counselors are of limited usefulness because they don't deal specifically with the problems peculiar to couples in business together. They can't really help because their vision is too narrow. They deal with marriages with marital problems, not business problems.

CASE III: A Restaurant

> Married seventeen years before going into business together
> Five children
> Business going into fourth year

This couple felt that, because it is harder for a business to succeed in a rural area than, say, in the midst of Long Island, greater pressure is put on the business and the marriage. "Setting up the business always costs more than you expect it's going to, so just be prepared for it by having enough resources to live on for awhile until the business is really on its feet," he said.

Their family unit is very secure. The idea of a business failure breaking up the family was not even a remote possibility.

Even before going into business together, they had always been able to speak freely with one another. This feature undoubtedly helped their present set-up.

"It's important to involve the children in the business," they said. "You've got to know your family beforehand. Our kids have always worked on family projects, so that their working here just came naturally. If your kids haven't worked before with such family projects, they're not going to suddenly change. You can't have kids who are prima donnas, who won't pitch in." They had originally planned to live off the premises, but immediately found that this was impossible.

She had said, before moving to their present home, that she'd never want to work together with her husband "because he's so dictatorial," she said with a laugh. Their respective roles have been maintained pretty much as they were before. Although they do follow a division of labor, "he has the final say-so," and they find that such an arrangement works smoothly.

"It's definitely harder on the woman," he said. "Not only does she run the household as before, but she's working full-time in the business as well." He added, "And the man is going to be putting in more hours than he ever put into anything before." Neither of them, however, has any reservations about having gone into business for themselves. She spoke about having a better self-image now. "I'm dealing with people more; I'm more than 'just a housewife.' "

He now has a chance to do more fathering. He said that his relationship with his last child is wholly different from those with all the other children, who'd been young while he was away at work.

The restaurant is going into its fourth year, and things have been going quite smoothly and, routinely; great amounts of time are now freed up. The first year, though, was very trying. She had hated the whole idea because she was afraid that the business would permanently disrupt family life. "You've got to realize it'll only last a short time."

"You're going to be doing it all yourself," he said. They laughed when they mentioned that they had thought a staff could be hired to run the show.

"You must be tremendously desirous of doing it—tough; one-tracked; persistent; optimistic. . . . It's that total commitment that bridges you over."

He is the more enthusiastic of the two—"*too* optimistic," she said—while she is the more cautious, the source of "stability." A certain balance between optimism and pessimism has to be struck.

They feel the urge to get away from the business, but not from each other. Besides, the various tasks in the family and in the business lead them in separate directions for portions of the day. One of the prime motivations for their decision to go into such a venture as this was so that the family could be together more.

CASE IV: A Hardware Store

Married seven years before going into business together
Two children
Business in second year

"There tends to be either of two extremes when a couple goes into business together," he said. "Either everything runs *so* smoothly you start getting suspicious—'How come nothing's wrong?'—or the whole thing is full of problems. We simply have so few problems, many fewer than before we worked together."

They decided to work together and for themselves because they spent too little time together before. They both wanted to be together—"We *like* being in each other's company all the time." Thus, such problems as privacy from one another are simply not an issue for them. Besides, there are always "stolen moments" when they are separated, such as during the slow hours of the day when one will watch the store and the other leave for home.

"You've got to *like* each other as well as *love* each other."

It is crucial, they said, to be able to carry on business discussions without having any bitterness overflow into the marriage, and vice versa. But, in a sense, they said, the very fact that you are living and working together so closely means that you automatically get along better. In an ordinary set-up, in which he works away from home, one can just walk off in a huff after an argument, and "that's that." Grudges build up. But in this sort of situation, the air must be cleared immediately. "There is no escape," they said. As a result, the immediacy of the problem and its resolution is a very healthy thing.

They had had a problem with taking business disagreements too personally during their first year. "The important thing is how you deal with it. We call each other up on it, and then we can laugh about it."

They believe that their marriage had already been characterized by open communication. "But now, in addition to that, there's understanding, because you're both there. When the husband's been away all day and the two of them sit down at the dinner table together, trying to convey to each other exactly how they felt during whatever situations occurred during the course of the day, half the time is spent just describing the preliminaries. The understanding is never complete." There is now, as well, no more thinking What did I do wrong this time? You know exactly what you did wrong, because you're both right there when it happens.

Some of their first-year headaches were caused by the fact that, because he'd been so used to being an employer before, he tended to treat his wife as an employee. "It's the problem of the male ego, being the boss," he said. The husband must be able to accept more equality, he added. "At the bottom line," however, she tends to accede to him.

They had a very interesting definition of *responsibility:* for instance, she is responsible for the household on a particular day in that she is the one who makes the plans for dinner or the laundry, even if both of them actually carry out the plans. The responsible person is "the one who makes sure something gets done," though this might involve delegating the task to the other person. In this sense, they are both willing to work equally hard at both the household and the business, although they "divide the responsibilities" differently.

They practice a certain amount of division of labor, but are not rigid about it. Their reason for such a division is for the sake of efficiency; if not, certain tasks would never be completed. Some areas clearly belong to one or the other; he, for instance, always does the bookkeeping.

One must be prepared to see a side of one's spouse in the business setting that ordinarily one would never see. "Sometimes you like what you see, and sometimes you don't."

They felt that if there are already serious marital problems beforehand, these problems will not be solved by the partners going into business together; rather, they will probably be aggravated.

Successful Marriage/Business Relationships

The four sample interviews suggest the following tentative list of characteristics in a marriage/business relationship that appear to lead to success.

1. Identifying as a *we*
2. Open communication lines
3. Insulating business conflicts from the marital relationship
4. Strong individual egos: self-esteem
5. Division of labor
6. Adaptability

This list does not deal with those characteristics necessary to successful marriage alone; marriage counselors deal with this. Nor does it trespass on the area best dealt with in the practical side of business ownership.

Other generalizations might be proposed from these interviews. Not all, however, seem to be necessarily fundamental to the success of the business/marriage relationship. More interviews would have to be conducted. For instance, every couple expressed a strong desire to be together for great portions

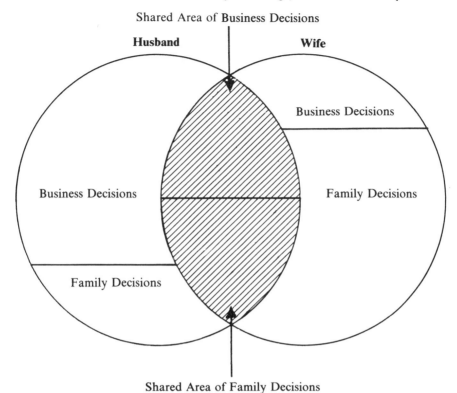

Figure 12.1 *A Successful Business/Marriage Relationship*

of time. Conceivably, if each of the partners needed a greater amount of privacy from the other, the couple could work out a situation in which these needs were satisfied, perhaps by using a division of labor.

It is obvious from the interviews that, although every couple used a division of labor, they all did so to differing degrees and for different reasons.

It is interesting that every couple had a different arrangement for designating which was in charge. There does not appear to be any general rule, except that, whatever the balance of power, both members are satisfied with it. When such an accord is not present, one of two destructive patterns occurs: either a harmful competition appears, a jockeying for power, or one member gradually assumes fewer and fewer of the responsibilities, leaving the other to pull the load. So, whether a couple has opted for equality or for one member being in charge, or whatever variations are possible, the important thing is that both the business and the marriage support the arrangement they both agree on implicitly and explicitly.

Figure 12.1 graphically shows a working premise for a successful business/marriage relationship. Note that each of the principal family members has unique areas of decision-making reserved for himself, for family decisions as well as business decisions. In general, the husband makes a few more of the business decisions on his own, whereas the wife makes a larger percentage of the family decisions. This relationship could certainly be reversed as long as both members feel comfortable with it. There is also a shared area of participation in which both members are involved.

When the two circles move closer together (that is, when they tend to overlap to a greater degree than is shown in Figure 12.1), there is too much overlap and not a sufficient amount of the division of labor either in the business area, the family area, or both. If the circles move so far apart that they do not intersect at all, there is no consultive decision-making, no check-and-balance system, and decisions tend to be made in a vacuum. This method of operation might represent a couple which fails to communicate often enough, and this failure to get together periodically will eventually spell doom for the business and may collapse the marriage as well.

Working as a couple in business where both of the partners are full-time with the venture means a true team-approach. There is no place for ego stroking and an "I'm right" attitude. Those games are fine for the large organizations since employees there have had practice in doing just that. In a small business, game playing and one-upping are wastes of time, drains on energy, and may be the precipitating forces that will end a potentially great partnership—in two respects.

CHAPTER THIRTEEN

The Future of Small Business

It is much less what we do than what we think, which fits us for the future.
Philip James Bailey

Employing crystal balls is always tricky. You can almost always be proved wrong, somehow, by someone. But we'll be bold enough to make a few predictions about some factors that will affect small business and the entrepreneur between now and the year 2000.

Money Matters

Inflation will not go away. Approximately every eight years, the dollar will lose about half its purchasing power. If you can build your business faster than the long-range projected inflation rate of 9 percent, then you will protect your financial future in a much sounder way than is ordinarily possible for someone collecting a salary. Also, if you can control your fixed expenses, such as rent, loan repayments, supplies, and taxes, your profit will increase at a greater rate than your sales.

The days of 5 percent money have vanished, never to be seen again. Interest rates might drop as low as 8–10 percent, but this will be temporary. The long-range rate will hover around 12 percent.

The United States dollar, however, will eventually stabilize against other world currencies.

Energy and Resources

One school of thought holds that there are no real shortages of energy sources, and that the planet can support a worldwide population of ten billion in comfort forever. At first this view seems that of a madman, though some of the evidence for it appears convincing. For the present, however, you should be prepared for shortages of one kind or another. Also, you should investigate alternative energy sources. Solar power is still very expensive, but a breakthrough is expected in the use of the solar cell, the small panel that collects the solar energy and converts it to electrical energy. Of course, in a rural setting, a wood stove is not only attractive and folksy, but it's also an energy source.

Your utility bills can be expected to continue to increase dramatically regardless of any effort on your part to conserve energy usage. As an example, during the years from 1973 to 1977, the total power output of Central Vermont Public Service (CVPS), an electrical utility serving most of that state and some of New Hampshire, remained constant, but revenues from the sale of electric power rose 55 percent.[1] Total consumption by retail customers actually declined slightly over the same period. While people struggled to conserve energy, utilities were granted multiple rate-increases by the state utility commissions whose sworn job it is to protect the consumer. Large shares of after-tax profit went to the benefit of the stockholders, not the power users. In 1973, CVPS actually paid out nearly twice its earnings to shareholders! [2] The future costs of telephone service will be increasing, too, especially for the smaller users. AT&T has lost its monopoly on long lines (an extremely profitable segment of the business), and, therefore, the little guy will be made to come up with the difference, or, as a phone company executive was once heard to say, go to the competition.

It is a reasonably safe assumption to say that we will solve our energy problems, but it won't be because of our government's efforts. Whether the source of future power will be the sun, the wind, the inside of the earth, matter conversion (fission/fusion), a combination of all of them, or an entirely new source, is impossible to predict. One thing is certain: there is a fixed and rapidly-diminishing amount of fossil fuel. Nature ain't makin' any more, at least quickly.

The Government

Small business will probably have to put up with increasing intervention by government—unfortunate but inevitable. Even with encroachment on the increase, however, the small businessman can expect to be a little safer from government interference than his brother in big business; unless, of course, government at all levels vastly increases its manpower. With over 13 million enterprises in the United States, mostly small, government regulating agencies, such as the IRS, FTC, SEC, FBI, and the others, will continue to devote most of their time and effort to the large corporations, especially multinationals. A quotation by Sam W. Tinsley, director of corporate technology at Union Carbide Corporation, seems to sum up the role of the government in business, large and small:

> Government officials keep asking us, "Where are the golden eggs?" while the other part of their apparatus is beating hell out of the goose that lays them.[3]

Education, Age, and Technology

The educational level of entrepreneurs has been steadily rising for years. Certainly, the majority of new small-business owners possesses at least some

[1] *Annual Report,* CVPS, 1977.
[2] Earnings were $.69 per share, whereas dividends paid were $1.28.
[3] "Vanishing Innovation," *Business Week,* July 3, 1978, p. 46.

college training. The trend toward more highly educated entrepreneurs will continue, and the age level of people taking the entrepreneurial plunge will drop. From the 1950s to the 1970s, the age of the average entrepreneur dropped from the low forties to the low thirties. In the last years of this century it will probably drop into the twenties, although there will be a new surge of owners in their fifties and sixties.

Sophisticated technology is already with us in small business, both in terms of hardware and software. More complex, less expensive electronic devices such as cash registers and computers will be seen in small business as well as the systems techniques formerly employed only by big business.

We are the last major country in the world to go metric. Although the transition will be a slow one, it is occurring now and will probably be complete in fifteen years. Out will go the pound, the foot, and the quart, and in will come the kilogram, the meter, and the liter. No more 12 inches to the foot, 3 feet to the yard, and 1,760 yards to the mile. Now it will be 100 *centi*meters to the meter and 1,000 meters to the *kilo*meter. Easy, huh?

Life-Style

With continued research in medical science, our life-style will change. We will live longer and be healthier while we do live, assuming, of course, that some nut doesn't plunge us into a world war or that we don't fill our atmosphere and our oceans with industrial waste. We predict that most types of cancer will be either curable or preventable by the year 2000. We further forecast that no cure will be found for the common cold during the lifespan of anyone reading this book. A secondary, and equally important, effect will be an increase in leisure time. The average work-week in the United States is now under forty hours, and this will slowly decline, to level out at about thirty-two hours per week by the end of the century. These two phenomena, a longer, better life coupled with more disposable time, will mean steady growth in nearly every product and service that occupies our free time—travel, eating out, garden implements, porno magazines, motorcycles, burglar tools, musical instruments, bedding, books, fishing rods, new types of television, boats, building materials (especially do-it-yourself), picture windows, casual wear, liquor, golf clubs, education, dogs, government forms, art supplies, sneakers, soft chairs, and an unimaginable array of electronic gewgaws and gimcracks, some useful, some not.

Assuring Future Success

Some experts seem to believe that small-business operation will become more and more difficult in the future because of a long list of problems and hurdles. This view can be supported if (1) the effects of the current problems in the world intensify, and (2) people do not change and adapt. Our particular view is that the chances of success for small businesses will actually increase in the years to come. There will be a change in the way that individuals accomplish goals in life and make choices about what they want in and for their lives. In addition, people who become entrepreneurs should guide their business lives according to a new gospel which springs from sound business policies as well as a deep awareness of the needs of their fellow humans.

The following seven areas of guidance have been provided by James Howard, the president of Country Business Services,[4] as general success characteristics of the *new* small business of the eighties and nineties.

Based on a CONCEPT

This concept is that of a delivery system put in place by an entrepreneur with vision and a real desire to serve. The concept comes partly from a personal recognition on the part of the business owner of what their true purpose is in life and becoming aligned with that purpose ("Right Livelihood"). The other side of the concept is a realization that business ownership, *per se,* is neither "right" nor "wrong." It is the conduct of the business, through the actions and the beliefs of the owner that may deem a business a worthy or faulty pursuit.

Oriented to the MARKETPLACE

Future products and services that are not provided to satisfy a need are doomed to ultimate failure. Period.

Supported by INFORMATION

As we mentioned in an earlier chapter, this is the age of information. Information comes from data and it becomes the base upon which to build knowledge and wisdom. Wisdom may be the only near-tangible objective in life that is a satisfactory end unto itself.

Managed According to a METHOD

The exact method used from one small business to another will vary just as one individual differs from another individual, but the successful enterprises and their owners will focus on the objectives (goals) that they want and allow the methods to develop that will bring about these goals.

[4] From a seminar entitled "The Right Way to Buy a Small Business."

Guided by *PERSONAL VALUES*

Good ventures have always become the lengthening shadows of those that own and operate them. Those of us who constantly study and observe small businesses now know that the real winners among them are built upon the ever-lasting foundation of personal integrity, conformance to the highest values of ethical conduct, trust, and love.

Directed by a *PLAN*

If you, the reader, have followed through this book carefully and have paid attention to what has been said, this statement is both anti-climatic and obvious. The idea of a business plan and what it does for a small business is so interwoven with the operation itself that we can say that the business, the business owner, and the business plan are ONE!

Committed to *QUALITY*

Many people have wearied of the cheap, the shoddy, and the impermanent. The large manufacturers of the world who run their businesses with "bottom line" philosophy (one of the most damaging and callous views ever proposed) will have to re-think their business principles in the next twenty-five years, or, like the dinosaurs before them, face extinction. If one element of business enterprise has been viewed as being relatively immune to economic cycles and consumer whimsy, it is the entire issue of lasting quality and enduring value.

The Entrepreneurial Revolution

"When I was growing up, you married early, found the right job, and were resolved to spend the rest of your life living morally." [5]

Years ago, many entrepreneurs were people with less than a high school education. College-trained young people headed for large companies, law firms, or investment houses. Success was the rolltop desk. Not so today. The new entrepreneurs (see Chapter 1) are highly educated, knowledgeable, and creative. Their venture is their love affair. They choose it; they're not forced into it. As we said earlier, the new entrepreneurs will, on the average, be younger than their predecessors, but we foresee a massive increase in senior entrepreneurs, those over fifty-five. There will also be more women in the ranks.

[5] Hugh Heffner, National Press Club Interview, January 12, 1979.

There will be an executive exodus in the next twenty years. It has already begun. Just how far it will go is anyone's guess. Certainly, there isn't room for a million middle- and top-management people to suddenly leave their jobs and get into their own businesses, but the number will be significant. This will be a healthy move for everyone, since most personnel experts who are looking at the executive market ten years from now claim that there will be a glut of managers due to nonmandatory retirement and the generation of the World War II babies reaching its midforties. In 1999, the children of the war babies will be in the twenty to thirty-five age-group, a new wave.

We are often asked whether or not big business is doomed. The word "doomed" in this context takes on an entire array of meanings, but consider the following quotation in a British journal which poses an interesting thesis:

> The world is probably drawing to the end of the era of big business corporations. These institutions were virtually created during 1875–1910. During 1975–2010 they may virtually disappear in their present form, and the interesting question is what will replace them.[6]

What will replace them, indeed? We believe that the corporate monoliths that have been built during the first eighty years of this century will change significantly over the last twenty years of the century so that with the passing of the millennium, smaller, more efficient business units will emerge. There will be exceptions, especially in the areas of basic commodity processing, but the general trend will be towards decentralization of both decision-making and enterprise.

As we reach the end of the twentieth century, both businesses and people will change. That change, which began in the early 1960s, is already underway. From the *me generation* of the 1970s, we will evolve into the *us generation* in the 1980s. The concern of many people will stretch beyond the limited sphere of self and will extend toward helping others. This effect alone may give even more impetus to the growing number of small-business owners. Probably by the late 1980s (certainly by 1990), one of our major interests will be man's spiritual nature.

We will close this chapter, and this book, with a statement made by Robert Schwartz.[7] Bob was asked by interviewer Sam Keen to comment on the following:

> Bob, we seem to be at a point in America today where there is a conflict between two separate cultures. The old culture says, "Money makes the world go round," and the new culture turns its back on that and says, "It's love that

[6] Norman Macrae, "The Coming Entrepreneurial Revolution: A Survey," *The Economist,* December 25, 1976, p. 41.
[7] "American Business Needs You," *New Age,* March 1976, p. 18.

makes the world go round." At least in the recent past, there has been a battle between these two cultures, and I see you as a person who bridges the gap between them. What do you feel will be the outcome of this battle?

Bob's answer was:

Actually, I sense a great potential kinship arising between the new culture and a new kind of entrepreneur that is developing out of the old form: an entrepreneur whose goals are to market ideas, services, and products at a scale more closely related to the love idea of the new generation than to the mechanical, money-oriented goals of the older generation. I see money becoming more of a lubricant to make things happen in the marketplace than a goal in itself, and I think the entrepreneur is in fact the ultimate agent for change in making the transition to a new way of living.

In case the reader missed the entire point of this book, and the philosophy of being in control of your chosen life's work as it relates to operating your own business, it is love first and financial well-being second.

The Apparent Contradiction:
Exxon Enterprises Inc.

It has been a theme of this book that the gulf between large and small business is so wide that there can be little real cooperation between the two. When the venture-capital market was running wide open, it attracted all kinds of funding sources that never should have entered the market. Banks, wealthy individuals, insurance companies, and large businesses all sought to find the next Digital Equipment Corporation that American Research and Development backed. There are very few success stories that can be retold today. The rush to get into venture financing with little or no thought given to the future viability caused most of these moneyed subsidiaries to lose their investments. A secondary problem was that the wrong kind of people were put in charge of the investment strategy and portfolio management. According to Harry Healer of First Capital Corporation of Boston, "Many venture capital operations were put under the control of 'bean counters' who would panic when they saw red ink."

The third problem, especially affecting large corporation backing the small venture, is a dichotomy between the methods and systems of the two types of operations. "They take too much time making decisions crucial to the young company and either fail to offer the kind of management assistance neophytes need or exert so much control that they quench the flame of enterprises." [1]

In the 1960s, Exxon Corporation joined this flock of investors to find the rough diamonds of the business world. If we knew what we know today about what was going to happen to the venture-capital market, we would not have bet that the world's largest corporation could have possibly succeeded backing entrepreneurial ventures. The timing was wrong (two recessions were ahead), everyone was in the market, and Exxon could have been estimated to fail in the area only because of size alone.

Exxon Enterprises lives on today. Its portfolio companies, with names like Qume, Vydek, Zilog, and Daystar are in business and growing. Companies like Eaton, Dow, Ford, and GE have either eliminated or severely redirected their venture operations, although several large firms seem to show interest in venturing again.

One very interesting observation made by Exxon Enterprises President Gene McBrayer may have helped Exxon understand just what it was getting into. "For every ten venture capital investments, we expect at least three to fail," he said. "Three will be what we call 'the living dead' and three might be marginally successful. If we're lucky, we will have one real, howling success. So, in oil industry parlance, there's a high dry-hole ratio." [2]

Exxon Enterprises has in-house start-up ventures as well as straight equity investments. Policy limits initial investments to $500,000 which generally results in an equity share of 10–40 percent.[3] In a personal and recent interview with Tom Castagna, financial and planning manager for Exxon Enterprises, some very interesting facts came to

[1] Bro Uttal, "Exxon Has Its Eye on More Than Oil," *Fortune,* April 1977, p. 167.
[2] Interview with Gene McBrayer, "Profile" (monthly publication for employees), vol. 16, no. 5, May 1977, p. 16.
[3] Michael Goodwin, "Exxon's Innovative Little Offshoot," *New York Times,* March 14, 1976.

light. Exxon spent time researching markets before it made any untoward moves regarding investment or new product introduction into any market. They then brought experts from those fields aboard to aid in either the internal development or the search for a venture in the field of choice. Once the venture is either selected or nurtured, one of the Exxon executives sits on the board and takes an active role in counseling the company. Like any good venture capitalist, Exxon supplies more than capital.

One other significant point came out of the interview. Exxon Enterprises appears to have copied some of the more effective methods of her operational parent. According to Castagna, Exxon has treated its affiliates somewhat as independent operating units. This is a real key to managing the portfolio companies within a venture-capital firm. It means guidance, but it also means having the guts to weather a rough financial storm when the product and the team is a sound one.

One question we leave unanswered. Can future entrepreneurs, even those not in high technology manufacturing, look to larger enterprises for financial succor?

SBA Field Offices

New England States

Boston, Massachusetts 02203
John Fitzgerald Kennedy Federal Bldg.

Holyoke, Massachusetts 01040
326 Appleton Street

Augusta, Maine 04330
Federal Building
U.S. Post Office
40 Western Avenue

Concord, New Hampshire 03301
55 Pleasant Street

Hartford, Connecticut 06103
Federal Office Building
450 Maine Street

Montpelier, Vermont 05601
Federal Building
2nd Floor
87 State Street

Providence, Rhode Island 02903
702 Smith Building
57 Eddy Street

Mid-Atlantic States

New York, New York 10007
Room 3930
26 Federal Plaza

Newark, New Jersey 07102
Room 1636
970 Broad Street

Syracuse, New York 13202
Hunter Plaza
Fayette & Salina Streets

Buffalo, New York 14203
Federal Building
Room 9
121 Ellicott Street

Albany, New York 12297
91 State Street

Philadelphia, Bala Cynwyd, PA 19004
1 Decker Square

Wilmington, Delaware 19801
U.S. Customs House
6th and King Streets

Baltimore, Maryland 21201
1113 Federal Building
Hopkins Plaza

Clarksburg, West Virginia 26301
Lowndes Bank Building
119 N. 3rd Street

Charleston, West Virginia 25301
3410 Courthouse & Federal Bldg.
500 Quarrier Street

Pittsburgh, Pennsylvania 15222
Federal Building
1000 Liberty Avenue

Richmond, Virginia 23240
Federal Building
400 N. 8th Street

Washington, D.C. 20417
1405 I Street, N.W.

Southern States

Atlanta, Georgia 30309
1401 Peachtree St., N.E.

Birmingham, Alabama 35205
908 S. 20th Street

Columbia, South Carolina 29201
1801 Assembly Street

Jackson, Mississippi 39205
245 E. Capitol Street

Gulfport, Mississippi 39501
2500 14th Street

Jacksonville, Florida 32202
Federal Office Building
400 W. Bay Street

Louisville, Kentucky 40202
Federal Office Building
600 Federal Place

Miami, Florida 33130
Federal Building
51 S.W. 1st Avenue

Tampa, Florida 33602
Federal Building
500 Zack Street

Nashville, Tennessee 37219
500 Union Street

Knoxville, Tennessee 37902
502 S. Gay Street

Memphis, Tennessee 38103
Federal Building
167 N. Main Street

Midwestern States

Chicago, Illinois 60604
Federal Office Building
219 S. Dearborn Street

Springfield, Illinois 62701
502 Monroe Street

Cleveland, Ohio 44199
1240 E. 9th Street

Columbus, Ohio 43215
50 W. Gay Street

Cincinnati, Ohio 45202
5026 Federal Building
550 Main Street

Detroit, Michigan 48226
1249 Washington Blvd.

Marquette, Michigan 49855
502 W. Kaye Avenue

Indianapolis, Indiana 46204
36 S. Pennsylvania Street

Madison, Wisconsin 53703
25 W. Main Street

Milwaukee, Wisconsin 53203
238 W. Wisconsin Avenue

Eau Claire, Wisconsin 54701
510 S. Barstow Street

Minneapolis, Minnesota 55402
816 2nd Avenue S.

Kansas City, Missouri 64106
911 Walnut Street

Des Moines, Iowa 50309
New Federal Building
210 Walnut Street

Omaha, Nebraska 68102
Federal Building
215 N. 17th Street

St. Louis, Missouri 63102
Federal Building
210 N. 12th Street

Wichita, Kansas 67202
120 S. Market Street

Southwestern States

Dallas, Texas 75202
1309 Main Street

Albuquerque, New Mexico 87101
Federal Building
500 Gold Avenue, S.W.

Los Cruces, New Mexico 88001
1015 El Paso Road

Houston, Texas 77002
808 Travis Street

Little Rock, Arkansas 72201
377 P. O. & Courthouse Building
600 W. Capitol Avenue

Lubbock, Texas 79408
Federal Office Building
1616 19th Street

El Paso, Texas 79901
109 N. Oregon Street

Marshall, Texas 75670
505 E. Travis Street

New Orleans, Louisiana 70130
124 Camp Street

Oklahoma City, Oklahoma 73102
30 N. Hudson Street

San Antonio, Texas 78205
301 Broadway
Lower Rio Grande Valley

Harlingen, Texas 78550
219 E. Jackson Street

Corpus Christi, Texas 78401
Post Office & Custom House Building

Mountain States

Denver, Colorado 80202
721 19th Street

Casper, Wyoming 82601
300 N. Center Street

Fargo, North Dakota 58102
653 2nd Avenue N.

Helena, Montana 59601
Power Block Building
Main & 6th Avenue

Salt Lake City, Utah 84111
2237 Federal Building
125 S. State Street

Sioux Falls, South Dakota 57102
National Bank Building
8th and Main Avenue

Far Western States

San Francisco, California 94102
Federal Building
450 Golden Gate Avenue

Fresno, California 93721
Federal Building
1130 O Street

Honolulu, Hawaii 96813
1149 Bethel Street

Los Angeles, California 90014
849 S. Broadway

Las Vegas, Nevada 89101
300 Las Vegas Blvd. S.

San Bernardino, California 92401
532 N. Mountain Avenue

Phoenix, Arizona 85004
122 N. Central Avenue

Tucson, Arizona 85701
Federal Building
155 E. Alamenda Street

San Diego, California 92101
110 W. C Street

Seattle, Washington 98104
506 2nd Avenue

Anchorage, Alaska 99501
1016 W. 6th Avenue

Fairbanks, Alaska 99701
510 3rd Avenue

Juneau, Alaska 99801
Federal Building

Boise, Idaho 83702
216 N. 8th Street

Portland, Oregon 97205
921 S. W. Washington Street

Spokane, Washington 99210
Courthouse Building
Room 651

Territories and Possessions

Hato Rey, Puerto Rico 00919
255 Ponce De Leon Avenue

Agana, Guam 96910
Ada Plaza Center Building

U.S. Department of Commerce Field Offices

Albuquerque, New Mexico 87101
U.S. Courthouse
Room 316
(505) 843-2386

Anchorage, Alaska 99501
412 Hill Building
632 6th Avenue
(907) 272-6531

Atlanta, Georgia 30303
75 Forsythe Street, N.W.
Room 400
(404) 526-6000

Baltimore, Maryland 21202
415 U.S. Customhouse
Gay and Lombard Streets
(301) 962-3560

Birmingham, Alabama 35205
Suite 200–201
908 S. 20th Street
(205) 325-3327

Boston, Massachusetts 02203
John F. Kennedy Federal Building
Room 510
(617) 223-2312

Buffalo, New York 14203
504 Federal Building
117 Ellicott Street
(716) 842-3208

Charleston, South Carolina 29403
Federal Building
Suite 631
334 Meeting Street
(803) 577-4171

Charleston, West Virginia 25301
3000 New Federal Office Building
500 Quarrier Street
(304) 343-6181, Ext. 375

Cheyenne, Wyoming 82001
6022 O'Mahoney Federal Center
2120 Capitol Avenue
(307) 778-2220, Ext. 2151

Chicago, Illinois 60604
New Federal Building
Room 1486
219 S. Dearborn Street
(312) 353-4400

Cincinnati, Ohio 45202
8028 Federal Office Building
550 Main Street
(513) 684-2944

Cleveland, Ohio 44114
666 Euclid Avenue
Room 600
(216) 522-4750

Dallas, Texas 95202
1100 Commerce Street
Room 3E7
(214) 749-3287

Denver, Colorado 80202
New Customhouse
Room 161
19th and Stout Streets
(303) 837-3246

Des Moines, Iowa 50309
609 Federal Building
210 Walnut Street
(515) 284-4222

Detroit, Michigan 48226
445 Federal Building
(313) 226-6088

Greensboro, North Carolina 27402
258 Federal Building
P.O. Box 1950
West Market Street
(919) 275-9111

Hartford, Connecticut 06103
Federal Office Building
Room 601-B
450 Main Street
(203) 244-3530

Honolulu, Hawaii 96813
286 Alexander Young Building
1015 Bishop Street
(808) 546-8694

Houston, Texas 77002
1017 Old Federal Building
201 Fannin Street
(713) 226-4231

Jacksonville, Florida 32202
P. O. Box 35087
400 West Bay Street
(904) 791-2796

Kansas City, Missouri 64106
601 E. 12th Street
Room 1840
(816) 374-3141

Los Angeles, California 90024
11201 Federal Building
11000 Wilshire Blvd.
(213) 824-7591

Memphis, Tennessee 38103
147 Jefferson Avenue
Room 710
(901) 534-3214

Miami, Florida 33130
City National Bank Building
Room 821
25 W. Flagler Street
(305) 350-5267

Milwaukee, Wisconsin 53203
Straus Building
238 W. Wisconsin Avenue
(414) 224-3473

Minneapolis, Minnesota 55401
306 Federal Building
110 S. 4th Street
(612) 725-2133

New Orleans, Louisiana 70130
909 Federal Office Building, S.
610 South Street
(504) 527-6546

New York, New York 10007
Federal Office Building
41st Floor
26 Federal Plaza
Foley Square
(212) 264-0634

Philadelphia, Pennsylvania 19107
Jefferson Building
1015 Chestnut Street
(215) 597-2850

Phoenix, Arizona 85025
5413 New Federal Building
230 N. 1st Avenue
(602) 261-3285

Pittsburgh, Pennsylvania 15222
431 Federal Building
1000 Liberty Avenue
(412) 644-2850

Portland, Oregon 97204
217 Old U.S. Courthouse
520 S. W. Morrison Street
(503) 226-3361

Reno, Nevada 89502
2028 Federal Building
300 Booth Street
(702) 784-5203

Richmond, Virginia 23240
2105 Federal Building
400 N. 8th Street
(703) 782-2246

St. Louis, Missouri 63103
2511 Federal Building
1520 Market Street
(314) 622-4243

Salt Lake City, Utah 84111
1201 Federal Building
125 S. State Street
(801) 524-5116

San Francisco, California 94102
Federal Building
Box 36013
450 Golden Gate Avenue
(415) 556-5864

San Juan, Puerto Rico 00902
Post Office Building
Room 100
(809) 723-4640

Savannah, Georgia 31402
235 U.S. Courthouse & Post Office
   Building
125–29 Bull Street
(912) 232-4321

Seattle, Washington 98104
8021 Federal Office Building
909 1st Avenue
(206) 442-5615

Values for Discounted Cash Flow Analysis (present rate of $1.00)

Effective Percentage Rates

Yr.	4%	5%	6%	7%	8%	9%	10%	11%	12%	14%	16%	18%
1	.9615	.9524	.9434	.9346	.9259	.9174	.9091	.9009	.8929	.8772	.8621	.8475
2	.9246	.9070	.8900	.8734	.8573	.8417	.8264	.8116	.7972	.7695	.7432	.7182
3	.8890	.8638	.8396	.8163	.7938	.7722	.7513	.7312	.7118	.6750	.6407	.6086
4	.8548	.8227	.7921	.7629	.7350	.7084	.6830	.6587	.6355	.5921	.5523	.5158
5	.8219	.7835	.7473	.7130	.6806	.6499	.6209	.5935	.5674	.5194	.4761	.4371
6	.7903	.7462	.7050	.6663	.6302	.5963	.5645	.5346	.5066	.4556	.4104	.3704
7	.7599	.7107	.6651	.6227	.5835	.5470	.5132	.4817	.4523	.3996	.3538	.3139
8	.7307	.6768	.6274	.5820	.5403	.5019	.4665	.4339	.4039	.3506	.3050	.2660
9	.7026	.6446	.5919	.5439	.5002	.4604	.4241	.3909	.3606	.3075	.2630	.2255
10	.6756	.6139	.5584	.5083	.4632	.4224	.3855	.3522	.3220	.2696	.2267	.1911
11	.6496	.5847	.5268	.4751	.4289	.3875	.3505	.3173	.2875	.2366	.1954	.1619
12	.6246	.5568	.4970	.4440	.3971	.3555	.3186	.2858	.2567	.2076	.1685	.1372
13	.6006	.5303	.4688	.4150	.3677	.3262	.2897	.2575	.2292	.1821	.1452	.1163
14	.5775	.5051	.4423	.3878	.3405	.2992	.2633	.2320	.2046	.1597	.1252	.0985
15	.5553	.4810	.4173	.3624	.3152	.2745	.2394	.2090	.1827	.1401	.1079	.0835
16	.5339	.4581	.3936	.3387	.2919	.2519	.2176	.1883	.1631	.1229	.0930	.0708
17	.5134	.4363	.3714	.3166	.2703	.2311	.1978	.1696	.1456	.1078	.0802	.0600
18	.4936	.4155	.3503	.2959	.2502	.2120	.1799	.1528	.1300	.0946	.0691	.0508
19	.4746	.3957	.3305	.2765	.2317	.1945	.1635	.1377	.1161	.0829	.0596	.0431
20	.4564	.3769	.3118	.2584	.2145	.1784	.1486	.1240	.1037	.0728	.0514	.0365
21	.4388	.3589	.2942	.2415	.1987	.1637	.1351	.1117	.0926	.0638	.0443	.0309
22	.4220	.3418	.2775	.2257	.1839	.1502	.1228	.1007	.0826	.0560	.0382	.0262
23	.4057	.3256	.2618	.2109	.1703	.1378	.1117	.0907	.0738	.0491	.0329	.0222
24	.3901	.3101	.2470	.1971	.1577	.1264	.1015	.0817	.0659	.0431	.0284	.0188
25	.3751	.2953	.2330	.1842	.1460	.1160	.0923	.0736	.0588	.0378	.0245	.0160

Sources of Information for Specific Businesses

Many sources of information are available to the entrepreneur. Here are five different sources that make reports available to persons desiring them: (1) the Small Business Administration (SBA), (2) the United States Department of Commerce (USDC), (3) The Bank of America, (4) International Entrepreneurs Association (IEA), and (5) miscellaneous references.

Small Business Administration (SBA)

The Small Business Administration (SBA) has two types of reports available: Small Business Biographies (SBB's), which are free, and the Starting and Managing Series (SMS), which are available for a nominal charge (about one dollar). Consult your local SBA office (shown in Appendix B) and be certain to ask for SBA Rubs 115A (free material) and 115B (for-sale material).

SBB's

1. Handcrafts and Home Business, SBB No. 1
2. The Nursery Business, SBB No. 14
3. Restaurants and Catering, SBB No. 17
4. Variety Stores, SBB No. 21
5. Laundry and Dry Cleaning, SBB No. 22
6. Food Stores, SBB No. 24
7. Drugstores, SBB No. 33
8. Hardware Retailing, SBB No. 35
9. Jewelry Retailing, SBB No. 36
10. Mobile Homes and Parks, SBB No. 41
11. Bookstores, SBB No. 42
12. Plumbing, Heating, and Air Conditioning Shop, SBB No. 43
13. Job Printing Shop, SBB No. 44
14. Men's and Boys' Wear Stores, SBB No. 45
15. Woodworking Shops, SBB No. 46
16. Soft-Frozen Dessert Stands, SBB No. 47
17. Furniture Retailing, SBB No. 48
18. Apparel and Accessories for Women, Misses, and Children, SBB No. 50
19. Trucking and Cartage, SBB No. 51
20. Hobby Shops, SBB No. 53
21. Interior Decorating, SBB No. 54
22. Painting and Wall Decorating, SBB No. 60
23. Sporting Goods, SBB No. 62
24. Photographic Dealers and Studios, SBB No. 64
25. Real Estate Business, SBB No. 65
26. Motels, SBB No. 66
27. Discount Retailing, SBB No. 68

28. Machine Shop—Job Type, SBB No. 69
29. Retail Florist, SBB No. 74
30. Pet Shops, SBB No. 76

SMS (Each title below is prefaced by "Starting and Managing a . . .")

1. Service Station, SMS No. 3
2. Small Dry Cleaning Business, SMS No. 12
3. Retail Flower Shop, SMS No. 18
4. Pet Shop, SMS No. 19
5. Small Retail Music Store, SMS No. 20
6. Small Retail Jewelry Store, SMS No. 21
7. Employment Agency, SMS No. 22
8. Small Drive-In Restaurant, SMS No. 23
9. Small Shoe Store, SMS No. 24

United States Department of Commerce (USDC)

The United States Department of Commerce (USDC) publishes a series of pamphlets called *Urban Business Profiles* (UBP's). These are available either at local field offices listed in appendix C or from The Superintendent of Documents, U.S. Government Printing Office, Washington, DC 20605. The cost is less than one dollar.

UBP's

1. Real Estate Brokerage, UBP No. 74T
2. Furniture Stores, UBP No. 75T
3. Contract Construction, UBP No. 76T
4. Beauty Shops, UBP No. 77T
5. Industrial Launderers and Linen Supply, UBP No. 78T
6. Machine Shop Job Work, UBP No. 79T
7. Catering, UBP No. 80T
8. Children and Infant's Wear, UBP No. 81T
9. Bowling Alleys, UBP No. 85T
10. Dry Cleaning, UBP No. 86T
11. Contract Dress Manufacturing, UBP No. 87T
12. Building Service Contracting, UBP No. 88T
13. Photographic Studios, UBP No. 89T
14. Convenience Stores, UBP No. 90T
15. Pet Shops, UBP No. 91T

The Bank of America

The Bank of America (Box 37000, San Francisco, CA 94137) also produces a series of low-cost reports (two to three dollars) on small businesses called *The Small Business Reporter* (SBR).

SBR:	Title	Vol.	No.
1.	Apparel Stores	12	2
2.	Auto Supply Stores	13	5
3.	Bars and Cocktail Lounges	11	9

4.	Bookstores	11	6
5.	Building Contractors	14	3
6.	Building Maintenance	12	3
7.	Camera Shop	12	7
8.	Handcrafts	10	8
9.	Toy and Hobby Stores	12	10
10.	Gift Store	13	4
11.	Hairgrooming/Beauty Shop	12	9
12.	Health Food Store	11	2
13.	Home Furnishings	11	1
14.	Liquor Store	11	4
15.	Mail Order Enterprises	11	7
16.	Mobile Home Parks	13	6
17.	Plant Shops	12	4
18.	Property Management	13	10
19.	Consumer Electronics Store	13	3
20.	Restaurants and Food Services	12	8
21.	Sewing and Needlecraft	11	10
22.	Shoe Stores	12	5
23.	Dry Cleaning Service	13	2

International Entrepreneurs Association (IEA)

The International Entrepreneurs Association, Inc. (IEA) (631 Wilshire Blvd., Santa Monica, CA 99401), headed by Chase Revell, has a series of reports relatively expensive by the standards of the first three categories; prices can run as high as thirty-five dollars per report. Some of these documents are well worth the price; others are not. The number following the title represents IEA's Report Number.

	Title	*Report No.*
1.	Plant Shop	2
2.	Pet Shop	7
3.	Furniture Store	11
4.	Instant Print Shop	13
5.	Mail Order	15
6.	Cheese Shop	19
7.	Bicycle Shop	22
8.	Liquor Store	24
9.	Equipment Rental	28
10.	Antiques Are Hot	32
11.	Pet Hotel	33
12.	Janitorial Service	34
13.	Dry Cleaners	37
14.	Photocopy Shop	38
15.	Miniware Houses	42
16.	T-Shirt Shop	43

Robert Morris Associates

As mentioned in Chapter 7, Robert Morris Associates (RMA) (Philadelphia Bank Building, Philadelphia, PA 19107) publishes an annual compilation title *RMA Annual Statement Studies*, which gives comparative ratios and other data on a great number of construction, manufacturing, wholesaling, retailing, and service businesses. The book is available from RMA, and the cost—about $20—is a bargain for any entrepreneur (see Figure E.1).

Miscellaneous References

Besides the four organizations listed, many authors who have become experts in a particular field (and who have, therefore, usually made a significant amount of money) will write a book on what they've learned. The usual pattern is that they make even more money from the book and leave you with very little usable material, since their success was due primarily to their own drive, personality, and risk toleration (which you might not possess). Coupled with these qualities was an unusual combination of intelligent market-planning and insight (Ford's Mustang in 1965) as well as timing, which some people like to call luck.

To catalog all the books that have been written on specific businesses would be a nearly impossible task. Here are some places to go for help:

Libraries. If you have access to the New York Public Library or the library of any large city, you're really in luck. Their card catalogs, by subject heading, will get you going. If your library is small, it may have a correspondent relationship with a larger one. Don't forget college and university libraries as well.

Trade Associations and Magazines. Most libraries will carry a copy of one of the three reference volumes that list all the trade and professional associations in the United States. Write to the one that most closely represents your business. Another reference that most libraries have also lists all United States periodicals. Write to the managing editor of the periodical. (You may also want to subscribe to and advertise in a particular publication.)

Bookstores. Most knowledgeable bookstore owners, being good entrepreneurs, cannot only help you with references (with a copy of *Books in Print*), they can also order the book for you.

RETAILERS - RESTAURANTS   253
SIC# 5812

Current Data						Comparative Historical Data			
338(6/30-9/30/78)		361(10/1/78-3/31/79)				6/30/76 3/31/77	6/30/77 3/31/78	6/30/78 3/31/79	
0-250M 237	250M-1MM 264	1-10MM 161	10-50MM 37	ALL 699	ASSET SIZE / NUMBER OF STATEMENTS	ALL 561	ALL 624	ALL 699	
%	%	%	%	%	**ASSETS**	%	%	%	
12.4	10.6	9.2	9.5	10.8	Cash & Equivalents	10.9	11.4	10.8	
4.2	5.1	4.4	5.7	4.7	Accts. & Notes Rec. - Trade(net)	5.1	5.2	4.7	
8.4	5.4	7.0	6.6	6.9	Inventory	7.3	7.0	6.9	
2.6	2.0	2.8	1.6	2.4	All Other Current	2.4	2.1	2.4	
27.6	23.0	23.4	23.5	24.7	Total Current	25.7	25.8	24.7	
56.0	57.9	61.2	60.2	58.2	Fixed Assets (net)	58.3	57.0	58.2	
4.8	5.2	3.1	3.3	4.5	Intangibles (net)	4.4	4.1	4.5	
11.5	13.9	12.3	13.0	12.7	All Other Non-Current	11.6	13.1	12.7	
100.0	100.0	100.0	100.0	100.0	Total	100.0	100.0	100.0	
					LIABILITIES				
9.8	4.9	3.1	1.4	6.0	Notes Payable-Short Term	5.0	5.7	6.0	
6.0	5.9	6.3	3.6	5.9	Cur. Mat.-L/T/D	5.8	5.8	5.9	
13.9	11.4	12.4	9.9	12.4	Accts. & Notes Payable - Trade	12.8	12.7	12.4	
8.4	7.8	7.9	5.4	7.9	Accrued Expenses	7.7	8.1	7.9	
7.4	4.3	2.2	2.9	4.8	All Other Current	4.6	4.1	4.8	
45.6	34.3	32.0	23.2	37.0	Total Current	36.0	36.5	37.0	
33.9	33.0	35.3	31.8	33.7	Long Term Debt	29.2	30.0	33.7	
3.2	1.3	2.9	4.7	2.5	All Other Non-Current	2.1	2.7	2.5	
17.4	31.4	29.9	40.4	26.8	Net Worth	32.7	30.9	26.8	
100.0	100.0	100.0	100.0	100.0	Total Liabilities & Net Worth	100.0	100.0	100.0	
					INCOME DATA				
100.0	100.0	100.0	100.0	100.0	Net Sales	100.0	100.0	100.0	
46.9	44.6	51.0	51.9	47.3	Cost Of Sales	47.3	47.4	47.3	
53.1	55.4	49.0	48.1	52.7	Gross Profit	52.7	52.6	52.7	
48.8	50.3	44.6	40.3	48.0	Operating Expenses	48.3	46.9	48.0	
4.3	5.1	4.3	7.8	4.8	Operating Profit	4.4	5.6	4.8	
2.0	1.7	1.6	1.3	1.8	All Other Expenses (net)	.3	2.0	1.8	
2.3	3.3	2.7	6.5	3.0	Profit Before Taxes	4.2	3.6	3.0	
					RATIOS				
1.1	1.1	1.0	1.3	1.1	Current	1.2	1.2	1.1	
.7	.6	.7	1.0	.7		.7	.7	.7	
.3	.3	.4	.8	.4		.4	.4	.4	
7	8	6	9	7	Quick	8	8	7	
(234) 3	4	4	7	(696) 4		(553) 4	(619) 4	(696) 4	
.1	.2	.2	.4	.2		.2	.2	.2	
0 INF	0 INF	1 549.1	3 116.9	0 INF	Sales/Receivables	0 INF	0 INF	0 INF	
0 INF	3 141.2	3 135.6	6 65.0	2 209.8		2 186.3	2 207.8	2 209.8	
4 83.3	8 45.1	7 48.9	15 24.8	7 52.6		7 51.1	7 54.0	7 52.6	
9 42.4	8 43.8	9 39.4	11 33.7	9 42.3	Cost of Sales/Inventory	9 40.5	9 41.8	9 42.3	
14 26.8	13 27.9	14 26.3	23 15.7	14 26.4		15 23.9	14 25.5	14 26.4	
23 15.7	22 16.3	27 13.6	35 10.3	24 15.1		25 14.6	23 15.8	24 15.1	
114.3	148.4	±INF	28.4	118.0	Sales/Working Capital	74.7	62.7	118.0	
-35.3	-26.9	-23.5	455.2	-30.8		-34.1	-33.1	-30.8	
-11.2	-10.4	-12.2	-29.3	-11.5		-11.9	-11.3	-11.5	
8.7	7.7	5.5	8.2	7.3	EBIT/Interest	10.4	8.0	7.3	
(195) 3.3 (230)	3.2 (135)	2.4 (35)	4.4 (595)	3.2		(450) 4.2 (502)	3.3 (595)	3.2	
.9	1.2	1.4	2.9	1.3		1.9	1.4	1.3	
4.1	3.7	3.2	12.1	3.7	Cash Flow/Cur. Mat. L/T/D	4.3	3.6	3.7	
(68) 1.9 (132)	2.1 (120)	2.0 (30)	2.6 (350)	2.1		(275) 2.2 (298)	1.9 (350)	2.1	
.8	1.2	1.1	1.6	1.1		1.2	1.1	1.1	
1.1	1.1	1.2	1.2	1.1	Fixed/Worth	1.1	1.1	1.1	
2.4	2.1	2.1	1.6	2.1		2.0	2.0	2.1	
-19.9	7.8	5.2	2.7	9.0		5.6	6.1	9.0	
1.1	1.1	1.3	1.0	1.1	Debt/Worth	9	1.0	1.1	
3.5	2.5	2.4	1.5	2.6		2.2	2.3	2.6	
-32.8	10.8	6.1	3.3	12.3		7.5	7.4	12.3	
101.2	67.3	49.1	43.7	64.2	% Profit Before Taxes/Tangible Net Worth	65.6	65.6	64.2	
(171) 40.7 (221)	31.3 (149)	27.6 (36)	32.6 (577)	33.0		(482) 34.3 (540)	33.3 (577)	33.0	
9.5	11.2	12.7	15.6	12.0		12.9	11.9	12.0	
23.8	16.5	14.1	15.7	16.8	% Profit Before Taxes/Total Assets	20.0	17.6	16.8	
9.6	7.6	7.0	12.3	7.9		10.1	8.2	7.9	
-.2	1.5	2.0	6.0	1.5		3.5	1.8	1.5	
14.2	7.5	6.2	3.9	9.1	Sales/Net Fixed Assets	10.0	9.9	9.1	
7.7	4.4	3.8	2.7	4.6		4.6	4.8	4.6	
3.3	2.6	2.6	2.1	2.6		2.7	2.8	2.6	
5.7	3.5	3.3	2.2	3.9	Sales/Total Assets	4.0	4.0	3.9	
3.8	2.6	2.4	1.7	2.7		2.7	2.7	2.7	
2.3	1.7	1.8	1.4	1.8		1.9	1.8	1.8	
1.6	2.2	2.2	2.2	2.0	% Depr. Dep. Amort./Sales	1.8	2.0	2.0	
(219) 2.5 (249)	3.0 (151)	3.0 (36)	3.1 (655)	2.9		(519) 2.8 (582)	2.8 (655)	2.9	
4.1	4.2	3.8	4.2	4.1		3.8	3.9	4.1	
3.1	2.9	2.2	2.0	2.9	% Lease & Rental Exp/Sales	2.4	2.5	2.9	
(179) 5.2 (182)	5.1 (95)	4.1 (19)	3.7 (475)	4.9		(390) 4.9 (402)	4.7 (475)	4.9	
8.1	7.2	6.3	5.2	7.1		7.2	6.8	7.1	
3.5	3.3	1.9		3.1	% Officers' Comp/Sales	3.2	3.0	3.1	
(129) 5.8 (131)	5.1 (39)	3.3		(301) 4.9		(270) 5.2 (287)	4.9 (301)	4.9	
9.3	7.8	4.5		8.1		8.3	7.7	8.1	
128428M	375037M	1369112M	1741231M	3611808M	Net Sales ($)	3039675M	3329711M	3611808M	
32083M	138493M	532541M	951805M	1654922M	Total Assets ($)	1371108M	1538797M	1654922M	

©Robert Morris Associates 1979   M = $thousand   MM = $million
See Pages 1 through 10 for Explanation of Ratios and Data

Figure E.1 *A Sample Page from* RMA Annual Statement Studies, *Robert Morris Associates*

Dun & Bradstreet.   A rather complete bibliography is published by Dun & Bradstreet called *Management Source Publications for Small Business.* The booklet is free in single quantities. Write to

Dun & Bradstreet Publications
P.O. Box 1770
Church St. Station
New York, NY 10008

Final Exam

Most books on small business contain a checklist for beginning the entrepreneurial journey, but most do not require the reader to answer questions in anything other than an
affirmative or a positive way. Our final exam is simply a series of thought-provokers
which, though not totally inclusive, are meant to cause the reader to think through some
significant areas of business before starting.

I.   Based upon all that you have read, especially Chapter 1, can you honestly say
     that you possess enough of the requisite characteristics to be a successful entre-
     preneur?

                    Yes _____   No _____

   A.   If you answered no, quietly close this book, open a beer, and recompute
        your pension benefits. If you answered yes, what makes you think you're
        so good? List specific areas of strength.

        1.

        2.

        3.

        4.

        5.

        6.

        7.

        8.

   B.   Now list items which need improvement, beginning with the weakest
        areas first.

        Where I need help   *What I need to improve*
        1.   1.

        2.   2.

        3.   3.

        4.   4.

5.	5.
6.	6.
7.	7.
8.	8.

II. What are the *real* reasons for your wanting to become an entrepreneur?

III. Reviewing your personal balance sheet in Chapter 7, what is the realistic maximum amount of money that you can invest in the business?

$ _____

IV. Do you plan to start a business or to buy a going concern?

A. Start _____   B. Buy _____

A. In starting or buying a business, how will you allocate beginning cash?

1.

2.

3.

4.

5.

6.

B. To buy a business, what do most banks require as a minimum down payment?

1. _____%
2. Express item 1 in decimal form: 0._____

3. Divide the decimal value in item 2 *into* your investment from III.

$$\frac{\$ _____}{0._____} = \$ \_\_\_$$

Your answer is the purchase price.

4. Now subtract the investment from the purchase price just determined:

$$\text{\$} \qquad - \text{\$} \qquad = \text{\$}$$

The answer is what you'll have to borrow.

5. Call a bank commercial officer and get the going loan percentage rate for businesses:

_____%

and ask him or her to calculate the monthly payment on the amount in (4) at the above rate for

5 years $_____

10 years $_____

15 years $_____

20 years $_____

V. Beyond your own funds and a bank, what other sources of capital are available to you?

Source	Amount
A.	$
B.	$
C.	$
D.	$
E.	$
F.	$

VI. If you plan to use partners, what strengths do they bring to the venture?

Partner A:

Partner B:

Partner C:

Do these strengths seem complementary or do they overlap somewhat?

VII. How much do you (and your family) need to live on per year? Note: This figure should be "tight-belt" financing.

$ _____

VIII. According to either research data or estimates from other entrepreneurs, what rate of return (profit) can this business be expected to generate?

_____%

IX. Express the value in VIII decimally:

0._____

X. Divide the answer to item VII by the answer to item IX.

$$\frac{\$ \rule{3cm}{0.4pt}}{0.\rule{1.5cm}{0.4pt}} = \$$$

Your answer is the approximate annual sales required to generate your living expenses. Can your business do this?

Yes _____   No _____

If the answer is no, you'd better do some more calculations or wait until you have a larger down payment to sponsor a larger firm.

XI. What positive factors will affect your future sales—i.e., what are several items that would increase your revenue?

A.

B.

C.

D.

E.

F.

XII. What could cause sales to decline?

A.

B.

C.

D.

E.

F.

XIII.   What primary customer group(s) will you serve? (You may check more than one.)
    A.   Industrial
        1.   Durable goods
        2.   Nondurable goods
        3.   Services
    B.   Governmental
        1.   Federal
        2.   State
        3.   Local
    C.   Foreign
    D.   Consumer
        1.   Low income
        2.   Middle income
        3.   High income
    E.   Other _____

XIV.   What makes you think that the customer base that you have selected will accept another business like yours?

XV.   How will you sell your products and services?
    A.   Me
    B.   My family
    C.   Salespersons (employees)
    D.   Representatives or agents
    E.   Distributors
    F.   Mail
    G.   Other _____

XVI.   What advertising media will you use and with what frequency (daily, weekly, once only)?

	Media	*Frequency*
A. Radio		
B. TV		

C. Newspapers
D. Magazines, Trade Publications
E. Shows
F. Yellow Pages
G. Billboards
H. Mail
I. Other_____

XVII. What are the perceived strengths and weaknesses of your competition?

Strengths	*Weaknesses*
A.	A.
B.	B.
C.	C.
D.	D.
E.	E.
F.	F.

XVIII. Now make a list of potential new products and services that you might add over the next few years:

A.

B.

C.

D.

E.

F.

G.

H.

XIX. Whom will you use for outside help?

A. Bank and banker:

B. Attorney and firm:

    C.   Accountant:

    D.   Consultant:

    E.   Ad Agency:

    F.   Others:

XX. What are some of the good and bad points about your location?

Good	Bad
A.	A.
B.	B.
C.	C.
D.	D.
E.	E.

XXI. What major assets will you have to buy or lease to begin operations?

    A.

    B.

    C.

    D.

    E.

    F.

    G.

    H.

    I.

    J.

XXII. What taxes will you be paying?
    A.   Income
    B.   Sales and use
    C.   Property

      D.   FICA
      E.   Self-employment
      F.   Unemployment
      G.   Workman's Compensation
      H.   Special license fees
      I.   Other _____

XXIII. What types of insurance will you carry?
      A.   Life
      B.   Health and accident
      C.   Liability (premises)
      D.   Liability (product)
      E.   Fire and theft
      F.   Extended coverage (vandalism)
      G.   Flood
      H.   Business continuation
      I.   Key person
      J.   Bad check and fraud
      K.   Other _____

XXIV. For the next five business years, what major goals have you set for yourself, either personally, professionally, or both?

      A.   Year 1.

      B.   Year 2.

      C.   Year 3.

      D.   Year 4.

      E.   Year 5.

XXV. Do you *want* to own and operate your own venture?

            ____Yes   ____No

Bibliography

ALBERT, KENNETH J. *How To Pick the Right Small Business Opportunity.* NY: McGraw-Hill, 1977.

BANGS, D. H. & OSGOOD, W. R. *Business Planning Guide.* NH: Upstart, 1978.

BATY, GORDON. *Entrepreneurship—Playing to Win.* VA: Reston Publishing, 1974.

BAUMBACK, C. & MANCUSO, J. R. *Entrepreneurship and Venture Management.* NJ: Prentice-Hall, 1975.

BAUMBACK & KELLY. *How To Organize and Operate a Small Business,* 6th ed. NJ: Prentice-Hall, 1979.

BROOM, H. & LONGENECKER, J. *Small Business Management.* OH: South-Western, 1975.

BUSKIRK, R. & VAUGHN, P. *Managing New Enterprises.* MN: West Publishing, 1976.

DAMCO, LEON A. *Beyond Survival.* OH: University Press, 1977.

DIBLE, DONALD. *Up Your Own Organization.* CA: Entrepreneur Press, 1974.

DIBLE, DONALD M., ed. *Winning the Money Game.* CA: Entrepreneur Press, 1975.

GREENE, GARDINER G. *How To Start and Manage Your Own Business.* NY: McGraw-Hill, 1975.

HOSMER, COOPER & VESPER. *The Entrepreneurial Function.* NJ: Prentice-Hall, 1977.

JOHNSTON, J. P. K. *Success in a Small Business Is a Laughing Matter.* NC: Moore Publishing, 1979.

KOBERG, D. & BAGNALL, J. *The Universal Traveler.* CA: William Kaufman Inc., 1978.

LILES, PATRICK. *New Business Ventures and the Entrepreneur.* IL: Irwin, 1974.

MANCUSO, JOSEPH R. *Fun & Guts—The Entrepreneur's Philosophy.* MA: The Entrepreneur's Club, Unltd., 1973.

MANCUSO, JOSEPH R. *How To Start, Finance, and Manage Your Own Business.* NJ: Prentice-Hall, 1978.

MANCUSO, JOSEPH, R. *Sources of Help for Entrepreneurs.* MA: Center For Entrepreneurial Management, 1979.

METCALF, BUNN, & STIGELMAN. *How to Make Money in Your Own Small Business.* CA: Entrepreneur Press, 1977.

RAGAN, R. & ZWICK, J. *Fundamentals of Recordkeeping and Finance for the Small Business.* CA: Entrepreneur Press, 1978.

STEGALL, STEINMETZ, & KLINE. *Managing the Small Business.* IL: Irwin, 1976.

STEINHOFF, DAN. *Small Business Management Fundamentals.* BNY: McGraw-Hill, 1978.

SULLIVAN, DANIEL. *Small Business Management: A Practical Approach.* IA: Brown Co., 1977.

TATE, MEGGINSON, SCOTT & TRUEBLOOD. *Successful Small Business Management.* TX: Business Publications, 1978.

TIMMONS, SMOLLEN & DINGEE. *New Venture Creation.* IL: Irwin, 1977.

WALKER, ERNEST. *The Dynamic Small Firm.* TX: The Austin Press, 1975.

WHITE, RICHARD M., JR. *The Entrepreneur's Manual.* PA: Chilton, 1977.

Formation of Partnership

Partnership agreements are often necessary as supporting documents for business plans (see Chapter 4). The following is a sample agreement establishing a partnership in the State of New York. For any legal peculiarities affecting the partnerships in his own state, the entrepreneur should check with his lawyer, and/or the office of his state's Secretary of State.

ARTICLES OF PARTNERSHIP

This contract made and entered into on the 1st day of March 19XX by and between Partner A and Partner B.

Witnesseth that the said parties have from this day formed a partnership for the purpose of engaging in and conducting a Marina sales and service business and the doing of all things necessary and incident thereto, under the following stipulations which are made part of this contract.

1. Said partners shall commence on the 2nd day of March 19XX and continue from and after said date for a period of ten years at the pleasure of said partners; and shall be otherwise terminated by the death, bankruptcy, insolvency, or disability of any of said partners thereto, or under the provisions under such act hereinafter set forth.

2. The business shall be conducted under the firm name of B & T Marina at 100 East Road, Penn Yan, New York 14927.

3. The investments are as follows, Partner A and Partner B each agree to contribute to the capital of the said partnership the sum of $20,000. Which shall be paid on the date of the execution of this agreement, and by the execution thereof by said partners the receipt of the same is hereby acknowledged.

4. All profits and losses arising from said business shall be shared equally.

5. Each of said partners shall devote his entire time, skills, labor, and experience to advancing and rendering profitable the interests and business of said partnership,

-1-

and neither partner shall engage in any other business or occupation whatever on his individual account during the existence of said partnership without the written consent of the other partner.

6. The accounting of said partnership shall be based on the accrual method. All books of accounts and all contracts, letters, papers, documents, and memoranda belonging to the partnership shall be open at all times to the examination of any of the partners. On December 31 hereafter, a statement of the business is to be made, the books closed, and each partner credited with the amount of the gain or charged for his share of the loss. A statement may be made at such other times as the partners agree upon.

7. Each partner shall furnish to the other, on request, full information and account of any and all transactions and matters relating to the partnership within his knowledge.

8. All moneys received by or paid to said partnership shall be daily deposited to the Security Trust Bank of Penn Yan, N.Y., except a change fund of $50.00 and a petty cash fund of $100.00. All disbursements of partnership moneys in excess of $10.00 shall be made by check on said partnership bank account. Checks for amounts drawn on the partnership account may be drawn only with signatures of the two said partners.

9. Each partner shall promptly pay his individual debts and liabilities and shall at all times indemnify and save harmless the partnership property therefrom.

-2-

10.   Each partner shall have a salary of $800.00 per month, the same to be withdrawn at such time or times as he may elect.   No partner is to withdraw from the business an amount in excess of his salary without the written consent of the said partner.

11.   The duties of each partner are defined as follows:

Partner A: Accounting and Bookkeeping

Partner B: Sales and Rentals and Service

Each partner is to attend to such other duties as are deemed necessary for the successful operation of the business.

12.   One partner may, at any time, dissolve said partnership by written notice of his intention to do so delivered or mailed to the other partner, and said partnership shall be dissolved at the expiration of sixty days after the giving of such notice.

13.   At the time of notice giving the dissolution of said partnership, or any other termination thereof as set out in the first stipulation above, an inventory and appraisement of all assets and property of said partnership shall be made by three disinterested parties engaged in the same or similar business in this vicinity, to be chosen by the partners to this agreement or their legal representatives, at the true value to the business thereof; and an account shall be taken of all assets and liabilities.   After payment of all debts and liabilities of said partnership, the assets and property so remaining shall be divided between the partners, their heirs and assigns, in the proportion in which the capital of said

-3-

partnership has been contributed by each. Provided, however, that, if either of the original partners to this agreement desires to carry on the said business, he shall have the first option to take over said business at the net value as calculated from the account so made and assume all operations thereunder in their own right and relieve the other partner, his heirs and assigns from all liabilities. Said option to be enforced shall be exercised within ten days after the accounting of the partnership has been made. Each partner for himself, his heirs and assigns hereby agrees to execute all instruments necessary or proper to invest the others with the property, real, personal, or mixed, so taken over by him.

14. No changes, alterations, additions, modifications, or qualifications shall be made or had in terms of this contract unless made in writing and signed by all of the partners.

IN WITNESS WHEREOF, the parties have hereunto set their hands to quadruple copies hereof, the day and year first above written.

Signed in the presence of:

_____   _____

_____   _____

STATE OF NEW YORK
COUNTY OF YATES

-4-

Personally appeared before me, a Notary Public within and
for said State and County, the above named, Partner A and
Partner B, the parties of this contract, who each
acknowledged the signing thereof to be his voluntary
act and deed, for the purposes therein mentioned.
IN WITNESS WHEREOF, I have hereunto set my hand and seal
this second day of March, 19XX.

Notary Public, Yates County, New York

-5-

Two Business Plans

In this appendix we present sample business plans for two operations: a full-service restaurant and a manufacturing concern. The businesses and the plans are real (but the names are changed) and are used with the permission of their authors.

Business Plan I: Patrick Esterhazy Designs, Inc.

This plan is interesting because it involves manufacturing. The device to be produced, although relatively sophisticated, is not proprietary or unique. The success of the venture would depend upon the marketing skill that the founders could muster. Even though the plan is totally hypothetical, the general concept makes for interesting reading.

The reader will note that the amount of retained cash is excessive, but some sound, realistic financial planning would bring it into line rather quickly.

PATRICK ESTERHAZY DESIGNS INCORPORATED
87 MERCER STREET
NEW YORK, NEW YORK

Business Proposal
by: Patrick Esterhazy and
Daniel McGillivary
April 30, 1978

-1-

STATEMENT OF PURPOSE

This Business Plan has been prepared by the management of PATRICK ESTERHAZY DESIGNS, INC., with respect to the sale of up to 200 (two hundred) shares of common stock of the corporation to a limited number of people at $1,000 dollars per share.

The business in which PATRICK ESTERHAZY DESIGNS, INC., is engaged is highly speculative in nature and involves a high degree of risk, and neither PATRICK ESTERHAZY DESIGNS, INC., nor any officer or director thereof makes any warranties or representations as to the potential success thereof. In addition, each prospective investor should consider the sections on Risk Factors, The Offering, and Management of PATRICK ESTERHAZY DESIGNS.

-2-

Table of Contents

-3-

SUMMARY

The principal business of PATRICK ESTERHAZY DESIGNS, INC., (PEDI) is the development, production, and marketing of a concealed-camera surveillance system, known as the Quiet Eye Surveillance System.

The Quiet Eye Surveillance System is a camera mounted inside a glass-mirrored sphere, cylinder, or box which is capable of surveillance without betraying its existence. The system can operate efficiently in less light than conventional concealed camera systems. By the use of a time-lapse shutter and 4X movie film, the Quiet Eye Surveillance System is capable of seventy-two hours of uninterrupted operation.

PEDI has begun the marketing of the Quiet Eye Surveillance System to architects, planners, designers, engineers, security consultants, and other users, such as banks, retailers, hotels, schools, government installations, hospitals, office and apartment buildings, and transportation terminals.

Capital for the company will be raised through common stock offerings at the rate of one thousand dollars ($1,000) per share. Two hundred shares are offered for sale in order to raise needed working capital for PEDI. The shares of stock will be offered to a limited number of prospective investors.

-4-

INTRODUCTORY STATEMENT

PEDI is involved in the production and marketing of the
Quiet Eye Surveillance System. The Quiet Eye Surveillance
System is composed of a camera concealed within a mirrored-
glass container in the shapes of spheres, cylinders, and boxes.
The mirror-like coating is unique in that it permits one
narrow portion of the visible spectrum to penetrate the
coating while reflecting the rest of the light. The narrow
portion of the spectrum allowed to pass through the coating,
that which the standard vidicon tube uses in conventional
black-and-white closed-circuit television cameras, is most
sensitive. For this reason, the Quiet Eye Surveillance System
can operate efficiently with less light than conventional
concealed camera systems. Film cameras are less expensive to
install than closed-circuit television, and, by using 4X
movie film and a time lapse shutter, one movie cassette can
last up to seventy-two hours, thereby requiring less maintenance.
The 4X movie film requires at least fifteen foot-candles of
light to record a clear image. Conventional lighting in most
commercial areas of business such as banks is approximately
forty to fifty foot-candles. Conventional one-way mirrors
could not be used to conceal the cameras since the amount of
light passing through them would be well below the required
fifteen foot-candles. The unique mirrored coating, however,
allows sufficient light to reach the concealed cameras to
record a clear picture. The management of PEDI believes that

-5-

this unique feature makes the Quiet Eye Surveillance System
the first mirror-concealed camera system that can use film
cameras. In addition, by using a variety of container shapes
and camera sizes and shapes, the system is designed to offer
maximum concealment, flexibility, and design aesthetics.
The use of empty containers (dummies) is useful in case someone
is familiar with this type of system. The individual looking
at the outside of the system cannot determine whether or not
there is actually a concealed camera.

-6-

The Quiet Eye Surveillance System is a new product. Only two other companies are known to produce anything similar. One of the companies has discontinued manufacture of its units and has begun placing orders with PEDI for the Quiet Eye Surveillance System. The other company has not been able to produce the same quality units. Their unit requires more foot-candles, lighting, and is not completely discreet.

It is the expert opinion of Martin T. Bombeck that "The Quiet Eye Surveillance System is the most refined and advanced system of its kind." Mr. Bombeck has been involved with the security field for thirty-four years and is thought to be an expert in his field. He presently is chairman of the board of Hutchins Guard Company.

-7-

MARKETING PLAN

PEDI has retained a national marketing concern, P.D.T. Industries, Inc., (PDT), to assist in establishing a nationwide sales and service organization for the Quiet Eye Surveillance System and other PEDI products. The agreement PEDI has with PDT is to last an initial term of one year expiring April 31, 1979, with a clause to permit renewal each year providing each party is in agreement. The terms of the agreement with PDT are 2.5 percent to 5 percent (declining percentage based on volume) of the gross sales of the Quiet Eye System, PDT owns five (5) shares of the company's common stock and has an option to purchase an additional five (5) shares at a price per share of $1,000 payable in cash and services, and PDT has informed PEDI that it intends to exercise such option prior to September 30, 1979.

PEDI, in conjunction with PDT, is in the process of selecting distribution-installers and architectural sales representatives for the Quiet Eye Surveillance System. PEDI has had meetings with Pri-Zon Research, Inc. (PZR) of Westport, Connecticut, and intends to appoint PZR as PEDI's master distributor for New England and as a dealer-installer for the State of Connecticut. PZR has agreed to furnish the cameras and other components for the Quiet Eye Surveillance System to PEDI at cost plus 10 percent. PZR will receive a fee of from 1 percent to 2 percent of PEDI's net sales from

-8-

the Quiet Eye Surveillance System. In addition, PZR has received an option to purchase up to ten shares of PEDI's common stock at a price of $1,000 per share. The agreement shall also be automatically renewable unless terminated by either party. PEDI has entered into an agreement with Crabtree TV (CTV) of Denville, New Jersey, appointing CTV its dealer-installer for the state of New Jersey, eastern Pennsylvania, and metropolitan New York City. The agreement with CTV is for a term of one year starting April 30. 1978, and is automatically renewable unless terminated by either party. PEDI has also entered into an agreement with Capitol Video Resources (CVR) of Silver Springs, Maryland, appointing CVR its dealer-installer for Washington, D.C., and Baltimore, Maryland. The agreement with CVR is also for a one-year term renewable unless terminated by either party.

The pricing policy of PEDI is based on the cost of labor, parts, materials, damages, advertising, shipping, and packaging materials. It is figured that out of every twelve units made, an average of two will be broken in production or shipping. Taking all expenses into account, we then multiplied that figure by two to get our list price.

-9-

CREDIT TERMS

The management of PEDI has agreed to extend credit to its customers on thirty-day terms.

OPERATIONS

PEDI proposes to sell up to two hundred shares of its common stock without par value at a price of $1,000 per share. PEDI was incorporated under the laws of the State of New York on April 30, 1978, and is in the process of commencing commercial operations. PEDI is engaged primarily in the design, development, and marketing of hidden-camera surveillance systems, designer lighting, and remote control painting devices.

On April 30, 1978, PEDI purchased a unique and specially designed vacuum-metalizing machine to be used in the manufacture of the mirrored-glass containers for the Quiet Eye Surveillance System. The purchase price of the machine was $9,000 and it was designed and made by an inventor of custom machinery.

PEDI holds the patents and prototypes for other Patrick Esterhazy inventions and has future plans of marketing some of these other devices as soon as the company's capital allows for this. Expansion is planned in order to keep up with the future demand for the Quiet Eye Surveillance System.

-10-

Other products for growth are:

The Esterhazy Robot: The Esterhazy Robot, a working prototype of which is available for inspection at the Esterhazy Designs Studio, is a device which can be pointed by remote control in virtually any direction. The Esterhazy Robot accomplishes this without complicated wiring (commutator rings are unnecessary) or electronics and is of simple design and construction. Flexible electrical wiring, or hollow tubes carrying water or gas,will not be crimped or broken while the Esterhazy Robot is in operation. It is the intent of PEDI to license the robot for use by third parties.

The Ubiquitous Energy System: The Ubiquitous Energy System, a working prototype of which is available for inspection at the Esterhazy Designs Studio, is a portable, spot-energy distribution device that can deliver light, sound, heat, air-conditioning, and other materials to a demand payload area. For example, it can be moved manually or by remote control to any horizontal position within an area thirty feet in diameter (706 sq.ft.), and, like the Esterhazy Robot, does not require complicated wiring or electronics. It uses no gears and is of simple design. The system is comprised of a horizontal pole connected on one end to a vertical support and on the other end to a second pole of substantially equal length to which the payload is attached. The first pole rotates 355 degrees around the vertical support and the second pole rotates

-11-

355 degrees around the opposite end of the first pole. There is no proof that the Ubiquitous Energy System will prove commercially viable. It is the intent of the management of PEDI to eventually license the system for use by third parties.

Risk Factors: In addition to the risks inherent in any new enterprise, Esterhazy Designs considers the major uncertainties and speculative factors affecting its business to include the following:

1. Esterhazy Designs has many potential competitors, most of which are better established companies, possessing greater funds and technical resources than PEDI. There is no guarantee that Esterhazy Designs will be able to successfully compete with these other companies.

2. Esterhazy Designs has not paid and does not have any present plans to pay dividends on its common stock. The declaration and amount of any dividends which may be paid in the future depend largely upon earnings, financial position, decision of the board, and the needs of PEDI.

3. The management of PEDI also recognizes that PEDI might need additional working capital in the near future depending upon sales. The management of PEDI intends to secure these additional funds through either borrowing, further sales of its common stock, or both. There is no assurance that PEDI will be

-12-

able to raise this additional capital.

Insurance: Insurance for PEDI has been obtained through the Hazzard Insurance Agency, New York City. The agreement has been set up at a fixed rate for furniture and equipment at Esterhazy Designs, 87 Mercer Street, New York, New York. There is also a provision in the agreement for a floater which is included in the policy. When deemed necessary by the management of PEDI, the floater will cover unanticipated increases in parts and merchandise up to $20,000. This floater shall be included in the fixed premiums of $1,800 per year.

-13-

MARKETING RESEARCH

The customers of PEDI are those needing a sophisticated system to fulfill their needs. Some of the applications of its use are sophisticated environments (i.e., embassies, theaters, museums, better stores), where surveillance can go on without offense to clientele or patrons; contemporary structures (i.e., offices, apartment buildings, hotels, shopping malls, banks, government buildings) where the surveillance function can be performed without compromising design standards; private environments (i.e., hotels, bars, motels, restaurants, etc.) where visible camera presence affects guests' and customers' feelings of privacy; environments for observation of behavior (i.e., psychiatric wards, test education, and rehabilitation programs) where overt camera presence would alter behavior); environments used for measurement of employee performance in sensitive areas (i.e., assembly lines, offices, warehouses, etc.) where overt systems single out employees and create employee/union tension. A Quiet Eye Surveillance System, properly applied, will increase employee performance and afford an excellent return on investment. Difficult theft-prevention problem areas (i.e., department stores, banks, jewelry stores, supermarkets, stockrooms, warehouses) where direction and field of scope of overt camera systems is not an effective enough deterrent to theft will be more efficiently protected.

Our customers realize that our system is far superior

-14-

in both technology and uses to any other discreet system produced. The management of our company feels that this is why our system is chosen above all others.

There are many uses for the Quiet Eye Surveillance System. Because of this, the Quiet Eye Surveillance System is marketed in all areas of retail and wholesale business including security.

Our major goal is to market the Quiet Eye Surveillance System in all of the major cities of the United States through marketing companies. This allows for a large market because of the high population rates in each city.

Customers will be attracted by (1) the direct approach of the marketing companies, and (2) a nationwide advertising campaign, covering technological magazines and trade journals.

-15-

COMPETITION

The management only recognizes two current competitors because of recent advances in the discreet surveillance field. New systems have not been refined to the point which ours has. Our two major competitors are the following:

1. Oversight Systems--This concern developed a system similar to the Quiet Eye Surveillance System, but was unable to refine its processes to prevent flaking of the mirroring under both hot and cold conditions. Oversight has since scrapped its process and is now purchasing its glass containers from PEDI.

2. Sutton Incorporated--This concern has provided a product similar to the Quiet Eye Surveillance System but lacking in its sophistication. With this system, more foot-candles are required to get a clear image through the glass surface. The other problem plaguing this product is that an observer can see into the sphere from the outside, therefore enabling a person to see if there is a camera present and where it is scanning.

The available market of the Quiet Eye Surveillance System is large and is difficult to gauge because of the age of the product. The market increases every day, making our available market large at present. The applications of our system are vast; it is used for security and checking employee performance,

-16-

to name a few. Documented evidence shows that the shoplifting rate has risen above the four-billion-dollar mark as of 1977; therefore, our business is a necessity in our society. Estimates show that 60 percent of all shoplifting is internal, done by employees, or caused by bookkeeping errors, assigning only 40 percent of all shoplifting to the consuming public. This evidence shows that there is a need for discreet systems not only to watch shoppers but also to watch employees. Because of increasing evidence that discreet systems are needed, PEDI has plans for expansion of its facilities to accommodate an increase in future sales. PEDI has developed other products for future marketing. The management has future plans for marketing its new products as soon as more working capital is made available from the sales of the Quiet Eye Surveillance System.

Location

PEDI is currently leasing the first floor of a stone and cement building at 87 Mercer Street, New York, New York. The total square footage of the combined studio and production area is 6,000 square feet, the studio, 3,000 square feet and the production area, 3,000 square feet. The area shall be leased to PEDI at a rate of $1.25 per square foot, which totals $7,500 a year or $625 a month. The area at 87 Mercer Street is zoned for commercial use only.

Personnel

PEDI will hire one employee to help the production of the Quiet Eye Surveillance System when the work load is too much for Mr. Esterhazy to handle. The person chosen to work with Mr. Esterhazy is the inventor of the vacuum-metalizing machine, who will work as an independent contractor at the rate of five dollars an hour.

Employment Agreement

Patrick Esterhazy has entered into an employment agreement with Esterhazy Designs for a period of two years pursuant to which Mr. Esterhazy has agreed to devote his time and efforts to the business of Esterhazy Designs as soon as possible. During such periods, Mr. Esterhazy will initially receive a salary from Esterhazy Designs of fifty dollars a week, and will be reimbursed for out-of-pocket expenses. Should Esterhazy Designs begin to generate income, it is intended that Mr. Esterhazy will receive salary increases in accordance with conservative business practices.

During the period of his employment, Mr. Esterhazy has agreed not to engage in any activity that is competitive with Esterhazy Designs and, in addition, has granted to Esterhazy Designs a right of first refusal with respect to the development and licensing of new concepts and inventions developed by him during the period of his employment with Esterhazy Designs.

Daniel McGillivary will be compensated on a time basis as his services are required and will receive sales commissions on sales consummated and delivered due to his efforts.

FINANCIAL SECTION

The Offering: Shares of Esterhazy Designs Common Stock are being offered and sold at a purchase price of $1,000 per share, pursuant to an exemption from the registration requirements of the Securities Act of 1933, as amended (the act), and cannot be resold by a purchaser thereof unless such shares are subsequently registered under the act or an exemption from such registration is available. No registration rights have been granted by Esterhazy Designs, and each purchaser of Esterhazy Designs must represent, among other things, that he has acquired the shares for his own account for investment purposes and not with a view to the distribution thereof. Accordingly, a purchaser of Esterhazy Designs shares must bear the economic risk of his investment for an indefinite period of time. The Board of Directors of Esterhazy Designs has adopted resolutions which are intended to qualify the proposed offering of common stock as being offered for the sale as Section 1244 stock. Pursuant to section 1244 of the Internal Revenue Code, as amended, if the shares being offered hereby so qualify, any individual stockholder sustaining a loss on the disposition of the shares can treat such loss as an ordinary loss rather than a capital loss. It is the suggestion of the board that each prospective purchaser consult his tax advisor to ascertain whether the benefits of section 1244 stock are available to him. A subscription agreement attached to and part of this business plan sets forth transfer restrictions and should be studied carefully by each prospective purchaser of Patrick Esterhazy Designs shares. All investments in Esterhazy Designs are subject to acceptance by the Esterhazy Designs board of directors which reserves the right to accept or reject any subscription in whole or in part.

FINANCIAL STATEMENTS
FEDI
PRO FORMA INCOME STATEMENT
FISCAL YEARS BY QUARTER

	First Quarter 40 UNITS		Second Quarter 45 UNITS	
Sales of units @ $400		$16,000.00		$18,000.00
Cost of goods sold		8,000.00		9,000.00
GROSS MARGIN		$ 8,000.00		$ 9,000.00
Operating expenses:				
Selling expenses:				
Sales salaries	$ 600.00		$ 600.00	
Utilities	1,200.00		1,200.00	
Supplies	900.00		900.00	
Advertising	600.00	$3,300.00	600.00	$3,300.00
Administrative expenses:	$1,875.00		$1,875.00	
Rent (plant)	600.00		600.00	
Legal fees	600.00		600.00	
CPA fees	900.00		900.00	
Auto	450.00		450.00	
Miscellaneous	450.00		450.00	
Insurance	6.25		6.25	
Safety deposit box	294.75		294.75	
Depreciation—equipment	66.25		66.25	
Depreciation—furniture & fixtures		$5,242.25		$5,242.25
Total operating expenses		$8,542.25		$8,542.25
Income before taxes		$ (542.25)		$457.75
Taxes (20%)		-0-		
Net profit (loss)		$ (542.25)		$366.20

FINANCIAL STATEMENTS
PEDI
PRO FORMA INCOME STATEMENT
FISCAL YEARS BY QUARTER

	Third Quarter 55 UNITS		Fourth Quarter 75 UNITS	
Sales of units @ $400		$22,000.00		$30,000.00
Cost of goods sold		11,000.00		15,000.00
GROSS MARGIN		$11,000.00		$15,000.00
Operating expenses:				
Selling expenses:				
Sales salaries	$ 600.00		$ 600.00	
Utilities	1,200.00		1,200.00	
Supplies	900.00		900.00	
Advertising	600.00	$3,300.00	600.00	$3,300.00
Administrative expenses:				
Rent (plant)	$1,875.00		$1,875.00	
Legal fees	600.00		600.00	
CPA fees	600.00		600.00	
Auto	900.00		900.00	
Miscellaneous	450.00		450.00	
Insurance	450.00		450.00	
Safety deposit box	6.25		6.25	
Depreciation--equipment	294.75		294.75	
Depreciation--furniture & fixtures	66.25	$5,242.25	66.25	$5,242.25
Total operating expenses		$8,542.25		$8,542.25
Income before taxes		$2,457.75		$6,457.75
Taxes (20%)		491.55		1,291.55
Net profit (loss)		$1,966.20		$5,166.20

-23-

FINANCIAL STATEMENTS
PEDI
PRO FORMA INCOME STATEMENT
FISCAL YEARS BY QUARTER

	Fifth Quarter 100 UNITS		Sixth Quarter 100 UNITS	
Sales of units @ $400		$40,000.00		$40,000.00
Cost of goods sold		20,000.00		20,000.00
GROSS MARGIN		$20,000.00		$20,000.00
Operating expenses:				
Selling expenses:				
Sales salaries	$ 600.00		$ 600.00	
Utilities	1,200.00		1,200.00	
Supplies	900.00		900.00	
Advertising	600.00	$3,300.00	600.00	$3,300.00
Administrative expenses:				
Rent (plant)	$1,875.00		$1,875.00	
Legal fees	600.00		600.00	
CPA fees	600.00		600.00	
Auto	900.00		900.00	
Miscellaneous	450.00		450.00	
Insurance	450.00		450.00	
Safety deposit box	6.25		6.25	
Depreciation--equipment	294.75		294.75	
Depreciation--furniture & fixtures	66.25	$5,242.25	66.25	$5,242.25
Total operating expenses		$8,542.25		$8,542.25
Income before taxes		$11,457.75		$11,457.75
Taxes (20%)		2,291.55		2,291.55
Net profit (loss)		$9,166.20		$9,166.20

-24-

FINANCIAL STATEMENTS
PEDI
PRO FORMA INCOME STATEMENT
FISCAL YEARS BY QUARTER

	Seventh Quarter		Eighth Quarter	
	125 UNITS		125 UNITS	
Sales of units @ $400		$50,000.00		$50,000.00
Cost of goods sold		25,000.00		25,000.00
GROSS MARGIN		$25,000.00		$25,000.00
Operating expenses:				
Selling expenses:				
Sales salaries	$ 600.00		$ 600.00	
Utilities	1,200.00		1,200.00	
Supplies	900.00		900.00	
Advertising	600.00	$3,300.00	600.00	$3,300.00
Administrative expenses:	$1,875.00		$1,875.00	
Rent (plant)	600.00		600.00	
Legal fees	600.00		600.00	
CPA fees	600.00		600.00	
Auto	900.00		900.00	
Miscellaneous	450.00		450.00	
Insurance	450.00		450.00	
Safety deposit box	66.25		66.25	
Depreciation—equipment	294.75		294.75	
Depreciation—furniture & fixtures	66.25	$5,242.25	66.25	$5,242.25
Total operating expenses		$ 8,542.25		$ 8,542.25
Income before taxes		$16,457.75		$16,457.75
Taxes (20%)		3,291.55		3,291.55
Net profit (loss)		$13,166.20		$13,166.20

PEDI
BALANCE SHEET
STARTING DATE APRIL 1, 1978

Current assets		
Cash		$70,735.00
Fixed assets		
Equipment		10,525.00
Furniture & Fixtures		1,740.00
Total assets		$83,000.00
Liabilities		
Capital stock		$83,000.00
$1,000 par value		
200 authorized		
83,issued and outstanding		
Total liabilities		$83,000.00

PEDI
BALANCE SHEET
YEAR END, APRIL 30, 1979

Current assets

Cash		$68,691.35*
Receivables (30% of 4Q sales)		9,000.00
Total current assets		$77,691.35

Fixed assets

Equipment	$10,525.00	
Less: accumulated dep.	1,179.00	
Furniture & fixtures	$1,740.00	
Less: accumulated dep.	1,265.00	
Net book value-equipment, furniture & fixtures		$10,821.00
Total assets		$88,512.35

Liabilities

Shareholders equity:

Capital stock - $1,000 par value 200 authorized, 83 issued outstanding	$83,000.00
Retained earnings	5,512.35
Total shareholders equity	$88,512.35

-27-

PEDI
BALANCE SHEET
YEAR END APRIL 30, 1980

Current assets

Cash		$107,356.15
Receivables (30% of 4Q sales)		15,000.00
Total current assets		$122,356.15

Fixed assets

Equipment	$10,525.00	
Less: accumulated dep.	2,358.00	
Furniture & fixtures	1,740.00	
Less: accumulated dep.	530.00	
Net book value-equipment, furniture & fixtures		9,377.00
Total assets		$131,733.15

Liabilities

Shareholders equity

Capital stock - $1,000 par value 200 authorized, 83 issued & outstanding	$ 83,000.00
Retained earnings	48,733.15
Total shareholders equity	$131,733.15

-28-

*Please note that no business would ever accumulate this amount of cash, as it would be a wasteful use of liquid asset. As we said in the main text, however, these plans were altered very little from those prepared by would-be entrepreneurs.

PEDI
CASH FLOW SUMMARY
FOR THE SECOND FISCAL YEAR MAY 1, 1979 TO APRIL 30, 1980

| | QUARTERS | | | |
	First (May-Jul)	Second (Aug-Oct)	Third (Nov-Jan)	Fourth (Feb-Apr)
Beginning balance	$ 68,691.35	$ 74,857.55	$ 84,023.75	$ 94,189.95
Add: 70% current sales	28,000.00	28,000.00	35,000.00	35,000.00
30% previous quarter	9,000.00	12,000.00	12,000.00	15,000.00
Total receipts	$ 37,000.00	$ 40,000.00	$ 47,000.00	$ 50,000.00
Total cash available	$105,691.35	$114,857.55	$131,023.75	$144,189.95
Less: Expenditures				
Purchases	18,800.00	18,800.00	23,800.00	23,800.00
Direct labor	1,200.00	1,200.00	1,200.00	1,200.00
Operating expenses	8,542.25	8,542.25	8,542.25	8,542.25
Income taxes	2,291.55	2,291.55	3,291.55	3,291.55
Fixed assets	0	0	0	0
Total expenditures	$ 30,833.80	$ 30,833.80	$ 36,833.80	$ 36,833.80
Ending balance	$ 74,857.55	$ 84,023.75	$ 94,189.95	$107,356.15

PEDI
CASH FLOW SUMMARY
FOR THE FIRST FISCAL YEAR MAY 1, 1978 TO APRIL 30, 1979

| | QUARTERS | | | |
	First (May-Jul)	Second (Aug-Oct)	Third (Nov-Jan)	Fourth (Feb-Apr)
Beginning balance	$83,000.00	$65,392.75	$65,158.95	$65,925.15
Add: 70% current sales	11,200.00	12,600.00	15,400.00	21,000.00
30% previous quarter	0	4,800.00	5,400.00	6,600.00
Total receipts	$11,200.00	$17,400.00	$20,800.00	$27,600.00
Total cash available	$94,200.00	$82,792.75	$85,958.95	$93,525.15
Less: Expenditures				
Purchases	6,800.00	7,800.00	9,800.00	13,800.00
Direct labor	1,200.00	1,200.00	1,200.00	1,200.00
Operating expenses	8,542.25	8,542.25	8,542.25	8,542.25
Income taxes	0	91.55	491.55	1,291.55
Fixed assets	12,265.00	0	0	0
Total expenditures	$28,807.25	$17,633.80	$20,033.80	$24,833.80
Ending balance	$65,392.75	$65,158.95	$65,925.15	$68,691.35

PEDI
Capital Equipment List

Major equipment:	Cost:
Vacuum-metalizing machine	$9,000.00
Water purifier	180.00
Craftsman lathe	430.00
Woodsman tool bench	85.00
	$9,695.00

Minor shop equipment:	
Fluorescent light fixtures	$ 80.00
Work chairs	60.00
Assembly tables	120.00
Assorted power tools	150.00
Tool box & assorted hand tools	260.00
File cabinets	100.00
Miscellaneous parts	60.00
	$ 830.00

Furniture for the studio:	
Bed	$ 80.00
Rug	40.00
Dining table	250.00
Dining-table chairs	200.00
Couch	300.00
Chairs	50.00
Lighting fixtures	200.00
Stereo (panasonic)	180.00
Pictures & mirrors	95.00
End table	145.00
	$1,740.00

Capital equipment total: $12,265.00

-31-

EQUITY POSITIONS

Marketing company	5 shares	$ 5,000
Patrick Esterhazy	25 shares	25,000
Daniel McGillivary	25 shares	25,000
D.B. McGillivary	8 shares	8,000
L. Plumber	5 shares	5,000
C. O'Toole	2 shares	2,000
M. Rodriguez	3 shares	3,000
A. Esterhazy	5 shares	5,000
C. Nakamura	5 shares	5,000
Total:	83 shares	$83,000

200 shares of stock being offered at $1,000 a share

83 shares issued and 117 still to be sold

-32-

MANAGEMENT

The officers and directors of PEDI are as follows:

Patrick Esterhazy	President and Director
Daniel McGillivary	Vice President, Secretary, Treasurer, and Director
D.B. McGillivary	Director
Linton Plumber	Director

Patrick Esterhazy, age thirty-two, has a business degree from Flood College, Burlington, Vermont. For the past two years, Mr. Esterhazy has, among other activities, devoted substantially all of his time to the development of the Quiet Eye Surveillance System and other inventions. Prior to that time, Mr. Esterhazy was involved as a trader on the floor of the New York Stock Exchange for six years, working for Esterhazy and Company.

Daniel McGillivary, age thirty-five, has a business degree from Flood College. For the past four years, Mr. McGillivary has been the executive vice president of Acme Manufacturing Co. Four years previous to that, Mr. McGillivary was involved as chief of advertising for Mind Magazine.

Linton Plumber, president of Linton Plumber and Associates, business consultants, has been associated with the firm for the past seven years. His experience has been primarily in the garment and textile industries. Prior to the formation of Plumber Associates, Mr. Plumber was active in the management

-33-

sector of various children's sportswear companies for more than twenty years.

D.B. McGillivary is the chief executive of Georgetown Air Rifles, Inc. In addition, he is the president of a venture capital firm, presently based in Florida.

Both Mr. Esterhazy and Mr. McGillivary are in good health and believe that their abilities will enable them to make PEDI a success. Mr. Esterhazy has the ability to produce and market the Quiet Eye Surveillance System, whereas Mr. McGillivary's training has resulted in superior abilities in the management field. Mr. Esterhazy's job is to produce and market the Quiet Eye Surveillance System. Mr. McGillivary, because of his experience, will be in charge of managing the firm of PEDI. All decisions regarding the company are to be made jointly.

Salary for Mr. Esterhazy will be set at fifty dollars a week. Mr. McGillivary has agreed to be compensated on a time basis at the end of the year in stock options.

In order to augment the skills of Mr. Esterhazy and Mr. McGillivary, the company has retained the services of Martin Rodriguez, CPA, and Dennis Longfellow, Esq.

D.B. McGillivary, a venture capitalist, has agreed to serve on the board and will provide ongoing management review. Linton Plumber has also agreed to serve on the board and will provide consulting services when deemed necessary.

-34-

SUBSCRIPTION AGREEMENT
(Sample)

The shares being offered for sale in this subscription are not registered under the Securities Act of 1933 and may be sold, transferred, or otherwise disposed of by an investor only if in the written opinion of counsel to or approval by Esterhazy Designs such proposed transfer is consistent with all applicable provisions of the Securities Act of 1933 and the rules and regulations thereunder, as well as any applicable "Blue Sky" or similar state securities laws.

This plan constitutes an offer only to the person whose name appears in the space provided below:

_____

Notary Public Signature and Seal   Name of Officer

_____
Date

Business Plan II: The Gastropod

This business plan for The Gastropod is extremely well done considering the relatively simple nature of the operation. The venture is nothing more than a small family restaurant and ice cream stand to be located in eastern Massachusetts.

This plan should be an example to any entrepreneur who claims that his enterprise is too basic for the preparation of a formal plan, especially the financial statements and data.

THE GASTROPOD
Ayer Road
Harvard, Massachusetts

Business Proposal By
George Host and
Paul Guest

-1-

STATEMENT OF PURPOSE

THE GASTROPOD is seeking $125,000 for the purchase of
equipment, land, and building on Ayer Road, Harvard,
Massachusetts. THE GASTROPOD will be a family restaurant
and ice cream stand. It will be owned and operated by
the partnership of George Host and Paul Guest. Each
partner will invest $20,000 ($40,000 in total) for the
initial cash outlays and to provide for adequate working
capital. THE GASTROPOD has no direct competition in town.
The customers will be a mixture of tourist and regular
clientele. THE GASTROPOD will be a profitable operation
within the first year of operation.

-2-

TABLE OF CONTENTS

-3-

THE BUSINESS

THE GASTROPOD will be a family-style restaurant and ice cream stand. It will be purchased and operated by the partnership of Paul Guest and George Host. THE GASTROPOD was so named because it is located in the middle of the Nashoba Valley, Massachusetts, which is known for its snail farms. The business is somewhat seasonal, which causes sales to fluctuate accordingly. When the business first opens, most of the customers will be tourist and street people. However, the partnership hopes to build up a solid base of regular customers. THE GASTROPOD will open for business on January 1, 1979. It will be open seven days a week. The hours will vary according to the time of year.

THE GASTROPOD will serve good quality food at a higher than average price. The specialty of the house will be apple pie, baked fresh daily. The menu for the restaurant will consist of typical breakfast items, a normal variety of sandwiches, a selected variety of dinners, daily specials, pizza, the normal beverages (coffee, tea, milk, soda), dessert (pies, pudding, cake, pastry), and any ice cream product available from the ice cream stand. The restaurant will also sell various bakery products (pies, doughnuts, pastries, cakes, cookies), and half-gallons of ice cream on a retail basis. The restaurant will also offer a take-out service. The menu for the ice cream stand will be ice cream cones, frappes, shakes, sundaes, banana boats, freezes, floats, and frozen yogurt.

-4-

The restaurant industry is part of the overall service industry. The service industries are presently growing and are expected to continue to grow into the future. Restaurant sales have been growing at a rate of 8 to 11 percent a year. It has been estimated that Americans spend $50 billion a year in restaurants. Also, it has been estimated that one meal out of every three is consumed away from home. It has been projected that by 1985, one out of every two meals will be eaten away from home. Therefore, from our market research we feel confident that our business will succeed, grow, and prosper.

MARKETING RESEARCH

THE GASTROPOD's market and customers can be divided into four different groups. The first group would be classified under the category of tourism. The tourists are in the area for different reasons depending on the season. During the spring, people travel to the area to view the blossoms on the region's many apple trees. During the summer, people are on vacation, creating a high volume of traffic on the roads. During the fall, tourists are in the area to pick apples at the nearby orchards (Nashoba Valley). Tourists are also in the area to view the fall foliage. This market is fairly steady from year to year.

The second group would be residential, the people living in the town of Harvard. The town has a population of approximately 3,700. The town has been growing at an accelerated rate. A new housing development was just started. Harvard is a bedroom community of Boston. The average family income is upper middle-class. There is a shopping center being built across the street from the restaurant. This should create a lot more traffic in the area. This is the market that we would like to increase as the business goes on.

The third group would be the Fort Devens Army Base market. Fort Devens has a population of approximately 15,000. The main gate is approximately five miles from THE GASTROPOD. This market should increase as THE GASTROPOD's reputation becomes better known.

The fourth group would be categorized as OTHER. This group would include people who live outside but patronize THE GASTROPOD on a consistent basis. Also included in this group would be the street people (truckers, salesmen, delivery men). Another part of this group would be the people who work in or around the town.

There is no direct competition in town with THE GASTROPOD. However, there is some competition outside of town.

Restaurant Competition

Deliquescent Dairy Bar--located in the town of Ayer, about two miles away from THE GASTROPOD. The building is old and somewhat shabby in appearance. It has about the same menu as THE GASTROPOD. It has a limited seating capacity of about thirty-five.

Downtown Restaurant--located in the center of Ayer, about five miles away from THE GASTROPOD. Its major drawback is that there is very little parking space because of its location in the center of town.

Fortified Diner--also located in the center of Ayer. It has the shape and metal appearance of a diner. It also has a reputation as a greasy spoon restaurant.

Ice Cream Stand Competition

Jones's--located in Littleton, about ten miles from THE GASTROPOD. It is the most efficiently run ice cream stand in the area. It has a tremendous following of customers. THE GASTROPOD will not focus on the market it serves.

The future looks bright for THE GASTROPOD. The tourism business is fairly steady from year to year. The town of Harvard is growing and should continue to grow in the future. Fort Devens is expected to absorb some of the troops that are being relocated out of South Korea. THE GASTROPOD is also in the unique situation of having no direct competition in town.

MARKETING PLAN

THE GASTROPOD's general marketing strategy is to provide good quality and good service. The reason for this is that the partnership feels that, if people are generally pleased with the food and service, they will come back again to eat. A satisfied customer is also going to recommend the place to friends. The prices may be a little higher than the going rate, but the partnership believes that people are willing to pay a little more when the quality of food and service is good. The long-term goal is to develop a regular clientele.

THE GASTROPOD's employees will be friendly and polite at all times to the customers. The customer will be waited on promptly. Food will be prepared quickly by the kitchen help. THE GASTROPOD will have a neat and clean appearance, and will have a friendly atmosphere where people can sit down, relax, and enjoy a good meal. The customer will always be thanked for his patronage before leaving.

Most of THE GASTROPOD's advertising will be in two local newspapers. The newspapers are The Public Spirit located in Ayer and The Harvard Post located in Harvard. Both papers are weekly. THE GASTROPOD will place half-page ads in both papers during the first two weeks of operation in January. Also, half-page ads will be placed in the papers when the ice cream stand opens in April. Ads will be placed in the papers every week.

-9-

These ads will be drawn up by the advertising agency of Adways, Inc., Newton Centre. The agency will also design and print the menus, 5,000 paper copies of which will be sent to all the homes in Harvard.

Sales Forecast

First year

January	$ 12,000.
February	$ 13,000.
March	$ 13,500.
April	$ 16,000.
May	$ 24,000.
June	$ 28,000.
July	$ 38,000.
August	$ 38,000.
September	$ 38,000.
October	$ 22,000.
November	$ 14,000.
December	$ 14,000.
Total	$256,500.

Second year

First Quarter	$ 48,000.
Second Quarter	$ 76,000.
Third Quarter	$125,000.
Fourth Quarter	$ 61,000.
Total	$310,000.

Third year

$340,000.

-10-

OPERATIONS

We will choose the partnership form of business ownership mainly for its advantages of financial strength, as well as improved credit standing, and simplicity of organization.

Partnership Contract

1. Name of Partners: Paul Guest, George Host
2. Name of Partnership: THE GASTROPOD
3. Type of Business: Restaurant and Ice Cream Stand
4. Location: Harvard, Massachusetts
5. Length of agreement: One year
6. Amount of capital for initial investment:

   Mr. Guest: $20,000

   Mr. Host: $20,000
7. Division of profits and losses: 50/50
8. Limitations of withdrawals: No money will be withdrawn except in the event of poor health, in which case it is not to exceed $5,000.
9. Compensation:

   Guest: salary of $13,000.

   Host: salary of $13,000.
10. New Partners: New partners must invest a minimum of $20,000, and both present owners must accept the new partner.
11. Procedure for selling out: All assets will be sold and will be divided according to investment.

-11-

This is just a general outline of what the partnership agreement would look like. Before any actual investment by either partner, a lawyer would draw up a more formal agreement.

The business is located on Ayer Road, in the town of Harvard, which is part of Worcester County. The location is about two miles from Route 2 and about forty-five miles outside of Boston. The building is set about forty yards back from the road. However, it is all open area between the building and the road. The building is set on six acres of land. There is an extremely large parking lot in front of the building. On the sides and behind the building are lawns and fields. There are five picnic tables on the lawns.

The building is painted white and is approximately 3,000 square feet in overall size. The front of the building has three large picture windows and one door on the restaurant side. The building has six serving windows on the ice cream stand side. On the inside of the building, there is a partition separating the restaurant from the ice cream stand. The restaurant can seat approximately a maximum of 100 people.

The facilities and the equipment of the building are as follows:

1 counter with stools

8 booths

10 wooden tables with matching chairs

-12-

1 gas heating system
1 central air conditioning system
Carpeting under all eating areas
Built-in music system
2 walk-in freezers
2 walk-in coolers
4 dispensing freezers
2 soda fountains
2 milk dispensers
4 NCR cash registers
2 soda-dispensing machines
2 refrigerators
1 refrigerated sandwich table
2 grills
2 deep fat fryers
1 microwave oven
1 steam table
1 bread warmer
1 three-oven stove
1 pastry display case
1 coffee machine
2 ice machines
1 commercial dishwasher
2 metal desks and reclining chairs
1 dough mixer

1 meat slicer
1 adding machine
1 check writer
1 water bubbler
Silverware
Tableware
Glasses

Possible suppliers to THE GASTROPOD are as follows:

Watt and Son Dairy
Harvard, Mass.

S.S. Pierce
Boston, Mass.

Nashua Beef, Inc.
Nashua, New Hampshire

Albert Notine and Sons, Inc.
Lowell, Mass.

Prime Tobacco
Fitchburg, Mass.

Carlson Orchards
Harvard, Mass.

Coca-Cola
Lowell, Mass.

Tonken Paper
Fitchburg, Mass.

Holiday Linen Service
Boston, Mass.

A.O. Smith Co.
New Ipswich, New Hampshire

Consolidated Foods, Inc.
Nashua, New Hampshire

Nabisco Inc.
West Boylston, Mass.

May Gold Farms
Pomfret, Conn.

The personnel that THE GASTROPOD will have to hire in its first year of business is as follows:

One full-time baker

One full-time chef

One full-time assistant chef

One part-time chef trainee (working full time during the summer)

One full-time dishwasher (an extra one to be hired during the summer)

Numerous full-time and part-time waiters and waitresses (the number depending on the time of year)

The financial compensation for the employees can be found at the end of the financial plan.

Future expansion plans may include the development of a retail butcher's shop in the area where the dining tables are located. One of the reasons that we are considering a butcher's

-15-

shop is that there is none in the area. Before this expansion would take place, extensive research would be conducted. First, the use of the dining area would be monitored. One of the things we would look at is how much money is produced from people eating in this area. This figure would be compared to the estimated income the butcher's shop would produce.

Long-term expansion plans would be based on the town of Harvard going wet (allowing liquor to be sold in town). This expansion would be to add an addition to the present building. It would include formal dining area, lounge, and larger kitchen facilities. All this expansion would be based on THE GASTROPOD's receiving a liquor license.

The general nature of THE GASTROPOD's conduct would be that of trust, respect, and understanding. This conduct would be extended to the customers, employees, suppliers, and the community. THE GASTROPOD hopes to be treated in the same way. THE GASTROPOD also hopes to become an important part of the community, and to develop strong ties with the community. Part of THE GASTROPOD's commitment to the community would be THE GASTROPOD's involvement with local civic groups. THE GASTROPOD will do its best to serve the needs of the community. After all, THE GASTROPOD realizes it has a social responsibility to the community in which it is located.

The overall schedule of events is as follows: The door of the restaurant will open on the second day of January, 1979.

-16-

The reason for opening at this time is that the first four months of the year are the slowest. This gives the employees time to get used to the overall operation of the business and to work out any kinks in the operation before it gets busy in the spring. The restaurant will be open all year round. The ice cream stand will open on the first weekend of April. The hours of operation will increase as the weather becomes warmer. The ice cream stand will close on the last weekend of October.

Restaurant Hours

January, February, March, November, and December

Monday-Friday	6 A.M.	to 3 P.M.
Saturday and Sunday	7 A.M.	to 6 P.M.

April, May, September, and October

Monday-Friday	6 A.M.	to 7 P.M.
Saturday and Sunday	7 A.M.	to 7 P.M.

June, July, and August

Monday-Friday	6 A.M.	to 9 P.M.
Saturday and Sunday	7 A.M.	to 9 P.M.

Ice Cream Stand Hours

April

Monday-Friday	3 P.M.	to 7 P.M.
Saturday and Sunday	11 A.M.	to 7 P.M.

May

Monday-Friday	3 P.M.	to 8 P.M.
Saturday and Sunday	11 A.M.	to 8 P.M.

June

Monday-Friday	3 P.M.	to 9 P.M.
Saturday and Sunday	11 A.M.	to 9 P.M.

July and August

Monday-Friday	11 A.M.	to 10 P.M.
Saturday and Sunday	11 A.M.	to 10 P.M.

September and October

Monday-Friday	3 P.M.	to 9 P.M.
Saturday and Sunday	11 A.M.	to 9 P.M.

-17-

There are certain risks involved in opening this business. However, this is true of all businesses just starting out. One risk would be not developing a regular clientele. Another risk would be that the cost of food might go so high that people will not be able to afford to eat out, or an overall downward trend in the economy which would cause people to save more and spend less. Another risk, which is totally up to God, is the weather. If the summer or the weekends during the spring or fall are excessively cold or rainy, the tourist business will be destroyed. Most of these risks are out of the control of THE GASTROPOD's management. However, just recognizing these risks has minimized them somewhat. The reason for this is that management should be able to adjust to these risks as well as possible when they first appear.

-18-

FINANCIAL PLAN

SOURCES AND APPLICATION OF CASH

Sources:

Mortgage loan[1]	$125,000.00	
Owner's equity	20,000.00	
Total	20,000.00	$165,000.00

Applications:

Purchase building, land and equipment	$125,000.00	
Renovations[2]	1,000.00	
Legal fees[3]	500.00	
Inventory[4]	10,000.00	
Deposit on telephone[5]	200.00	
Installation of telephone[5]	40.00	
Deposit to gas company[6]	900.00	
Deposit to electric company[7]	1,500.00	
Insurance	5,704.00	
Advertising agency[8]	150.00	
Cash on hand[9]	20,006.00	
Total		$165,000.00

Explanation for Sources and Application of Cash

1. Mortgage loan for $125,000 for ten years at 10 percent interest.

2. General money used to spruce up the building since it has been closed for over a year.

3. The lawyer's fee would include the cost of drawing up the partnership agreement and legal advice on the purchase of the building.

4. Beginning inventory needed to start operation of the restaurant.

5. New England Telephone requires a $200 deposit on any business phone. It also charges $40 to install the phones.

6. The Boston Gas Company requires a deposit of double your average monthly bill.

7. Massachusetts Electric requires a deposit of double your average monthly bill.

8. Cost of having an advertising agency draw up an ad campaign.

9. Money placed in checking account. This would be the type of account where both partners' signatures would be needed for a check to clear.

THE GASTROPOD
Opening Day Balance Sheet

Assets		Liabilities	
Current assets:		Bank loan payable	$125,000.00
Cash	$ 20,196.00		
Inventory	10,000.00	**Equity**	
Prepaid utility	2,600.00		
Prepaid legal	500.00	G. Host	$ 20,000.00
Prepaid insurance	5,704.00	P. Guest	20,000.00
Total current assets	$ 39,000.00	Total liability and owners' equity	$165,000.00
Land, building, and equipment	$126,000.00		
	$165,000.00		

THE GASTROPOD
Balance Sheet
End of First Year

Assets		Liabilities	
Current assets:		Bank loan payable	$106,376.00
Cash	$ 44,852.00		
Inventory	10,000.00	**Equity**	
Total current assets	$ 54,852.00		
		G. Host	$ 20,000.00
Land, building & equipment	$125,000.00	P. Guest	20,000.00
Accumulated depreciation	6,240.00	Retained earnings	27,236.00
Value of land, building, and equipment	118,760.00	Total liabilities & equity	$173,612.00
Total assets	$173,612.00		

THE GASTROPOD
Pro Forma Profit & Loss
3 Year Summary

	Year 1	Year 2	Year 3
Sales			
Ice cream stand	$ 64,000	$ 78,000	$ 85,000
Restaurant[1]	192,500	231,000	255,000
Total sales	$256,500	$310,000	$340,000
Less cost of goods sold[2]	102,600	124,000	136,000
GROSS MARGIN	$153,900	$186,000	$204,000
Operating expenses			
Wages[3]	$ 82,801	$ 93,000	$100,000
Advertising[4]	800	1,000	1,200
Advertising agency[5]	150	-	-
Electric	9,000	9,000	11,000
Gas	5,100	5,400	5,500
Legal	500	300	300
Interest[6]	1,200	1,000	800
Repairs[7]	1,800	2,000	2,400
Uniforms[8]	330	390	420
Telephone[9]	600	600	600
Charities[10]	360	600	600
Office	1,200	1,200	1,400
Depreciation[11]	6,200	6,000	5,700
Accounting[12]	600	600	600
Property tax[13]	6,225	6,400	6,600
Miscellaneous	1,200	1,800	2,000
Total operating expenses	$118,306	$129,290	$138,720
Net profit before taxes	$ 35,594	$ 56,710	$ 65,280
Less income tax	10,460	22,200	28,410
Net profit after taxes	$ 25,134	$ 34,510	$ 36,870

-23-

Explanation of Pro Forma Profit and Loss

1. Not included in this figure is the 6 percent meal tax.

2. Cost of goods sold is figured at 40 percent of sales, which is around the industry average.

3. Turn to the end of the financial section for the cost of labor breakdown.

4. Cost of advertising in local newspapers.

5. Advertising agency used to produce first year's ads.

6. Interest paid on the mortgage loan of $125,000.00.

7. Any repair or maintenance work needed on the inside or outside of the building.

8. Cost of renting uniforms for waitresses or waiters.

9. Cost includes the $21.79 minimum charge plus any calls outside the minimum charge area.

10. Contributions to local organizations.

11. The depreciation of the building and equipment.

12. The cost of having the accounting firm prepare quarterly and yearly tax returns.

13. The tax that is paid to the town of Harvard. It is figured by taking 30 percent of the assessed value, then multiplying that by $166 per thousand.

-24-

Pro Forma Profit & Loss — THE GASTROPOD — First Six Months of Operation

	Jan.	Feb.	March	April	May	June
Sales						
Ice cream stand				$ 2,000	$ 5,000	$ 5,000
Restaurant	$12,000	$13,000	$13,500	14,000	15,000	23,000
Total sales	$12,000	$13,000	$13,500	$16,000	$20,000	$28,000
Cost of goods sold	4,800	5,200	5,400	6,400	8,000	11,200
GROSS MARGIN	$ 7,200	$ 7,800	$ 8,100	$ 9,600	$12,000	$16,800
Operating Expenses						
Wages	$ 5,620	$ 5,620	$ 5,620	$ 6,896	$ 7,025	$ 7,564
Advertising	100	100	100	100	50	50
Electric	750	750	750	750	750	750
Gas	450	450	450	450	450	450
Legal	42	42	42	42	42	42
Interest	1,000	1,000	1,000	1,000	1,000	1,000
Repairs	150	150	150	150	150	150
Uniforms	150	150	—	150	150	60
Telephone	30	30	50	50	50	50
Charities	100	100	100	30	30	30
Office	100	100	100	100	100	100
Depreciation	520	520	520	520	520	520
Accounting	42	42	42	42	42	42
Miscellaneous	100	100	100	100	100	100
Total operating expenses	$ 9,074	$ 8,954	$ 8,954	$10,230	$10,397	$10,908
Net profit before taxes	(1,874)	(1,154)	(854)	(630)	(1,603)	(5,892)

Pro Forma Profit & Loss — THE GASTROPOD — Second Six Months of Operation

	July	Aug.	Sept.	Oct.	Nov.	Dec.
Sales						
Ice cream stand	$15,000	$15,000	$10,000	$ 7,000		
Restaurant	23,000	23,000	18,000	15,000	$14,000	$14,000
Total sales	38,000	38,000	28,000	22,000	14,000	14,000
Cost of goods sold	15,200	15,200	11,200	8,800	5,600	5,600
GROSS MARGIN	$22,800	$22,800	$16,800	$13,200	$ 8,400	$ 8,400
Operating Expenses						
Wages	$ 9,287	$ 9,287	$ 7,321	$ 7,321	$ 5,620	$ 5,620
Advertising	750	750	750	750	750	750
Electric	750	750	750	750	750	750
Gas	450	450	450	450	450	450
Legal	42	42	42	42	42	42
Interest	1,000	1,000	1,000	1,000	1,000	1,000
Repairs	150	150	150	150	150	150
Uniforms	60	—	—	—	—	—
Telephone	150	50	50	50	50	50
Charities	50	30	30	30	30	30
Office	100	100	100	100	100	100
Depreciation	520	520	520	520	520	520
Accounting	42	42	42	42	42	42
Miscellaneous	100	100	100	100	100	100
Total operating expenses	$12,631	$12,571	$10,605	$10,605	$ 8,904	$ 8,904
Net profit before taxes	$10,169	$10,229	$ 6,195	$ 2,595	$ (504)	$ (504)

THE GASTROPOD
Pro Forma Profit & Loss
Year 2 in Quarters

	1st Quarter	2nd Quarter	3rd Quarter	4th Quarter
Sales				
Ice cream stand	$ —	$20,000	$ 48,000	$10,000
Restaurant	48,000	56,000	77,000	51,000
Total sales	$48,000	$76,000	$125,000	$61,000
Less cost of goods sold	19,200	30,400	50,000	24,400
GROSS MARGIN	$28,800	$45,600	$ 75,000	$36,600
Operating Expenses				
Wages	$18,000	$25,000	$ 30,000	$20,000
Advertising	250	250	250	250
Electric	2,250	2,250	2,250	2,250
Gas	1,350	1,350	1,350	1,350
Legal	1,000	1,000	1,000	1,000
Interest	1,000	1,000	1,000	1,000
Repairs	500	500	500	500
Uniforms	120	90	100	100
Telephone	150	150	150	150
Charities	150	150	150	60
Office	300	300	300	300
Depreciation	600	600	600	600
Accounting	150	150	150	150
Miscellaneous	450	450	450	450
Total operating expenses	$26,270	$33,240	$ 38,270	$28,210
Net profit before taxes	$ 2,530	$12,360	$ 36,730	$ 8,390

THE GASTROPOD
Pro Forma Cash Flow
1st Year by Month

	January	February	March	April	May	June
Cash receipts						
Ice cream stand	$ —	$ —	$ —	$ 2,000	$ 5,000	$ 5,000
Restaurant	12,000	13,000	13,500	14,000	15,000	23,000
Total cash receipts	$12,000	$13,000	$13,500	$16,000	$20,000	$28,000
Cash disbursements						
Cost of goods sold	$ 4,800	$ 5,200	$ 5,400	$ 6,400	$ 8,000	$11,200
Electric	450	450	450	750	750	750
Gas	1,652	1,652	1,652	1,652	1,452	1,652
Mortgage	1,120	1,120	1,652	1,660	1,652	1,620
Uniforms	500	50	50	60	50	50
Telephones	120	20	20	20	20	20
Charities	150	150	150	150	150	150
Repairs	100	100	100	100	100	100
Office	100	100	100	100	100	250
Accounting	100	100	100	100	100	100
Miscellaneous	—	—	—	—	—	100
Advertising	5,620	5,620	5,620	6,896	7,025	7,564
Wages	—	—	3,100	—	—	3,100
Total cash disbursements	$14,362	$14,192	$17,492	$16,728	$18,427	$25,546
Net cash flow	(2,362)	(1,192)	(3,992)	(728)	1,573	2,454
Cumulative cash flow	(2,362)	(3,554)	(7,546)	(8,274)	(6,701)	(4,247)

THE GASTROPOD
Pro Forma Cash Flow
1st Year by Month

	July	August	September	October	November	December
Cash receipts						
Ice cream stand	$15,000	$15,000	$10,000	$ 7,000	$ -	$ -
Restaurant	23,000	23,000	18,000	15,000	14,000	14,000
Total cash receipts	$38,000	$38,000	$28,000	$22,000	$14,000	$14,000
Cash disbursements						
Cost of goods sold	$15,200	$15,200	$11,200	$ 8,800	$ 5,600	$ 5,600
Electric	750	750	750	750	750	750
Gas	450	450	450	450	450	450
Mortgage	1,652	1,652	1,652	1,652	1,652	1,652
Uniforms	60	-	-	-	-	-
Telephone	50	50	50	50	50	50
Charities	20	20	20	20	20	20
Repairs	150	150	100	100	100	100
Office	100	100	100	100	100	100
Accounting	100	100	100	100	100	100
Miscellaneous	100	100	100	100	100	100
Advertising	9,287	9,287	7,321	7,321	5,620	5,620
Wages						
Quarterly tax	-	-	3,100	-	-	3,100
Total cash disbursements	$27,919	$27,859	$24,943	$19,443	$14,542	$17,892
Net cash flow	$10,081	$10,141	$ 3,057	$ 2,557	($542)	($3,892)
Cumulative cash flow	$ 5,834	$15,975	$19,032	$21,589	$21,047	$17,155

THE GASTROPOD
Pro Forma Cash Flow
Year 2

	Year 2
Cash receipts	
Ice cream stand	$ 78,000
Restaurant	232,000
Total cash receipts	$310,000
Cash disbursements	
Cost of goods sold	$124,000
Electric	9,000
Gas	5,400
Mortgage	19,824
Uniforms	330
Telephones	600
Charities	-
Repairs	2,000
Office	12,000
Accounting	-
Advertising	1,000
Wages	83,000
Property tax	6,400
Income tax	22,200
Legal	300
Total disbursements	$287,254
Net cash flow	$ 22,746

Break-even Analysis

First Year
$$\frac{\$118,306 - 102,600}{1 - \frac{102,600}{256,500}} = \$197,177 \text{ of sales are needed to break even.}$$

Second Year
$$\frac{\$129,290 - 124,000}{1 - \frac{124,000}{310,000}} = \$215,483 \text{ of sales are needed to break even.}$$

Third Year
$$\frac{\$130,300 - 136,000}{1 - \frac{136,000}{340,000}} = \$217,167 \text{ of sales are needed to break even.}$$

Break-even formula:
$$\frac{\text{Fixed costs}}{1 - \frac{\text{Variable costs}}{\text{Sales}}}$$

THE GASTROPOD
Breakdown of Wages
First Year Operation

Jan., Feb., Mar., Nov. & Dec.

(Restaurant)

2 partners	Salaries $250.00 each	$ 500.00
1 Baker	40 hrs/week Salary of	100.00
1 Chef	50 hrs/week Salary of	200.00
1 Assistant chef	40 hrs/week Salary of	135.00
1 Chef trainee	20 hrs/week @ $2.65/hr.	53.00
1 Dishwasher	40 hrs/week @ $2.65/hr.	106.00
2 Waitresses	40 hrs/week @ $1.50/hr.	120.00
2 Waitresses	15 hrs/week @ $1.50/hr.	45.00
4 Waitresses	16 hrs/week @ $1.50/hr.	96.00

Total for a week $1,405.00
X 4   4
Total wages/month $5,620.00

April (Ice Cream Stand)

2 Partners	Salaries $250.00 each	$ 500.00
2 Waitresses	24 hrs/week @ $2.65/hr.	127.20
2 Waitresses	16 hrs/week @ $2.65/hr.	84.80

(Restaurant)

1 Baker	40 hrs/week Salary of	150.00
1 Chef	50 hrs/week Salary of	200.00
1 Assistant chef	40 hrs/week Salary of	135.00
1 Chef trainee	30 hrs/week @ $2.65/hr.	79.50
1 Dishwasher	40 hrs/week @ $2.65/hr.	106.00
4 Waitresses	40 hrs/week @ $1.50/hr.	240.00
2 Waitresses	16 hrs/week @ $1.50/hr.	96.00
1 Waitress trainee	4 hrs/week @ $1.50/hr.	6.00

Total for a week $1,724.50
X 4   4
Total wages/month $6,896.00

THE GASTROPOD
Breakdown of Wages
First Year Operation

May (Ice Cream Stand)

2 partners	Salaries $250.00 each	$ 500.00
2 Waitresses	25 hrs/week @ $2.65/hr.	132.50
2 Waitresses	16 hrs/week @ $2.65/hr.	84.80
1 Waitress	10 hrs/week @ $2.65/hr.	26.50

(Restaurant)

Same expenses as April   1,012.50

                              Total for a week $1,756.30
                                    X 4

                              Total wages/month $7,025.20

June (Ice Cream Stand)

2 partners	Salaries $250.00 each	$ 500.00
2 Waitresses	30 hrs/week @ $1.50/hr.	90.00
2 Waitresses	14 hrs/week @ $1.50/hr.	42.00
2 Waitresses	12 hrs/week @ $1.50/hr.	36.00

(Restaurant)

1 Baker	40 hrs/week Salary of	150.00
1 Chef	50 hrs/week Salary of	200.00
1 Assistant chef	40 hrs/week Salary of	135.00
1 Chef trainee	40 hrs/week @ $2.65/hr.	106.00
2 Dishwashers	40 hrs/week @ $2.65/hr.	212.00
7 Waitresses	40 hrs/week @ $1.50/hr.	420.00

                              Total for a week $1,891.00
                                    X 4

                              Total wages/month $7,564.00

THE GASTROPOD
Breakdown of Wages
First Year Operation

July and August (Ice Cream Stand)

2 Partners	Salaries $250.00 each	$ 500.00
2 Waitresses	40 hrs/week @ $2.65/hr.	212.00
4 Waitresses	20 hrs/week @ $2.65/hr.	212.00
3 Waitresses	12 hrs/week @ $2.65/hr.	95.40
3 Waitresses	10 hrs/week @ $2.65/hr.	79.50

(Restaurant)

Same expenses as June   1,223.00

                              Total for a week $2,321.90
                                    X 4

                              Total wages/month $9,287.60

September and October (Ice Cream Stand)

2 Partners	Salaries $250.00 each	500.00
3 Waitresses	30 hrs/week @ $2.65/hr.	90.00
2 Waitresses	12 hrs/week @ $2.65/hr.	95.40
5 Waitresses	10 hrs/week @ $2.65/hr.	132.50

(Restaurant)

Same expenses as April   1,012.50

                              Total for a week $1,830.40
                                    X 4

                              Total wages/month $7,321.60

MANAGEMENT

Resume, George Host

Personal History: Born September 22, 1957, in Harvard, Massachusetts; member of the varsity soccer and basketball teams while in high school, graduated from high school in June, 1976. After graduating from high school, went on to Shotwell College in Albion, Maine. While at college, majored in Economics and Management with a concentration in Small Business Management. Graduated from Shotwell College magna cum laude in May, 1980.

Work History: Worked as a stock boy and clerk in a grocery store. Operated an ice cream truck for two summers. Managed a general store called The Nonesuch in Ayer, Massachusetts. Worked for the Director of College Relations at Shotwell College and was a Resident Assistant at the college for one and a half years.

Resume, Paul Guest

Born March 17, 1957, in Boston, Massachusetts and brought up in the resort town of Hyannis, Mass. Worked at the Bayfront Motel and restaurant: performed such duties as busboy, chef, and bartender. Acted as front desk clerk on a part-time basis. For a period of one year, was employed by the Short-Stay Motor Court in Hyannis as head of the kitchen, then went back to the Bayfront as full-time desk clerk.

-35-

Both partners are young, energetic, and willing to work the long hours that are necessary for a small business to be successful. Both partners have had management experience. Mr. Host's knowledge and understanding of the town of Harvard will complement Mr. Guest's background in the tourist business. Mr. Host will be responsible for accounting and purchasing. Mr. Guest will be responsible for personnel and customer relations. Both will be active in day-to-day operations. All major decisions and policies will be made jointly.

Both partners will have a yearly salary of $3,000 to start. Profits from the first year will either be split in half between the partners or will be left in the business. This will depend upon the cash flow situation of the business. The second year, compensation to each partner should be around $15,000, between salary and profits.

-36-

APPENDIXES

Supporting Professional Services

Fortune Insurance Agency
Stone Fence Road
Harvard, MA   01451

Robert Smith Associates
Public Accountants
1 Main Street
Leominster, MA   01453

Floyd Law Offices
The Terrace
2 South Street
Clinton, MA   01510

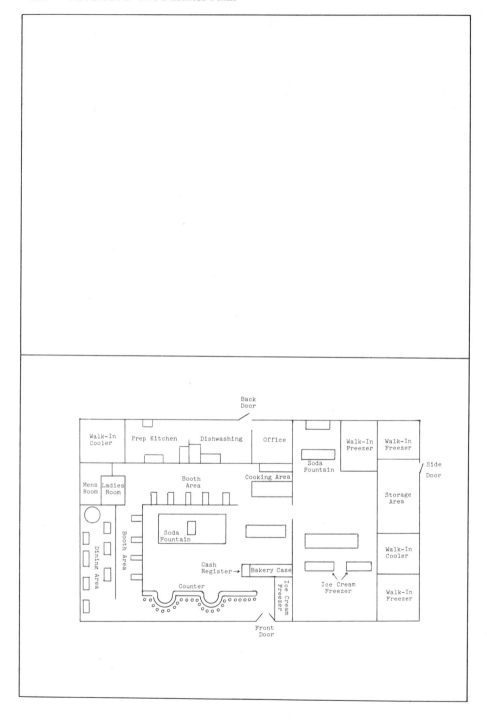

Index